The Church as
Moral Community

Lewis S. Mudge

THE CHURCH AS MORAL COMMUNITY

Ecclesiology and Ethics

in Ecumenical Debate

CONTINUUM • NEW YORK

WCC PUBLICATIONS • GENEVA

1998

The Continuum Publishing Company
370 Lexington Avenue
New York, NY 10017

World Council of Churches
WCC Publications
150 route de Ferney
1211 Geneva 2, Switzerland

Printed in the United States of America

Library of Congress Cataloging-in-Publication Data

Mudge, Lewis Seymour.
    The church as moral community : ecclesiology and ethics in
ecumenical debate / Lewis S. Mudge.
        p.   cm.
    Includes bibliographical references and index.
    ISBN 0-8264-1048-0
    1. Christian ethics.   2. Church.   I. Title.
BJ1241.M83   1998
241—dc21   98-15081
                                                                         CIP

WCC ISBN: 2-8254-1262-7

Printed in the United States of America

Contents

Preface

The Catholic novelist Georges Bernanos is remembered for having warned of the consequences that follow from posing questions the wrong way. "The worst, the most corrupting of lies," he is reported to have said, "are problems poorly stated."[1]

Sometimes the way we put the question *is* the question.[2] Today's contentious, fragmented, public world is not an easy setting in which to debate serious issues of any kind. Problems *may* be poorly stated simply out of inadvertence, ignorance, or incompetence. But public discourse—at least in the West—has now reached new levels of obfuscation, some of it, I fear, deliberate. Policy documents suppress facts that do not fit partisan preconceptions. Media barons turn public information into entertainment; arguments are egregiously politicized; single issues are isolated from their contexts; words fail to surmount cultural barriers; opposing parties attack each other with fear-driven meanness of spirit; candor and trust are in short supply. Health care, welfare, affirmative action, assisted suicide, abortion, the global market economy, the care of the earth: all these and a host of other matters are dealt with in expedient ways that typically avoid the truly important upstream questions.

Conditions of this kind signal a decline in the morality of discourse itself. Some public issues involve questions people typically label as "moral" because of their subject matter. Other topics seem morally neutral. But moral valence always attaches to the *way* questions are dealt with.

Behind the specific matters at issue in any debate there is always the further question of the quality of human community that the debate itself represents. The ways we treat one another in controversy often say as much as the decisions that issue from the fray.

Far from addressing such issues effectively, contemporary American Christians—and perhaps others as well—seem all too often to share the world's shortsighted, corrupting ways of framing and discussing controversial issues. Attempts by Christian communities to take distinctive moral positions in this chaotic world too often degenerate into legalism, single-issue politics, captivity to one side or another in current culture wars, or dancing with divergent ideologies that divide them internally and undermine their public credibility. Rarely do these struggles tap what Bryan Hehir calls the "premoral" convictions that Christian people ought to have in virtue of the fact that they are members of the community of faith.[3]

The premoral convictions we are failing to tap, I am convinced, belong primarily in the arena of ecclesiology. Contributions by churches to public discourse have become disconnected from the fabric of communal relationships in which Christians stand by virtue of the reconciling work of God in Jesus Christ. We argue individualistically, legally, ideologically, but seldom as members of a body for whom relationships of basic trust with others are fundamental.

This book seeks a strategy for recovering these missing connections. It asks how the community of faith as such can be both context and criterion for dealing with today's questions of shared life on earth, some of which involve threats to the continuation of life itself. The heart of the argument is that churches need to recover the vocation of providing primary moral formation, of shaping people's moral *identity*, long before politicized policy arguments begin.

One does not just sit down and *think* one's way from a vacuum of values to moral convictions. One begins one's thinking with as yet unspoken convictions already formed in principle by one's community of faith. This is true whether the community of faith is religious or secular, spiritual or rationalistic. In grasping this insight, moral reasoning in our time has become increasingly "communitarian." It has become reflection on the ways in which, as human beings, we have been shaped in communion with one another, and on the consequences of such primordial communion for making moral decisions.

As it happens, these matters have been the focus of a study process sponsored over the last four years by the World Council of Churches (WCC).[4] The pages that follow are one participant's "take" on that international dialogue on "ecclesiology and ethics." They are also an effort to contribute to the dialogue's next stage. If the WCC inquiry has produced a provisional conclusion, it is this: asking moral questions well begins when we learn to *be the church* well. And being the church well means becoming a formational community whose practices—liturgical and moral alike—arise from and are made possible by the gospel message. It is now necessary to press this conclusion further. How is such formation possible in today's fragmented, pluralistic cultures? Is it even plausible to talk about such a thing in an age of biblical illiteracy marked also by individualism, hedonism, consumerism, and organized greed?

And may not a moral reading of ecclesiology bring with it significant changes in the construal and pursuit of the ecumenical task? Here we are treading on controversial ground. Is this approach continuous or discontinuous with what ecumenism has meant to most of its participants up to now? I take the former position, but understand the concerns of those who think otherwise. With respect for the past, I join with others now to propose a new vision. Communities of Christian practice can here and now begin to make space in the midst of human affairs for an energizing, sacramentally real, presence of a larger, inclusively human, matrix of mutual moral obligation.

Adapting biblical language, we are calling this imaginatively and actively maintained space a "household of life." Churches living together as sponsors of such a moral household, open to relationships with other compatible secular and religious initiatives, could become a significant moral force in today's world. They could challenge the right of the global market economy and the system of national states to determine what life on earth is ultimately about. Congregations that knew themselves to be part of such a cosmopolitan community could hardly be content with privatized, limited understandings of faith.

But, as matters now stand, there is little consensus among the churches about the *relationship* between faith as believed and sacramentally shared, and the way congregations should understand themselves as moral communities in each place, let alone as members of a reconciling community spanning the globe. This lack of moral consensus is a serious matter: perhaps more serious even than the churches' continuing inability to reach agreement sufficient to achieve communion in matters of faith, sacraments, and ministry. It is serious because it means that the churches cannot make a common lived witness in the face of issues that today involve "justice, peace, and the integrity of creation."[5]

Can Christians even discern—from the places they now live—a comprehensive human solidarity to which all persons belong and are responsible? Can the shared life of churches disclose actual swatches of the fabric of relationships human beings need to have with one another in virtue of being fellow voyagers through a single historical process, members of a *communio viatorum?* Or are we content, with the politicians and diplomats, to treat questions of global human well-being as mainly *management* issues—that is, making sure at any given time that there is enough (likely *just* enough) caring, justice, peace, protection of the environment and all the rest to let us get on with *business*, which, for many, is what we are really here to do?

So I take my turn at wrestling with these enormous questions. I know that after six chapters I have not wrestled a single one of them to the ground, that every formulation has its drawbacks and dangers, and that I have blind spots for escape from which I need the help of collaborators at every turn. Of all this my interlocutors have not failed to remind me. Some, reading an earlier draft, found too little sense of sin and grace. One began with an assault on my title. He wrote, "To put it sharply, the church is not called to be a 'moral community.' The desire to be good is the sin of the Pharisee. The church is a community of forgiven sinners bearing witness to the one who redeems them and the world from self-centeredness. The word for that is not morality but love."[6] I understand very well what Charles West is saying, and I agree with it. But I try to come at the matter from a different, yet compatible, perspective.

The practices of the Christian community are enabled by the grace of God. They are not "good works" that generate merit to be exchanged for salvation. Yet love needs to be spelled out concretely *as* practice. Otherwise we risk forgetting Calvin's "third use of the law," which points to the role of Torah in the lives of the redeemed. Redeemed sinners still need practical guidance in the very behavior to which they are graciously empowered. They are liberated from guilt or self-righteous moralism to membership in a grace-enabled moral community. This community is then able to engage in ethical reflection, articulating positions and practices that constitute a distinctive witness to God-given possibilities beyond those yet realized in our global civilization.

The words *moral* and *ethical* can be confusing and deserve some brief further comment. In ordinary English, these terms are close to being interchangeable. If a distinction can be made, *morality* concerns the mores, customs, or, as I prefer to say, the practices in which persons are formed by primary communities. *Ethics*, on the other hand, is a field of inquiry which brings the content of such moral upbringing to critical and conceptual consciousness, perhaps extending it into new areas of concern. Neither is sufficient without the other. I use the word *moral* as much as I do because the central notion of this book has to do with the formation of congregations in practices that help manifest Jesus Christ—as Bonhoeffer said—"taking the form of a community."[7]

Indeed there is always a danger that morality will collapse into moral*ism*. We may all too easily come to suppose, as Glenn Tinder says, that we can be "good without God"[8]—as if goodness could *inhere* in us. But ethical reflection, properly practiced, can save morality from this fate. "Christian ethics" indeed begins when one realizes that integrity in the gospel no longer allows one *simply* to rest amid the mores of one's community or culture: when one stands before God and begins to take responsibility for one's life as a person both formed and free.

A second critical observation has to do with my forays into social and political philosophy. This book grafts perspectives from these fields into the customary codes of theological and ecumenical speech. This will no doubt cause discomfiture to methodological purists. But I think ecumenism from time to time needs a dash of sociological realism tempered by philosophical reflection. And this mixed mode could also invite the attention of readers who find unadulterated ecumenical language impenetrable and thus fail to give it the attention it deserves.

I hasten also to say that dealing with secular philosophies of society is not this book's primary agenda. I am trying to pursue that topic elsewhere. Here social philosophy is mainly a tool for envisioning the community of faith concretely. The theologian who cares what happens to the congregations today dare not work in intellectual isolation. There is much to be learned outside the field of theology as such. But making constructive use of human science disciplines need not mean being captured by these disciplines' worldviews. I trust that no such capture has occurred here.

Third, I am acutely aware that a variety of opinion warns against overly utopian pictures of what Christian congregations can become, pictures that do not deal realistically enough with what is going on in the world. "Don't make it too rosy," writes Anna Marie Aagaard, who also resists the dangerously totalizing implications of too much talk about Christian "globalization."[9] Lukas Vischer in effect shares the concern of the prophet that the day of the Lord may be "darkness, and not light" (Amos 5:20). Max Stackhouse, if I rightly understand him, thinks that envisioning the church as a moral counter-community is fundamentally the wrong way to go: that because there seems little alternative to the current world economic order we need to explore that order's own moral possibilities, including the possibilities of the life of the corporation.

I respect these views and, I trust, have learned from them. I will only say that if churches are to wrestle authentically with global issues alongside transnational corporations, NGOs, and governments, they must in the process also become communities that embody the kind of life they desire for everyone. Congregations become what they are in part by interacting with forces in their environments. Sometimes they do this by taking up provisional alliances with these forces, sometimes by resisting them, sometimes, in different respects, by doing both. Chapters 3 and 4 try to make this dialectic clear. I think that there is room in this picture for what Max Stackhouse wants to do.

Finally, while this is decisively an ecumenical book, some have noticed that it is also a very American one. The fact that I refer to political and social philosophers such as John Rawls, Alasdair MacIntyre, and others no doubt makes this plain, as if the numerous references to American theologians and church situations in the text did not do so already. If these pages had been written in some other part of the world, Larry Rasmussen reminds me,[10] religious pluralism rather than secular moral and political philosophy would likely have been the focus of attention. But the road to ecumenism lies through attention to the locality one knows best. Global issues always have their local manifestations. Local questions generally have their global implications. I trust that acknowledging my situatedness makes this book more, rather than less, authentic.

This is enough apology for now. It is time to express appreciation. These pages would not have been written at all had it not been for two invitations from the WCC to draft materials for the "ecclesiology and ethics" process: the first to write a preliminary essay on "formation," the second to act as principal drafter, with a committee, at the consultation in Johannesburg in June 1996. These tasks came to hand at a time when I was also working on drafts of related materials for my own Presbyterian Church (U.S.A.), and the U.S. National Council of the Churches of Christ. Later there was a drafting responsibility for the World Alliance of Reformed Churches. Some of the resulting texts were originally essays under my own name; some were drafts or parts of drafts designed to put words to the thoughts of others at conferences or consultations. Some of these pieces have already been or are about to be published. Others remain in manuscript form.[11]

Somewhere in this complex process I realized that I had the makings of a book. Besides, I needed a chance to pursue second thoughts, which I surmised might lead me to put certain things differently. This did not seem at first an overwhelming task. But accomplishing it took much longer than I originally expected. Reviewing copious notes taken during the WCC Johannesburg sessions disclosed insights I had missed. Notions that seemed cogent enough in groups of persons with similar convictions suddenly needed all kinds of explanation and support when forced to make their own way. New discoveries and new connections of ideas led me to rethink, reframe, and rewrite. More needed to be done to achieve a coherent voice and vision. And my dialogues with the good colleagues who read my penultimate draft—a text, as it turned out, rather far from the final result—were in many ways a continuation of the debates which began in the WCC meetings, seasoned by the reactions of others who came with fresh eyes to the process. This is now a considerably different book from the one I first set out to write. I hope the result moves the total discussion forward. Whether it does so or not, of course, is for others to judge.

I warmly thank the colleagues from whom I have learned so much over these three years, and especially those who were at the Johannesburg consultation. The latter will recognize passages they have seen before, especially in chapter 5. With permission from the WCC, I have borrowed a number of paragraphs of which I, with a committee, was the original drafter, giving them a somewhat new but still very recognizable shape.[12] I have also borrowed and revised a few paragraphs previously published under my name elsewhere. Places where this has been done are indicated in the endnotes. The effect, I think, is to keep the argument about these texts going: even to improve them almost as if the meetings that instigated them were still in session. Of course I realize that we are not still in session: it is not the same. I must now take sole responsibility for what I have done.

Special thanks go to Anna Marie Aagaard and Duncan Forrester, co-moderators of the WCC study, and to Alan Falconer, Thomas F. Best, and Martin Robra of the WCC staff. All five played major roles in the WCC effort and commented with penetrating wisdom on these materials in their various stages. Julio de Santa Ana, also of the WCC staff, read the entire penultimate text and shared with me his generous and engaging perspectives. Duncan Forrester's book on the ecclesiology and ethics process, *The True Church and Morality*,[13] was especially helpful, as was Ion Bria's *The Liturgy Beyond the Liturgy*.[14] Thanks, too, to chairperson Michael Kinnamon of the Ecclesiology Task Force of the U.S. National Council of the Churches of Christ, to Joseph Small of the Presbyterian Theology and Worship Unit, and to Milan Opocensky of the World Alliance of Reformed Churches. Their writing assignments for projects going on at the same time as this one led me to do work that has influenced this book.

Two teaching responsibilities along the way contributed to my thinking. The first was in the San Francisco Theological Seminary Doctor of Ministry program (headed by my estimable colleague Walter Davis) in the summer of 1996. In two seminar groups we read together the materials from Ronde and Tantur, as well as those being prepared for and issuing from Johannesburg (the latter meeting took place in the *middle* of the six-week seminar in San Anselmo), along with the work of other authors. I am glad to record the names of D. Min. students Musimbi Kanyoro and Marta Palma, of the Lutheran World Federation and WCC Geneva staffs respectively, who brought particularly impressive ecumenical experience and judgment to our task.

I also floated some of these ideas, with early scraps of manuscript, during the spring of 1997 in a study group at the remarkable Montclair Presbyterian Church in Oakland, California. I happily name my congregational co-conspirators: Sharon Noteboom, Austin Hoggatt, Jean Mudge, David Cudaback, Forrest Orr, Brad Hestir, Sarah Meyer, and Meta McAulay.

Two ethicist friends not involved in the WCC study, Max Stackhouse and Charles West, were good enough to comment in detail on the man-

uscript in its penultimate form. Jack B. Rogers and Loren Mead both read
and responded to an early draft of chapter 1. My son-in-law James Mit-
telberger, a geriatrician and medical ethicist, helpfully responded to a version of chapter 4. Lukas Vischer offered me a searching commentary on
chapter 6. Finally, Larry Rasmussen, himself one of the leading figures in
the ecclesiology and ethics study and principal drafter of the Ronde report
"Costly Unity," sent me detailed observations on the whole manuscript,
which proved transforming at several points. These friends saved me from
mistakes and helped me say what I wanted to say. Such colleagueship is
priceless, and I am grateful. The usual absolutions are declared. If I had
indulgences in my bag I would offer them freely too!

Norman Hjelm, in his incarnation as Senior Editorial Advisor for the
Continuum Publishing Company, was the one who encouraged me do a
book on this subject in the first place. I am grateful for his editorial acumen
throughout, and also for his encouragement at moments when I needed
it. Director Frank Oveis of Continuum had confidence in this project at
the start and was more than patient through delays at the end. Thanks,
too, to Marlin van Elderen and Jan Kok who made possible the WCC
co-publication arrangement. I am likewise grateful to the faculty and trus-
tees of San Francisco Theological Seminary, and especially to President
Donald McCullough and Dean Ronald White, for the sabbatical study
leave during which most of my writing was done.

My wife, Jean McClure Mudge, not only put up with this project, but
patiently let me go on much too long about it on innumerable occasions.
She also offered every kind of editorial advice, love, and support, all the
while working hard on a book of her own. My grown children Robert,
William, and Anne, and Robert and Anne's spouses Ingrid and Jim, looked
on indulgently and even asked me from time to time what I was doing.
Three more grandchildren have appeared since I mentioned Alison in the
foreword to *The Sense of a People*. They are Benjamin, Lillian, and Isaac.
Should Alison and they at some future time happen to come across these
pages, they will know I was thinking of them, too.

Lewis S. Mudge
San Francisco Theological Seminary and
The Graduate Theological Union, Berkeley

ONE

A Calling to Be Different

In a morally chaotic world, Christians need—somehow—to be different. One hears this judgment expressed today across a wide spectrum of theological and ethical opinion, both within the churches and beyond. Conservatives and liberals[1]—in accord on little else—tend now to agree that Western societies no longer represent (if they ever did) coherent orderings of life compatible as a whole with Christian faith. Despite welcome progress on many fronts—human rights and their implications, for example—these societies today seem devoted mainly to the pursuit of wealth and power for the few and media manipulation for the many. If churches are to play any worthwhile role in such a world they must first reclaim their calling to be distinctive, morally formative, communities.

Surely this is the import of much significant recent literature. Stanley Hauerwas first told us in 1977 that "the church does not have, but rather is a social ethic."[2] In a more recent book he compares the making of disciples with teaching people to lay brick.[3] Becoming a disciple, we read, is like painstakingly learning and practicing a skill. Many writers parallel Hauerwas's insights. The churches, they say, need to become communities of disciplined moral life if they expect to make any serious impact on our time. Similar views appear in the work of John Howard Yoder, Vigen Guroian, and many others. A striking new book, *Practicing Our Faith*,[4] edited by Dorothy Bass, makes the same point by lifting up the theme of shared practice. All speak of a need for practical and moral distinctiveness.

As Stephen Carter has more aggressively put it, churches need to become once more, as they were at the time of the Reformation, "a powerful independent moral force."[5]

One can even find this sentiment among thoughtful unbelievers, at least a few of whom guardedly wish the churches well. Critics such as Jeffrey Stout say they would like to hear theologians and religious ethicists speak more theologically in the full meaning of the word.[6] Others, such as Adam Seligman, are aware that Western societies have depleted their moral capital to the vanishing point, marginalizing the very institutions on whose formative activities they once depended for social cohesion.[7] While there is no new readiness to honor confessionally motivated arguments in the public arena—the old "church-state" dichotomy dies hard—one senses a feeling in many quarters that simply marginalizing and privatizing religious faith in Western societies has been a mistake. Many want the churches to find some way to speak up, without opening the door to theocratic political moves that could threaten religious freedom or lead to deeper public conflict among religious worldviews.

No one is quite clear about how this should be done. But even if the churches thought they knew in general terms, they are nowhere near agreement about what content a distinctive contemporary Christian witness should offer. On the right, the agenda has to do with responsible personal conduct, with family life, with sexual purity. On the left, embattled liberals are trying to regroup their forces around questions of economic justice, welfare, heath care, affirmative action, and the environment. And, as if to avoid both these agendas, many in the church and beyond are lapsing into new kinds of general individualistic religiousness that drain faith of distinct theological and moral content. Speeches and voting behavior in church assemblies tell the story: they tend to reflect cultural patterns in the larger society rather than serious theological reflection. All in all, the churches are missing what could be an important opportunity for recovering a distinctive identity and public voice because they cannot agree about what that identity should be and what that voice should say.

The root problem, this book maintains, is that there seems little *connection* in people's minds between the moral convictions to which they bear witness and the nature of the ecclesial community in which these convictions are nurtured. Ethics and ecclesiology are not seen as closely related. Yet the practice of Christian discipleship in the world is inevitably tied to the liturgical, storytelling, ministering fabric of Christian common life. It is tragic that so many brothers and sisters with strong opinions now seem bent on tearing that fabric to shreds in order to reweave it to their own specifications. Christian moral formation worthy of the name cannot be merely a reflection of opinions that happen at any moment to prevail; it must rather be an expression of the church's fundamental nature as a community of sinners forgiven by God in Jesus Christ and thereby providentially enabled to become an instrument of God's mission to humankind. To *be* the church in this sense, I claim, *is* the fundamental moral act on which all other forms of witness, all reflection in the categories of "Christian ethics," depend.

It follows that ethics must be understood ecclesiologically, and ecclesiology must be understood ethically. This seems simple enough to say, but the matter turns out to be not as simple as it seems. The World Council of Churches study of "ecclesiology and ethics" has sought to sort out the implications of the question.[8] The results deserve both critical attention and imaginative continuation. I suspect that our wrestling with these matters will go on for some time to come.

Ecclesiology and Ethics: The Fundamental Issues

What is the heart of the problem? At first glance, the notion that the church should be a moral community seems a truism. From the start Christians have assumed that professing the faith has moral implications and consequences. They have drawn on the rich moral implications of the Hebrew scriptures: Torah, prophets, and wisdom literature. They have taken to heart the Ten Commandments, passages such as Amos 5:24 and Micah 6:8, and the summaries of the Law in Deuteronomy 6:4 and Matthew 22:37-40. They have canonized a New Testament itself filled with passages of moral and ethical import: the Sermon on the Mount, other parables and sayings of Jesus, the admonitions of St. Paul, the guidance of the Pastoral Epistles. Moreover, the church over the centuries has produced an exceptionally rich tradition of ethical reflection and moral guidance, much of it designed to wrestle with the problems of "Christ and culture." This process has involved ongoing dialogue with, and much borrowing from, secular ethical perspectives: Platonic, Stoic, Aristotelian, Kantian, utilitarian, existential, and others.

Moreover, it is not the first time that moral tests have been taken as crucial to the distinctive identity and integrity of the Christian community. Tertullian's moral rigorism, the claims of Donatists and Novatians, prohibitions of the use of alcohol, the rejection of slavery, or torture, or atomic weapons: all these things have been taken at one time or another— at least de facto—as definitive of the church's being. This continues to be true. A simple test will do. Ask any group of Christians on what grounds, if any, they would be prepared to refuse eucharistic fellowship with some other Christian group. Moral issues are the ones most likely to be named. For one group the issue could be racism. For another it could be ordaining gay and lesbian persons. The point is that in all these cases moral issues— much more than the traditional "marks"—are taken to have ecclesiological implications. But the exact ways in which they do remain unclear.

Issues of this sort have now begun to affect the recognition or acceptance of particular communions within ecumenical fellowships.[9] When the Lutheran World Federation and the World Alliance of Reformed Churches both declare that the practice and theological defense of apartheid by white South African church bodies is a violation of the integrity of the faith which jeopardizes their relation *as communions* to the world bodies in question, the relationship between ecclesiology and ethics takes a new turn.[10] The same happens when the WCC Central Committee questions whether a church that fails to condemn violations of human rights in its own country has violated the expectations of ecumenical fellowship.[11] The same applies when a WCC Assembly debates whether a church's defense of peace and the rejection of the logic of deterrence should be, in effect, a criterion of ecumenical recognition.[12]

In all these cases the ecclesiological implications have been clear enough. But they have seldom been spelled out in terms of the churches' *core* self-understandings. Moral questions, especially controversial political ones, have been held at arm's length when it came to ecclesiastical definitions concerned with *esse* or fundamental "marks."[13] Konrad Raiser suggests that the churches have been able to fend off such questions, or fail to see their relevance, because they have assumed that their role was to defend some eternal, established, moral order however conceived, and to interpret its demands pastorally to the people.[14] The idea that moral order may depend upon, essentially inhere in, the churches reality and practices, that it may consist in the faith-community's own ordered response to God rather than in principles inherent in the general structures of human existence, is a perception that has come largely with the twentieth century.[15]

This realization is at least in part the result of cultural shifts whose nature it is important to grasp. People in Western cultures are experiencing a deterioration of generally shared moral standards, an evaporation of public notions of virtue. We are now living in many seemingly incommensurable moral worlds.[16] Different subcultures—including those of different generations—support diverse moral universes. These worlds have great difficulty communicating with one another. Purposeful action has become disengaged from the former matrix of meanings that allowed socially shared evaluation of its worth. Relations between persons have largely become "contacts" among autonomous, distinct and particular individuals acting out whatever values they happen personally to hold. Communities formerly based on shared, face-to-face expectations and fulfillments have decayed into societies governed by abstract statutes and distant regulatory agencies.

Moreover, the forms of "postconventional" ethical reasoning by which secular ethicists have sought to replace inherited notions of virtue are also in disarray. The notion that Enlightenment-style moral theories represent universal forms of human reasoning has collapsed in favor of the view that they merely reflect the cultures in which they have happened to appear. Think tanks and programs dealing with "human values" thrive in North American universities, but fail even to search for foundational moral principles. Rather they analyze the structures of moral arguments in relation to particular sets of circumstances. This work is not to be denigrated, for it can illuminate issues—say in medical ethics—human beings have not faced before. But when contemporary secular moralists seek out reasons—say, in some conception of the nature of the human being—for fighting slavery and torture or upholding human rights or defining the meaning of "informed consent"—they frequently arrive at formulas that are surprisingly shallow in relation to the conclusions drawn from them.[17] Indeed, most academic moral philosophers now try to keep their territory as "thin" and procedural, rather than substantive, as possible.[18]

In the face of such thin arguments we fall into a kind of rough pragmatism. People are saying that what does not turn into act has no value.

They are saying that only practice verifies theory, for reality has become identical with the historical world. All possibilities jostle, and whatever jostles to the top of the bowl rules so long as it can maintain its position. In place of virtue—whether of the classical Greek or Enlightenment variety—the West now lives with a loose set of working life-platitudes joining appropriate sets of technical rules within whose frame of reference any desired goal—personal, political, academic, economic as the case may be—may be pursued. In ordinary, nontechnical speech, this sort of pragmatism means adjusting our projects (as well as our opinions) to "what works." The pragmatic turn leaves society vulnerable to a relativism that honors whatever social practices may evolve within it.[19] Public morality—if such a thing exists—can then be grounded only in some contingent "sentiment of solidarity, in sympathetic identification with a form of life."[20]

All this would be bad enough in a stable, business-as-usual world. But our world is not stable. It is deeply threatened by its own frantic pursuit of productivity and profit. Ironically, as our public moral resources diminish the questions faced by our planetary civilization deepen. It is not only that persons are left to pursue their lives in a world without norms. In a morally fragmented time, we face questions of such radical scope and import that they can be dealt with only in collective ways. These issues have to do with the very continuation of life on earth itself. The ways issues of population, hunger, justice, peace, and the care of the environment are dealt with will determine the human future and perhaps the future of the planet. These are gigantic global policy issues, but they are also issues that impinge on personal behavior. From where will come the wisdom, and the courage, to deal with them?

These circumstances challenge the churches to become moral sources in themselves, not merely in the sense of giving good advice, but in their fundamental communal self-understandings. Already they are being challenged from within as well as from the outside. For some time now Christians of the southern hemisphere have been pressing those of the north to see that taking a stand against political oppression and economic injustice is of the essence of being the church, not merely a concern held by some within the church. Solidarity with the poor has virtually been elevated to the point of being a "mark" of the church alongside the traditional four. The same begins to be true of other issues, as it has long been of slavery. Who is prepared to recognize a church that practices institutional racism as a policy, or that countenances torture, or that is conspicuously indifferent to human rights?

The ecclesiological import of such questions deepens when the churches are understood as instruments of a *missio Dei* concerned with the fulfillment of God's purposes for life on earth. To the extent that the church *is* mission, and to the extent that one holds an eschatology that takes the moral content of history seriously, then the church is called to *embody*, not just offer opinions about, the justice and peace that are requisite to that divine–human fulfillment. The work of the WCC on "justice, peace and the integrity of creation" included an ecclesial dimension of this sort from the start. The churches at the Vancouver WCC Assembly of 1982 were called to engage in "a conciliar process of mutual commitment" with regard to these values. The ecclesial character of the needed moral reflection and action became patent then, and has continued to be so, even when occasionally forgotten, in the ecumenical movement ever since. "What is at stake," writes Konrad Raiser, "is no less than the reconstruction of ethics as such. The question is whether there is an independent entry point to ethics starting from the experience and reality of the church."[21]

That is the heart of the matter. Suddenly, one realizes that the issue no longer merely concerns what authority the churches have as such (as opposed to individual members or groups) for making moral and social pronouncements. That issue was fought out in North American Protestantism a generation ago.[22] The discussion now moves from what the church *says* to what the church *is*. How close to the heart of what has been believed about the church's essential being do moral issues now come?

The churches are not clear about this. The confessional traditions have a variety of conceptual resources that might be brought to bear, but these have hardly begun to be applied to the issues set forth here.[23] Ecumenical debate has wrestled with the matter in several ways. Is the church on the one hand a "mystery" and on the other a "prophetic sign," as Faith and Order has claimed? Is there a distinction between the church as "mystical body" on the one hand and the church as servant people of God on the other, as *Lumen Gentium* suggests? Do the Reformed and Lutheran notions of *status confessionis* help? What about the Vatican II formula by which the church is sign, sacrament, and instrument of the coming unity of humankind? Does a theological formula exist that defines the intrinsicality of the church's moral being without *reducing* the church to the particular moral positions it may advocate at any given time?

These distinctions are important, and perplexing. If the church is in its *very being* a moral community, then it becomes deeply vulnerable to internal moral conflict. One wonders how, and on what basis, its unity can be maintained.[24] The importance of the church's worldly moral role, stressed to the exclusion of all else, puts the church's own moral fabric at risk. The more moral responsibility the churches are called upon to take in modern society the more they become vulnerable at the core of their being to disruptive, maybe even schism-threatening, disagreements reflecting passions at work in that society. If, on the other hand, an attempt is made to isolate a core of the church's being independent of moral dispute, perhaps as a reconciling context for the dispute itself, then the church may preserve its unity at the price of irrelevance.

Put this another way. The more the churches take on responsibility for being primary moral communities in today's world the more some sense of a core ecclesial being *beyond* moral dispute is needed to sustain such a role. As the next section will show, in North America the churches have gone a long way toward letting moral questions determine the de facto limits of ecclesial fellowship, without considering the long-term implications of being in such a position. Thus, while I want to see the churches *be* moral communities in a profound sense, I do not want to see moral matters exhaust their being, for then they would represent no transcending reality giving them anything truly "different" to offer.

Clearly, more must be done to clarify these issues. How *should* we conceive the relationship between ecclesiology and ethics? That question occupies the rest of this book. But it is important on the way to that discussion to look at the actual situation, "on the ground," in at least one part of the church. Analyses of other corners of the vineyard would be welcome in response. No approach to our question that cannot speak to the complexities and tensions of actual church life is likely to have much value.

Moral Conflict in the Churches:
A North American Perspective

It is not as if pastors and people were thinking about all these things in the form they have been presented. For the most part they are not. But they are reacting to the same conditions the theologians are wrestling with. They are responding with revulsion to the disorder and shallowness of the life they see about them. They are at the same time trying to speak with a clear moral voice. But they cannot agree how to do so. The rancorous results amply illustrate the practical, not merely theoretical, difficulty of the issues raised in the preceding section.

The desired "difference" *from* the world most often plays out only as difference of opinion between partisan Christian groups that reflect different trends *within* the world. Far from being communities of independent moral witness, churches are becoming battlegrounds for rival communities of the morally like-minded. The resulting divisive rancor has overwhelmed, even replaced, thought about the fundamental nature of the church.

In North American churches, at least, one finds two primary moral agendas at work. In the Protestant context, Jack B. Rogers traces these worldviews back to historic nineteenth-century patterns still present, if somewhat modified, in the contemporary Christian life. On the right he finds the themes of naive realism, biblical literalism, separatism, revivalism, moralism, and millennialism. On the left emerge the themes of ecumenism, internationalism, denominational initiative, historical relativity, pluralism, interreligious dialogue, and social concern.[25] The Roman Catholic scene would need to be described differently, but comparable phenomena would no doubt emerge.

Of course such polarities are never absolute. Persons and even institutions may be conservative on some issues and liberal on others. One may both oppose abortion and support the death penalty. What matters is how one makes one's worldview coherent. Discerning that, of course, requires analysis that may itself become controversial. But pressures on people to follow party lines across the board despite possible personal reservations have been growing in the North American churches. This is true especially where matters of sexuality are concerned. Seldom today do divergent moral positions meet on common ground. Differences of worldview generate tensions that threaten the churches' unity, and even in some cases their continued existence.

Rather than attempt to *define* these different moral positions in their contemporary form, I think it best simply to offer some descriptive notes. These will suggest the current lay of the land. No one, of course, will be satisfied with the way her or his viewpoint is described. I apologize in advance, and do my best.

NOTES ON THE CONSERVATIVE AGENDA

A conservative communal morality agenda for the church is being acted out today in a variety of ways. North American Catholics and others feel the impact of John Paul II's reiterated opposition to birth control and abortion. He makes these prohibitions public touchstones of Catholic ethics and litmus tests of loyalty for bishops and priests.[26] The Southern Baptist Convention decrees a boycott against the Disney Corporation because of "gay days" at its theme parks and liberal personnel practices of that company with respect to "domestic partners." The Episcopal Church tries (and narrowly acquits) a retired bishop for having ordained a practicing homosexual man to the priesthood; then enacts a general prohibition of such ordinations. Subsequently this church narrowly rejects a proposal for drafting a liturgy for same-sex unions. Eastern Orthodox member bodies of the National Council of the Churches of Christ in the U.S.A. temporarily suspend their affiliation as a warning against even entertaining a membership application from the Association of Metropolitan Community Churches. American Presbyterians, by a narrow vote, enact an omnibus "fidelity and chastity" amendment[27] to their church's constitution. Its clear though unwritten intention is to prohibit the ordination of practicing gay and lesbian persons, but it actually opens the way for juridical investigation of candidates for ordination concerning their possible involvement in numerous kinds of behavior (one reader has counted over six hundred relevant passages) called "sin" in the church's confessional documents.[28] Groups such as the Moral Majority or the Christian Coalition seek to impose their sense of "difference" on the churches and to organize them for political purposes. They lobby among conservative Christians on the right wing of a whole range of issues: public welfare, abortion, health care, gun control, campaign finance, and even aspects of foreign policy.

These instances are of course extremely diverse. Each case tells a different story. Can one generalize in any useful way? The tendency of Christians to identify unreflectively with one side or the other in an ongoing struggle of worldviews in the broader culture obviously contributes to the sloganization of theological controversies inside the church. This in turn reduces faith convictions to simplistic and distorted "sound bite" dimensions. Concentrations of energy in "single issue" politics obscure the deeper interconnections of moral questions. The impulse to legislate moral difference either by making special rules and regulations for Christians, or by seeking to impose such standards on everyone, ironically tends to uphold the social order in whose terms the differences in question are defined. Seeing difference in legalistic and single-issue ways tends to blind people to the possibility of more visionary and transformative change for society as a whole.

One is reminded of the similar substitution of legislation and regulation for human judgment in many walks of life.[29] As mutual trust diminishes and mutual suspicion grows, both in the churches and in society at large, ever more elaborate regulations tie the hands of persons whose wisdom used to be trusted. There is more than a whiff of Donatism—that is, obsessive moral rigorism—in the claims now being pressed by conservatives who forget that Donatism was condemned finally as a heresy by the early church because it implicitly denied the doctrine of grace. The Donatist heresy carries with it a tendency to think of "sin" not as a condition of estrangement from God, but as consisting of particular, nameable, proscribed activities, hence sin*s*.

Many such presentations of moral difference all but abandon morality's deeper theological grounds. Of course public campaigns for moral rectitude always trample on nuance and complexity. Obsession with sexual matters and with legalistic means of dealing with them tends to block out of consciousness *other* moral concerns the churches—with the support of many conservative members—are simultaneously trying to communicate: concern for the environment, for economic justice, for care and compassion, for world peace. Ironically, few voices are calling for including such larger moral questions in manuals of church order or canon law. Few are urging that clergy and others be *disciplined* for conspicuous consumption, for contributing to economic injustice, or even for the sin of gluttony (which happens to be on the Presbyterian list).

But what difference can such proclamations of difference actually make?

Are they steps toward defining the *kind* of difference *from* the world that could truly make a difference *in* the world? One cannot help observing that many disciplinary pronouncements and enactments today, considering the way they are made and the subject matter they include, contribute more to internal division, acrimony, and mutual distrust than they do to effective witness. What the world sees is not churches taking the moral high ground but fallible human associations torn by internal dissent. Print and electronic media fasten on such conflict, amplify it, propagate it. The intended moral messages do not get through: only the impression that church leaders cannot be trusted to behave and that much of the time Christians cannot in any case agree what standards the gospel should require.

THE MUTED VOICE OF "LIBERALS"

One hears less today than a few years ago from the liberal or progressive side of the church, although it is unquestionably still there, and perhaps ready to become again more audible. It would be difficult to list a series of recent ecclesiastical legislative actions on the progressive side parallel to those representing conservative opinion. But nearly every church assembly endorses annually a series of pronouncements produced by the social action lobbies of the denominations concerned. These usually attract very little attention today, probably because they are regarded merely as politically correct rhetoric rather than indications of genuinely transformative intent. Yet some progressive initiatives still attract attention and have their impact.[30]

There exists a long and honorable tradition of progressive Christian thought that has yielded much insight of moral consequence. The most prominent historic achievement of Christian liberalism may have been its role in the nineteenth-century defeat of slavery. A generation later, progressive leaders took on the cause of quality of life in the inner cities. Today they lead the concern in the churches for justice, for human and civil rights including rights for women, minorities, gays and lesbians, affirmative action, environmental concern, peace-making, and the like. Without a small but determined left wing, the white South African churches would not have recognized their opportunity to join their black brothers and sisters in the struggle against apartheid in that country. They would have been in an even weaker position to offer moral leadership than they now are. Many other examples could be adduced. Significantly,

John Paul II—so conservative in many respects—finds himself on what can only be called the progressive side of many economic, human rights, peace-making, and environmental issues.

But much of the progressive communal agenda today increasingly exhibits traits that mirror-image the conservative ones: among them a tendency to reflect the contest of worldviews going on in the culture at large and a tendency to focus on single issues. An excessive individualism sometimes obscures equally important claims of social responsibility. While people of many political viewpoints favor laws to protect human rights, progressives sometimes expand the conception of rights that inhere in human beings by virtue of their humanity to create a situation in which rights legislation becomes nothing but the management of conflicting claims to entitlements of all kinds, both on the part of individuals and of ethnic, racial, occupational, and generational groups. Many progressives also believe that devotion to causes such as justice, peace, rights, environmental integrity, and the like generates an intrinsic moral integrity born of single-minded focus on the objective being sought. There is—it is argued—less need then for specific rules governing behavior in the community. As Johann-Baptist Metz has said, "If the church were more radical in the gospel sense it would probably not need to be so 'rigorous' in the legal sense."[31]

In all these traits, the contemporary progressive agenda, like the conservative program, tends in practice to come loose from its own rich theological sources. Sometimes this means adopting an academic, human-science, or political-philosophical approach to social issues rather than a predominantly theological strategy. The British theologian John Milbank says:

> Contemporary political theologians tend to fasten upon a particular social theory, or else put together their own eclectic theoretical mix, and then work out what residual place is left for Christianity and theology within the reality that is supposed to be authoritatively described by such a theory.[32]

He adds that for some of these writers "the faith of humanism has become a substitute for a transcendent faith now only half-subscribed to."[33]

A very similar critique of the liberal position in Christian ethics comes from the American religious studies scholar Jeffrey Stout. He is writing about the work of James Gustafson, an ethicist who stands in the tradition of Calvinist piety and the thinking of H. Richard Niebuhr, but who revises the tradition considerably according to his own lights. Stout asks:

> Is not Gustafson's theology distinguishable from a humane and recognizably secular vision only at the points at which he is also most elusive, where we have the most difficulty figuring out what he is saying and why he is saying it, where we have the most trouble discerning what the difference comes to and why he wants to maintain it?[34]

This is as much as to say that the progressive difference is today, at least on the surface of things, not very much of a difference at all. If conservatives have failed to articulate a genuine moral difference from the spirit of the age because of their bondage to existing secular conservative worldviews, their legalism and their obsession with sexual "sins," it appears that Christian progressives have done much the same thing in other ways. They, too, have taken sides in the contest of worldviews. They have confused human-science analysis with Christian ethics, and, above all, failed to bring the theological riches of their own tradition to bear on a whole range of issues of immense human importance. In short, they have too often resorted to forms of advocacy indistinguishable from those one encounters in secular left-wing politics. Do Christians deeply concerned about justice, peace, and the sustainability of a livable environment have to step outside the theological circle to find serious intellectual or moral companionship? It appears in many cases that today they do. The faith may thereby be diluted, or it may be enriched, by borrowings of this sort.

SEEKING PERSPECTIVE: DANGERS AND OPPORTUNITIES
This debate between the right and the left, in North American Protestantism at least, may now be assuming some characteristics of a classic "church struggle." While it is not yet comparable to the struggle over slavery or over the appropriate Christian attitude to Hitler's National Socialism, the outcome of the current debate could have serious consequences for the communions and denominations concerned. The whole question of Christian response to the moral fragmentation and emptiness of our time is being held hostage to the terms of reference of conflict involving divergent moral interpretations of the faith.

Indeed, this conflict is potentially church-dividing. As matters stand, there appears to be a de facto, if not de jure, readiness on both extremes to unchurch the opposition emotionally, rhetorically, and politically. There is little sense of *koinonia* between the two wings of opinion, little feeling of meaningful sharing even at the Lord's Table, despite the fact that both worldviews typically exist within communions fully united in the ecclesial and sacramental sense. These moral positions address the world in divergent ways. They do not build up the *whole* church as a moral community.

It is important to stand back for a moment and see all this in perspective. Factions in the church demanding that more attention be paid to certain moral questions or distinctive aspects of the faith are hardly a new phenomenon. Think of the Montanists, the Donatists, the Novatians, the radical reformers, the Puritans, even the early Methodists. The pattern is clear enough. Movements for greater moral or spiritual rigorism than "establishment" circles demanded have generally been sectarian in form. They have criticized Christian practices representing institutional "compromise" (Ernst Troeltsch's term) between the tradition of faith and its cultural environment. The "sect type" has repeatedly mounted a polemic against the looseness and worldliness of the "church type." Many dissenting movements over the centuries have left their impression on the "established" church bodies even as they have separated from them. They have sometimes provoked theological rejoinders of lasting importance as in the case of St. Augustine against the Donatists. They have preserved Christian culture, as in the case of St. Benedict and the monasteries. They have won over the church to new moral points of view, as in the eventual decision to outlaw slavery.

All these movements, and many others in their various ways, have initially conveyed the message that being the church authentically requires special moral discipline beyond what can be expected of ordinary "culture-Christians." Many of these groups have been willing to risk schism to transmit their message clearly. Sometimes schism has been the result, sometimes it has not. What are the odds of schism now? That the salient issue now has to do with sexuality means at least this much: that more people become passionately involved in controversy than would otherwise be the case. Because such a deep taboo attaches to homosexual practice in the minds of many the debate reaches beyond strong partisans of the right and the left into the center of church life, dividing some denominations almost down the middle. In their adamant opposition to ordaining gay and lesbian persons, the right has found a vehicle capable of winning far more votes for their reactionary agenda than that agenda would ordinarily attract on its merits. It has led people to suspect that every other moral issue the church may debate is a coded version of this one. The divisive potential of this question has fueled right-wing ambitions for institutional "takeover." It has escalated the perennial tension between Christian worldviews into a financial, political, and legal struggle for the control of several North American church bodies.

How can matters have come to such a pass? Can practicing the "wrong" sort of sexuality—even in permanent monogamous relationships—possibly be as important a matter as denying the faith under persecution, or holding slaves, or torturing children, or oppressing workers, or despoiling the environment? How has *this* issue become so central that in North American Protestantism it now eclipses all others, so divisive that it must be dealt with before any other moral question can seriously engage the attention of pastors and people? Moreover, is this question of sexuality and ordination destined eventually to tear churches in other parts of the world apart as well?

One can conjecture that this might happen anywhere today given the requisite cultural conditions. These could be circumstances of any sort in which people felt attacked or undermined in their personal identities as sexual beings. John Burgess has argued, following the French philosopher Michel Foucault, that what we used to call the "soul," meaning the sense of personal being or identity, has now become focused in sexuality. And this substitution of sexuality for soul impacts our theological and moral reasoning. Burgess writes:

> Without our being aware of it, the sexuality debate has become the vehicle for getting at the most basic questions of faith. In many ways the debate is not about sexuality at all, but about theological anthropology—that is, what it means to be human before God.[35]

And, further, "Because the church is no longer sure how to use the language of faith to clarify issues of sexuality, it is tempted to use the language of sexuality to clarify issues of faith and faithfulness."[36]

Sexual orientation has thus for many taken on a quasi-ontological meaning. Members of the majority culture are likely to feel that they fulfill the human *essence* in their heterosexuality. If such assumptions are challenged, as they are by many Christian liberals, not to speak of militant gay and lesbian groups, the entire heterosexual culture is also challenged. People will fight ruthlessly to maintain a status quo that gives them a sense of their own integrity and worth, perhaps the principal source of integrity and worth they are able to maintain in today's rapidly changing world.

The problem then is that the Christian community, polarized over the meaning of sexuality, becomes paralyzed about everything else. The churches, ironically, are then unable to be the sorts of communities needed to ground a sense of moral order in the midst of chaos. Congregations then have no reply to the conditions described earlier in this chapter. They have no reply to the decline of traditional public virtue, no reply to the shallowness and pluralism of postconventional ethical reasoning processes, no reply to a normless, platitudinous pragmatism. Yet the congregation is the source from which we seek coherent life-perspectives not otherwise easily available. Is there any hope for transcending the debates that make an individual's sexual orientation the measure of his or her selfhood toward a deeper sense of the church as moral community in which persons ground their selfhood in just, loving, inclusive relationships?

Diagnoses and Prescriptions

It is one thing to speculate philosophically about how the churches might escape from their current internal struggles, but quite another to find practical strategies for such an escape. I do not think that the present polarization of moral opinion in the churches will easily disappear, or even that the focus of debate can readily be shifted to more fruitful subject matter. But proposals for overcoming ideological polarization and moralistic obsession are in the field. These deserve attention on the way to the conclusions that close this chapter.

GETTING IN TOUCH WITH CONGREGATIONS

The proposals in question mainly have to do with correcting the failure of theologians and church leadership to make adequate contact with the moral and theological understandings—as well as the fears—shaping the lives of believers in local congregations. It is argued by the Roman Catholic critic J. Bryan Hehir, for example, that we must reconnect the church's public witness with the conceptions of faith held in ordinary parishes across the land.[37] Jack B. Rogers, somewhat similarly, wants to reactivate the faith and witness of the large majority of Protestants who stand in the church's "center," favoring neither the ideological right nor the ideological left.[38]

Both Hehir and Rogers believe, in somewhat different ways, that church leadership over the past few generations has failed to communicate effectively with people in the pew, leaving the latter vulnerable to the fearful divisiveness with which they are now afflicted. Hehir lays responsibility for this failure on the theologically sophisticated leadership that over two generations has sought to "sharpen the social edge of faith" without grasping the basics of congregational life. Figures such as John Courtney Murray, the Niebuhrs, and many others after World War II joined hands with ecumenical agencies to try, with little success, to bring congregations out of religious privatism to social consciousness. For Rogers, leaders of a "liberal" worldview came to dominate Protestant headquarters cadres, but failed either to appreciate or significantly influence the church's great middling majority. Today we have to deal with the wreckage wrought by disconnected leadership of this kind.

Rogers and Hehir would no doubt agree that such leadership took for granted that adequate primary formation in the essentials of faith was going on in local congregations. Leaders sought to move the churches toward more adventurous forms of social witness. But was this assumption about the adequacy of primary formation justified? It is not clear, for example, that Reinhold Niebuhr—so anxious was he to make distinctions between "moral man" and "immoral society"—asked himself often enough about the *connections* between personal moral issues and matters of public moral concern. Nor were the connections adequately made by most pastors. The theological base for social consciousness was not there. In fact serious theological training in the parish was being neglected because too many congregations and pastors took for granted—without putting it in so many words—that the surrounding culture provided the essentials of a "Christian" attitude to life. Such a culture, they seem to have thought, only needed to be gently interpreted by sermons making frequent references to football, TV advertising, and popular self-help literature.

I exaggerate to make a point, but only a little. American congregations seem often to have preferred to pick up a "gospel" *from* the surrounding culture rather than from leadership that might suggest formulating a message *to* that culture. In their captivity to culture they imbibed a very attenuated version of what the faith ought to mean. Christian symbols were and indeed are present in the culture, but in increasingly fragmented form, almost always secularized and politicized, ever more alienated from their original sources and often used for extraneous purposes. Congregations and people have resisted receiving specific teaching from theologians, church leaders, and pastors, *especially* where that teaching has sought to liberate them from their cultural captivity.

Douglas John Hall argues, indeed, that captivity to the moral and ideational norms of American society has left the people without any sense of a *need* to think theologically. Congregations—the very people in whom Rogers and Hehir place so much hope—are in Hall's view so reflective of the culture around them that they cannot think coherently about the faith. Hall argues that religious "simplism," by which he means the "oversimplification and sloganization of the faith" is the "ideational backbone of the culture-religion called Christianity."[39] This is true not only of the "center" but also of those who hold ideological tendencies to the right and to the left. On the right: shallowly grounded exclusivism, false pretensions to finality, tolerance but not real love for persons of other religions.[40] On the left: the liberal preoccupation with social issues, as if having the right position on each one were all that is needed to bear adequate witness.[41] Being part of the cultural establishment prevents congregations from seeing possibilities that are *there* for them, but in the present state of affairs unimaginable: like being part of a "global Christianity which has transcended the past and risen to the challenge of our common planetary future."[42]

Facing this situation, both Rogers and Hehir want to make the connections between theological leadership and the minds of the people not accomplished before: Hehir by getting in touch with people's "premoral" incarnational, sacramental, and social convictions; Rogers by restoring, in contemporary form, the balanced synthesis of evangelical piety which preceded a century and a half of ideological polarization. But one senses that neither strategy will be enough to bring churches out of the cultural captivity and accompanying strife over worldviews that divide them today. Neither proposal seems to articulate a new sense of mission to the contemporary world that would require both an astute analysis of what is going on in that world, and a vision for the churches' role in it.

Such a missionary objective calls for a strategy more profound than urging leadership to make greater efforts to listen to congregations while trying to sharpen their moral sensitivity. What is needed, rather, is an altogether new sense of what it *is* to be the church in the world today. But is there any *realistic* hope of escape from today's ideologically polarized, morally debilitating, culture-captivity into the bracing fresh air of God's mission to humankind? Only if by God's providence we are led into a new "definition of the situation." This present epoch in church history *will* pass. Could there be signs that even now it is beginning to give way to something new?

Among the several diagnoses and prescriptions in the field, Loren Mead's seems most aware that this question involves something beyond empathy and educational strategies. It involves the *missio Dei*, the question of the ends of human history in the light of Jesus Christ. In *The Once and Future Church*,[43] Mead argues the case that the mission frontier has come to the doorsteps of local congregations, whose members must now seek to discern for themselves what that mission in a fragmented and pluralistic world means. In Mead's analysis, the great denominational structures are associated with an older notion of mission: one in which churches in a Christian nation sent "missionaries" to nations overseas. Such "foreign" mission work was for the most part consigned to specialists supported by missionary societies or denominational boards. It was therefore not seen as the direct responsibility of congregations. But now the notion that North Americans live in "Christian nations" that need to evangelize other nations has been exposed as empty. The frontier of mission is now everywhere.

A "POST-WESTPHALIAN" WORLD

What could this mean? Writers such as Mead, Douglas John Hall, Stanley Hauerwas, and John Howard Yoder have been saying for some time that we are moving into an epoch properly called "post-Constantinian," "post-Christendom," or "postestablishment." These terms, probably too formulaic to begin with, have by now picked up a good deal of wear. The consequences they suggest are often too simplistically applied. To write as if sixteen hundred years of "Christendom" have been all one thing is to suggest that the present period is all one thing as well. In truth, as our authors well know, the past has been enormously variegated and complex, and the transitions taking place now at the close of the twentieth century likewise defy any simple summary. Change also proceeds at very different rates and in many different ways in different parts of the world.

But is there anything in the notion of a post-Constantinian, post-Christendom, or postestablishment world that can suggest hopeful strategies for churches that desire to discern the *missio Dei*, to bear genuine moral witness, in that world? Changes are taking place that will profoundly alter the churches' *role* in society. These changes are not just further instances of the phenomenon of secularization. Secularization of a sort *is* going on. Intellectuals and the media feel ever freer to dismiss "religion" as a significant factor in matters of public importance.[44] But, ironically, the culture is as "religious" as it has ever been, if not more so. Nicholas Lash speaks for Britain but his words apply equally to North America:

> A glance at any bookshop shows that—from astrology to witchcraft, from yoga to the enneagram—thick mists of something very much like "mysticism" in [Ernst] Troeltsch's sense, far from "evaporating," flourish with positively tropical luxuriance. And, almost without exception, it seems to be taken for granted in these circles that "religion," in *their* sense, has nothing to do with politics.[45]

The role of the classical Christian tradition as carried by the organized churches *has* changed and diminished. The Enlightenment saw a repudiation of theocracy, of a "tutelage" that made human beings less than their true selves. Nor is it as if a powerful hegemonic church were still manipulating the state for its own purposes.[46] Ecclesiastical power of this sort ended for all intents and purposes in the seventeenth century. What is beginning to weaken *now* is a certain broadly held understanding of the churches' role as legitimators of individualistic virtues and nationalistic values in secular states willing to grant "religious freedom" in return for unthreatening ideological support.[47] We have been living with an arrangement—an acted-out set of assumptions—concerning the role of the churches in private and public life, which began *not* with the Emperor Constantine but much more recently, in 1648, with the signing of the Peace of Westphalia, marking the end of the religious wars that had convulsed Europe for thirty years. Thinking in post-Westphalian rather than in post-Constantinian terms gives a much sharper focus to the discussion of mission for today. William T. Cavanaugh writes:

> What was at issue in those wars was the very creation of religion as a set of privately held beliefs without direct political relevance. The creation of religion was necessitated by the new State's need to secure absolute sovereignty over its subjects.[48]

In short, Westphalia marked the beginning of a process across Europe by which nationalism replaced religion as public focus for people's loyalties and religious faith itself became marginalized, privatized, and individualized in both conception and content.[49] The principle of *cuius regio eius religio* ("whoever the prince may be, his will be the prevailing religion") moreover marked a hardening of already developing confessional loyalties, whether to one or another form of Protestantism or to Roman Catholicism. In North America, in turn, these loyalties were among the factors supporting the growth of that strange ecclesiastical anomaly called the denomination.

Furthermore, by removing religion so far as possible from the sphere of public argument, Westphalia opened the way for an Enlightenment already dawning in the work of thinkers such as John Locke and René Descartes, and destined for full flowering a hundred years later in the thought of figures such as Voltaire, Immanuel Kant, James Madison, and Thomas Jefferson. The whole American problematic of "separation of church and state" was based on this outworking of Westphalian assumptions. Public debate was to be conducted in rational, religiously neutral, terms open to all educated persons. "Religion" came to be considered "a particular district of existence which people may inhabit if they feel so inclined."[50]

But now, as we have seen, the "grand narratives" of the Enlightenment are themselves collapsing, and with them all the other assumptions flowing from the Westphalian treaty. We are approaching an age beyond that of the taken-for-granted existence of secular sovereign states and privatized understandings of religion that have characterized European and then North American life since the mid-seventeenth century. Put differently, what is *really* ending here is not only "religion's" privatized, marginalized role in the modern world as defined by Enlightenment-oriented nation-states, of which the United States has been a particularly good example. What is really ending is the whole hour upon the stage of that "modern" world itself. Enlightenment culture and eighteenth-century nation states privatized and marginalized "religion" for intellectual and political purposes.[51] Today's secular elites essay to get along without "religion" in that sense altogether. But what is disappearing is the entire cultural synthesis that gave "religion" that privatized, crutch-for-those-interested-in-such-things role in the first place.

What the churches are losing in this cultural change, then, is a niche—a set of assumptions concerning their own nature and function. If "religion" seems to be becoming less influential, it is not only because of secularization in the media and the universities, not just because of the prestige of science, but also because cultural change is gradually eliminating religion's Westphalian social role. But such a niche, such a role, may not have been worth having. It essentially distorted the meaning of the gospel. One should not weep at *that* sort of loss. A genuinely post-Westphalian church would be free to stop playing the role assigned to "religion" by public principalities and powers, and begin to be *itself*, to receive the identity held out for it as a calling in Scripture.

GRASPING THE OPPORTUNITY FOR CHANGE:
POSTMODERN ANALYSIS

Thoughtful observers of many persuasions have sought to formulate what might be required for the churches to enter such a future.[52] In doing so many of them have availed themselves in various ways of the notions of "deconstructionist," "antifoundational" or, as more often expressed, "postmodern" thought. Here the term *postmodern* refers not only to the range of cultural phenomena previously described, but also to academic perspectives or methods that reflect these phenomena, finding in them insights which turn into analytical tools. The thinkers in question are also "deconstructionist" to the extent that they self-consciously refuse the grammars of institution maintenance—particularly the economic logic— of late twentieth-century societies. They are "nonfoundationalist" to the extent that they refuse the aid of philosophical visions of any kind that purport to ground theological reflection in broadly persuasive and legitimating reality propositions, metaphysical, scientific, or otherwise. They are "postmodernist" to the extent that they make a point of functioning intellectually in a world without given institutional grammars and philosophical foundations, either to celebrate its freedoms or to recover ancient traditions, or both.

These notions have been around for some time. Endless discussion has disclosed how slippery they are, at the same time rendering them trite. Yet they continue to have their uses. At the very least they point to an attitude, a mood. The Berkeley political philosopher Philip Selznick offers the best description of postmodernity that I have seen. He writes:

> Much of what is called postmodern in the arts, literary criticism, philosophy, and social theory is, above all, a challenge to coherence. Purported unities of self, community, culture, law, art, science and organization are exposed as inescapably plural, conflict-filled, dissociated. Whatever unity we may find is imposed, not natural or organic.[53]

It seems to me that such a situation and all that goes with it enables theologians to make two moves that improve their chances of envisioning a post-Westphalian world. The first is to declare independence from all assumptions belonging to the modern or late-modern universes of thought, to cast aside all that might otherwise claim some sort of inevitable or foundational character. The church does not *have* to be related to the society around it the way it has been ever since Westphalia. Those postures, and the controversies that go with them, are not intrinsic to the faith. The moral certitudes over which we are today so bitterly divided are seen to have no basis in the order of being, but only in the assumptions with which we happen to have been living for the last few hundred years.

Second, a postmodern stance enables these theologians to entertain the idea of a community of practices based on the Christian story that has as much right to constitute a moral universe as any set of socially established virtues or Enlightenment-style lines of argument. In the postmodern perspective, the church is free to be the church, without apology to reality definitions coming from elsewhere.

Could such a perspective help liberate the churches from the bewitchment of a culturally homophobic metaphysics of personhood? It has already done so for significant numbers of Christians. But whether such liberation becomes general depends on how the opportunities of the postmodern perspective are played out on the ground. On the one hand a postmodern sensibility *can* be read simply as permission for a new "lightness of being," including a promiscuous multiorientational sexuality. That is precisely what conservatives and many others fear, and claim to see in the agenda of the Christian left. But on the other hand a postmodern reading of the world could mean new freedom for the church to gather around its story and its traditions, and in faith to be what it will be. It could mean a recovery of the whole array of Christian practices free from the sort of foundational cultural demands that have in the past made such practices obsessive rather than free. The new perspective the postmodernist theologians see could help us receive the grace that confers freedom to be what we are, and yet be hospitable to others whose being-in-practice is different.

But, alas, it is one thing to envision possibilities and another thing to live them. The churches are not yet liberated enough from old assumptions to be able to grasp the new possibilities their thinkers set before them. We still live in a war of worldviews: premodern sensibilities are trying to defend themselves in a late-modern situation. Or perhaps this warfare represents the fracturing process (surface rifts indicating the crunching of tectonic plates far below) that occurs as an older vision begins to give way to a newer one.

Some will say that the conservative agenda really represents the older world and the progressive position the new. However satisfying it might be for one like myself to believe that, I rather think that the older situation is represented by the fact of the conflict itself. Apart from ideological conflicts rooted in the churches' Westphalian captivity, there is no reason why a concern for personal morality should be incompatible with bold social witness and vice versa. For either of these two to be authentic, the other is necessary. It should be possible for the church to combine, without ideological conflict, a due sense of personal fidelity and integrity in sexual as in all other matters with vigorous witness in the fields of justice, peacemaking, and the care of creation. How might such a possibility be realized?

A Primacy for Practice

The concluding section of Nicholas Lash's recent seminal essay "The Church in the State We're In" is titled, "Back to School." Lash goes on to ask, "how might the kind of 'people' that Christians (like Jews) confess themselves to be, acquire the discipline, sustain the culture, that would render us capable of 'speaking truth to power'?"[54]

Lash speaks here of an educational process that inducts successive generations into citizenship of a promised city destined to be achieved not by human effort alone but by the power of God. On the way to that city the people of God gain a wealth of "wisdom and experience in making and sustaining the ecosystems of the common life."[55] But before congregations can begin to do such duty they will need to be *formed* differently out of, and then back into, the world around them. The road to disestablishment, that is moving toward a new age in the history of the church, lies not merely in conceptualizing the difference between the old and the new, but in shaping congregations in new forms of communal practice, with a vivid awareness of what is at stake in doing so.

I am well aware, of course, how quickly some words become clichés. "Community" is an excellent example. It is, as one British critic has said, "the propaganda of optimists everywhere."[56] The same thing will no doubt soon happen to the new watchword, "practice." But this is a perennial intellectual phenomenon. A given terminology rises, seems apt, quickly becomes a fad, and disappears again, before we have had a chance to think about the realities it seeks to articulate. That could be the case here. Let us try very briefly to see what those who use these words actually make of them. More will be said about practice in chapters 3 and 4

Visions for gathering communities of Christian practice in a postmodern or post-Westphalian world are now being deployed in a variety of ways. One finds positions that repristinate aspects of the "left wing of the Reformation" (Stanley Hauerwas and John Howard Yoder), visions of religio-moral ethnicity in the Orthodox tradition (Vigen Guroian), "paleo-orthodox" stances focused on the testimony of the early councils and fathers of the undivided church (Thomas Oden), communities of scholars gathered around traditional catholic teaching (the "Pro Ecclesia" movement: Carl Braaten and Robert Jenson), journals such as *First Things* and *The New Oxford Review*, and much more. One encounters alliances between different sectors of this new theological-practical communitarianism, as between certain Protestant evangelicals and certain Roman Catholics. I would place in the same context—however different the theological content—proposals for theologically informed common life that center on different sectors of the women's movement as well as the Afro-American, Hispanic, and Asian communities.

These proposals draw near to one another because they are able to bring different theological traditions to bear on what believers *do* in practice. This is not "doctrine divides, service unites" (the unofficial motto of the 1925 Stockholm Conference on Life and Work) all over again. The doing in question now includes everything involved in acting out the faith: teaching the tradition, celebrating the sacraments, seeking justice, protecting the earth. Evidence that doctrinal traditions may converge in such a *comprehensive* understanding of doing can be found in the already mentioned book *Practicing Our Faith* edited by Dorothy Bass.[57] Here writers representing a wide range of backgrounds—Roman Catholic, Presbyterian, United Church of Christ, Methodist, Episcopal, Christian Methodist Episcopal, Lutheran, Society of Friends—present essays on some twelve sectors of Christian practice.[58] The spirit of communitarian moral formation is palpable throughout.

Not all forms of emphasis on practice, of course, stress *moral* practice. One may say that, in the whole range of practices mentioned in *Practicing*, some seem more "moral" in the ordinary sense of that word than others. But surely doing justice is a practice just as much as keeping the Sabbath or teaching the content of tradition. The line between the "moral" and the "ritual" (so beloved of an older generation of Pentateuch scholars) becomes increasingly blurred. It can be said today that the more one sees moral behavior as depending on specific communal allegiances rather than on publicly available forms of reasoning, the more the *whole* life of the *ekklesia*—doctrine, liturgy, personal spirituality, service, social witness— becomes a moral reality in its own right. If the community of faith is the primary source of moral consciousness, then *everything* about that community's life, not just specific commandments or ethical reflection as such, contributes to that end.

I believe it is also true that the more clearly it is seen that moral questions today involve the sorts of conduct that make for the well-being, or perhaps even the survival, of the human race, and not merely what it is proper for individuals to do in a world of stable social values, the more clearly moral in significance the *entire* life of the faith community becomes. There are situations in which simply *being* the church of Jesus Christ in a world like this one is the supremely moral act.

By whatever route the church may come to fulfillment as moral community, it cannot be content to be merely an organization located at some point along the worldly spectrum of social-political ideas. It belongs to a *different oikoumene*, and from that vantage point seeks to hold open space in which the world can come to itself. As Nicholas Lash writes:

> The church, God's gathered people, gives visible expression, sacramental utterance, to God's promised healing of the human race. This particular people finds its identity in the exercise of its vocation to narrate, announce, and dramatize, the origin, identity, and destiny of humankind as common life, *koinonia*, communion in God.[59]

But such communities of God's gathered people will pursue their vocations in a variety of different ways. They are likely to be just as diverse as the historic Christian confessions and communions are now. The new communities will need to be in communion with a larger church and with one another. Appropriating the creative energies of numerous communities of Christian moral practice will call for a profound new form of ecumenical visioning. Such relationships are going to be more, rather than less, critical than they have been up to now. Especially among highly energetic communities of this kind, one has to sort out what is authentic and destined to be lasting from what merely represents the current enthusiasms of theorists or leaders. Desperately needed is a larger context of church in which moral challenges of this kind can be received in their full impact, placed in context, subjected to criticism, abandoned if necessary, and—where appropriate—taken on board as permanent insight.

Thus, to the list of practices already named, *ecumenical* practice needs to be added. In fact, ecumenical practice needs to be the context of all the other practices. Whether this can come to be true in the average congregation is open to question. But, then, the issue has always been whether serious Christian commitment requires one to supplement ordinary congregational life with gatherings of the more adventurous. Is the issue of ecclesiology and ethics to be solved today, as it has been before, by there being two kinds of Christian societies, the one the worshiping congregation of ordinary, moderate, women and men, and the other the distinctive community of the particularly committed ones? Will some ecumenical version of the *ecclesiola in ecclesia*—the comunity of focused vision witnessing within the larger communion of the church—be the answer to the call for Christian difference today?[60]

However matters turn out, the period after the Westphalian Age will have a character of its own. What that will be depends on events yet to unfold. But once the churches are no longer in thrall to centuries-old politico-social arrangements, once they are no longer only organizations for helping individuals and families in their private lives, once they are no longer merely playing legitimating roles for declining nation-states, once they no longer represent sharply distinguished confessional groups owing their boundaries in part to the personal choices of seventeenth-century sovereigns, then anything is possible. What about a global household of practicing, witnessing, Christian communities? What about *all* that is implied in the word *oikoumene*?

TWO

Seeing the World
Through Ecumenical Lenses

Beyond the Westphalian compromise lies a new ecumenical perspective on the world. Although ecumenism achieved its present institutional form at the hands of churches living within the now waning modern paradigm, its greatest achievement has been to open windows for seeing beyond the Westphalian arrangements. Ecumenism has helped Christian faith communities imagine how they could live together toward the encompassing horizon of the *missio Dei*, of God's mission to humankind. It has only begun to achieve realizations of that vision.

I continue then to develop the argument that constitutes this book's central thread. In pursuit of God's mission, Christian faith communities of every sort are called to be anticipations of a coming, morally formed, *oikoumene* of humankind, a "household" so inclusive that at the end it becomes a "city" in which God, Godself, may come to dwell (Rev. 21: 3). An ecumenical mode of discourse thus offers the most promising context for many diverse communities of Christian moral practice to move in concert toward that fulfillment.

Institutional Ecumenism: A Weak Reed?

But is this a credible claim in the light of what the word *ecumenical* has, for many people today, come to mean? The word has in ordinary speech become loaded with institutional and sometimes also ideological overtones. It evokes thoughts of councils of churches, church unity negotiations, bilateral dialogues, and the like. But not everyone interested in the church as moral community is also interested in such arcane ecclesiastical matters. Furthermore the term in some circles has become (I think by deliberate intention of the movement's detractors) almost an antonym to the word *evangelical*. It has come to mean "liberal" in the pejorative contemporary sense of a left-leaning, free-spending, addiction to meddlesome social engineering that neglects saving souls in favor of (often unsuccessful) schemes for saving societies. Is *that* the kind of morality intended here? Some readers may wonder why they are being led in an ecumenical direction at all.

And are not the more conservative, less activist, forms of ecumenism—pursued mainly in various kinds of interinstitutional negotiations—themselves largely things of the past, their unitive projects underfinanced, confused, moribund? Is all this not a lost cause, an irrelevancy, a plaything of older, now discredited, church leaders, a needless drain on already hard-pressed church budgets? Do these enterprises not call for expensive structural changes to do what is being done perfectly well already? Some say today that the reality of friendship and cooperation among local congregations has simply overtaken formal ecclesiological categories. They say we should just declare that these things aren't problems anymore, and get on with our business.

In some ways the people who argue this case (and they are many) are ahead of the ecumenical dialoguers and negotiators, in some ways not. They are ahead in following the leadings of the Spirit, which simply ignore the lack of formal recognition between certain communions, which encourage a sheer neighborliness that naturally extends to sharing at the Table of the Lord. But these same people are often behind the dialoguers in that they do not grasp the total vision that animates ecumenical work. Neighborliness, amiable and even Spirit-filled as it often is, is frequently content to leave the status quo unchallenged and unchanged. But the divisions that remain among the churches, anachronistic and often technical as they are, block wholehearted pursuit *together* of an ecumenical vision for humankind.

Granted that enthusiasm for the institutional ecumenism the churches have known these many years has reached a low point. I argue here that the questions we are now addressing have it in them to help renew the ecumenical movement itself and set it on a new course. It is ironic that an effort to achieve some form of practical consolidation and theological concord—not to say organic unity—among the Christian churches of the world has gained momentum only in the final years of the Christendom mindset, at a point in time when the churches have already lost much of the cultural influence they once had.

The Christian ecumenical movement of the late nineteenth century and the first half of the twentieth could indeed be interpreted as the last gasp of a Constantinian or Westphalian form of Christendom as church leaders began to sense their accustomed position in the world crumbling under fragmenting, secularizing forces. Certainly the successful missionary efforts associated with that early ecumenism can now be seen as an unwittingly farsighted strategy to establish beachheads for the faith in the southern hemisphere against the day when the churches might lose their hold on the North and the West.

One doubts, however, that much of this fin-de-Christendom sense was in the minds of ecumenical leaders at the time. At the close of the nineteenth century the mood seems to have been, if not triumphalistic, at least highly confident. Kenneth Scott Latourette could speak of the nineteenth as "the great century," meaning the period of "abounding vitality and unprecedented expansion" between 1815 and 1914.[1] The Edinburgh World Missionary Conference of 1910 was a harvesting of the fruits of this "great" ecclesiastical and missionary epoch. It envisioned still greater harvests to come. It projected the entire human race as object of an evangelistic effort embodying God's mission to the world of that time. Many, if not most, of those present at Edinburgh appear to have believed that this evangelistic mission entailed a *cultural* Christianization of the world: that is, the conversion of peoples and nations to expressions of Christian faith resembling those of the West, at least in outward form and expression. Many believed, indeed, that the presentation of the gospel in these terms to every nation—if not a response by every individual—could be accomplished in their own generation.[2] This 1910 meeting not only gave an early platform to many persons who would turn out to be leaders in the twentieth-century ecumenical movement; it also saw the beginnings of the movements that would become "Faith and Order" and "Life and Work," not to speak of the International Missionary Council, integrated into the World Council of Churches only in 1961.

For many years after 1910, ecumenism in its actual embodiments remained essentially a North Atlantic phenomenon dominated by the leaders of established Protestant denominations. These leaders took for granted an influential role in the societies of which they were a part. It is instructive, for example, to read the minutes of the Oxford Conference on Life and Work of 1937, and to realize that the delegates assumed that the principal way in which the Christian witness for peace should be furthered in a world preparing for war was by high-level consultation with governments. Access to such circles on the part of leading Protestant "churchmen" was taken for granted. There is little sense in these debates that the very circumstances and assumptions that made such access and influence possible were even then beginning to crumble.

The more than sixty years that have followed these pre-World War II conferences have seen great achievements, notably in the Faith and Order and Life and Work movements out of which the present dialogue on ecclesiology and ethics has come. The fifty-year career of the World Council of Churches (founded in 1948) will be justly celebrated at Harare, Zimbabwe, in December 1998. Still, I believe that ecumenism has been institutionalized, however unavoidably, in models that tie it to an order of things now passing away.

This did not occur without warnings, notably from Karl Barth, who already at Amsterdam in 1948 pointed out the dangers of a *corpus Christianum* model. Nor did it proceed without keen recognition of the problem on the part of leadership. Still, the WCC become a reflection of social roles of its most influential member churches. We are *still* seeking to break out of the *corpus Christianum*. I agree with Geiko Müller-Fahrenholz when he writes:

> I am convinced that we are only at the beginning of what can truly be called an ecumenical movement, even though some people predict its imminent demise. The ecumenical structures that have emerged in the 20th century are only a first stage. If stagnation has set in, the main reason is that hitherto attempts have been made to merge two obsolete organizational models: the traditional church pattern as it has developed historically in its denominational and cultural location; and the global principle of international companies.[3]

It is becoming plain, among other things, that ecumenical bodies must do much more than furnish travel budgets and facilities for representatives of denominations interested in church union talks, conciliar agendas, and the like, carried on in the manner of the many other governmental and nongovernmental organizations with which the WCC is surrounded on its Geneva hilltop. I speak as one who has benefited from, and I hope contributed to, many an international consultation set up on this basis. I have learned enough from such meetings to know we need a new way. The churches are in a life-or-death competition with other global movements that lay claim to the human spirit. Evangelization of the nations, in the sense of cultural Christianization, is no longer a feasible goal. Radical religious and cultural pluralisms are here to stay. The *oikoumene* needs new formats for understanding and responding to God's mission to humankind.

The Missio Dei *at the Turn of the Millennia*

In many ways the churches are today in a position analogous to their stance on the eve of Edinburgh 1910, only with much less confidence and clarity of vision. They are evaluating the results of nearly a century of further missionary effort and ecumenical work, and again seeking to gather the results into some new initiative. But while the missionary effort prior to 1910 led, with great energy, toward institutional ecumenism as we have known it, the subsequent harvest has been meager in comparison. The present generation does not approach a new millennium with nineteenth-century enthusiasm, but rather with late-twentieth-century questions about where ecumenical mission has gone wrong and about what the future holds. Church unity negotiations have stalled. Support for ecumenical organizations has declined. Church leaders are far more aware than the Edinburgh delegates were of being at the end of a historical epoch, and more aware of the need to build an ecumenism that is decisively new. "Movements which [seem] to threaten the very existence of the faith" are again "calling forth all [our] inner resources."[4] Beset by debilitating disagreements, the churches are looking for a vision of the world persuasive and powerful enough to help project a new sense of *oikoumene*, a new action-oriented vision of humanity in the light of the gospel, in which people can believe and which can once again give coherence to their actions.

What is the mission of God to the human race today? A substantially new ecumenical situation calls for efforts to rethink the whole point and purpose of the calling to be part of this mission.[5] I find congenial several aspects of David Bosch's vision in *Believing in the Future.*[6] Bosch's argument that a missiology of Western culture must be ecological, countercultural, ecumenical, contextual, lay-oriented, and local is right on the mark. So is his emphasis on cultural analysis of the postmodern scene. Konrad Raiser's earlier book, *Ecumenism in Transition,*[7] offers guidelines which remain important. Among other things, Raiser proposes the vision of humanity as God's "household of life," a notion then enriched in the work of Geiko Müller-Fahrenholz and developed still further in this book, especially in chapter 6.

As Raiser indicates, a key to the ecumenical future may well lie in renewed appreciation for the range of meanings and derivations connected with the Greek word *oikoumene.* This term obviously existed long before it was taken up by the movement of Christian churches that has given it its primary contemporary meaning.[8] The word is derived from the root *oikos,* meaning "house" or "household." The Greeks understood the *oikoumene* as the household of civilization as they understood it. Beyond its borders were barbarians who shared neither the language nor the culture of Mediterranean civilization. The ancient Roman Empire understood its *oecumenicus* or "inhabited world" as the sphere of its political, military, and economic jurisdiction, and hence as the space of an imperial intention. Ancient usage already shows that *oikoumene,* while it literally means "the inhabited world as a whole" and occurs only in the grammatical singular, can in actual usage mean many different things depending on the ways in which it is interpreted. It is the world of human beings seen as having a certain coherence expressive of the observer's intentionality, that is, his or her construal of the world as a space for action.[9]

The ancient Greek interpretation of the *oikoumene* (linguistic, cultural, literary) differed from the Roman one (military, legal, administrative). And, increasingly today, human enterprises of every kind have "ecumenical" intentions in the sense that they see the whole inhabited world as a field for product marketing, for cultural conquest, for scientific discourse, for military planning, or for any one of several other objectives. Each person, one could even say, has some sense of the whole world of other persons: hence a kind of personal *oikoumene* in which others are seen as fellow voyagers through life, or as objects of antipathy, avarice, concern, or love, as the case may be.

The contemporary world has been and continues to be the crossroads of many such "ecumenical" visions.[10] The communist *internationale*, while it existed, was both a vision for the inhabited world, and a world of values for its adherents to inhabit. Today there are new *internationales:* the world as seen and inhabited by transnational corporations, as seen and inhabited by international bankers, as seen and inhabited by environmental scientists, as seen and inhabited by military planners. The list could go on. Should not the churches project a similar, yet far more profound, vision of an *oikoumene* of fulfillment of God's purposes for the human race? And do the churches not need institutions, of some sort, for trying to make the vision concrete?

The ecumenical question for today then is not only one concerning the effectiveness or usefulness of certain interchurch organizations, important as they may be. Nor is it simply a matter of the kind of political activism that some associate with "ecumenism." It is whether Christian faith itself, by its very nature, involves some vision of the coherence of the human realm in the light of God's intentions for it. And, if so, how should that idea find its fulfillment in the contemporary world?

A number of answers to this institutional question have been, and continue to be, given: from loose linkages among essentially independent "evangelical" congregations to various sorts of high-level ecclesiastical geopolitics. This book argues that one vital strand in any such fulfillment must be a moral intentionality. And conversely, if the church is to be a moral community at all, it must be so in an ecumenical way. And that requires pursuit of further meanings of the term *oikoumene*. It will turn out that it also means the global "household" in which people live, and that in turn this "household" requires a certain kind of "economics" or "household management." Only at this global, inclusive level of understanding can one grasp what the church's fundamental moral nature *is*, and what it can therefore mean for humankind.

It follows that a conception of the *missio Dei* for today must bring together all these seemingly disparate subject matters into one complex vision. It must concern churches in their ecumenical relationships, but also the ethics of the human household. It must be about international economics, and also about care for the global human environment, or ecology. All these terms are derived from the same Greek root. One properly understands ecumenism in the Christian sense only when one realizes that it is a moral alternative to the *oikoumene* understood in other, exploitative or militaristic ways. To speak of the church as moral community one must understand all these matters in their interactions. Not only are they linked linguistically—which is, after all, an accident of the way the Greek language has deployed the derivatives of one very valuable root—they are also related in actual, practical encounters. Christian ecumenism thus needs to be seen as a path one can choose to follow among the alternative spiritualities—that is, ways of envisioning and living out the perceived meanings of life—available in our time.

The most important alternative spiritualities today are other transnational visions, rival interpretations of the *oikoumenes*, which threaten to "colonize," indeed to occupy as if militarily, human life-worlds in every nation, on every continent. There is a new "systems" colonialism abroad on the earth; and churches, far from traveling *with* a vigorous colonialism, as was the norm in 1910, need to stand *against* the new colonialisms of our own time.

Any strategy for being part of the mission of God to humankind thus needs to be based on cultural, economic, and political analyses of what is going on in the world: on some vision of what is going on with human beings. Chapter 1 has already begun to offer such an analysis, exploring both the challenges and possibilities of postmodernism, arguing that morality must arise primarily from the cultures of faith communities, and suggesting that humanity is now in a situation in which moral awareness has become a matter of life or death for the race itself. This makes the relationship between ecclesiology and ethics a central question for our time: for that question has to do with the very nature of ethics and the very being of the church, simultaneously considered.

The Rise of the Great World Systems

I offer now a very compressed, and necessarily selective, sketch of the changed conditions under which we must now conceive the church's task of furthering the *missio Dei*. I have spoken of many rival interpretations of the *oikoumene* as a human action field. Now is the time to speak further of some of these rival interpretations, and of the impact of what they do upon human well-being, indeed upon the well-being of the whole created order of which we human beings are a part.

ENLIGHTENMENT LEGACIES

I argued in chapter 1 that Enlightenment thought buried the ethics of virtue only to discover that its own philosophical foundations as a universal form of human life are crumbling. The resulting moral pragmatism offers little defense against the consequences of contemporary social practices. In fact, two Enlightenment legacies are very much alive in this postmodern time. They are, first, the ideal of human autonomy as such, and, second, the technological capacities by which human beings may exercise their autonomy as they wish. From these sources the West has derived a capacity to develop many specialized fields of expertise and activity. These become global communities of practice, which quickly become independent value-worlds with their own rules, methods, procedures, and goals. Such global systems of human activity move forward without serious concern for human consequences that lie outside their operational frames of reference. The industrial-economic consequences of the Enlightenment are today in the saddle with virtually no meaningful moral restraints to keep them from compromising basic values of human life as such.

I am referring, of course, to transnational corporations, global communications systems, the world of international banking, the systems of governmental agencies, and even the worlds of science and technology. Each of these realms of practice sees the world principally as a supplier of human and material resources to be exploited for purposes of the system in question. These global universes of practice are juggernauts. They are not restrained merely by external critical analyses or by political protests. From within any one of these worlds, thoughts belonging to other worlds appear nonsensical: they "do not compute." Each deserves to be called a self-contained and often self-sufficient interpretation of the *oikoumene* because, for those involved, the "inhabited world" quite simply *is* what the system in question makes of it.

Furthermore, each of these systems has its own internal "morality," its own internal rules of good practice. A term such as "business ethics" *could* mean the study of how businesses should be accountable to public standards of moral behavior, if applicable public standards existed. But in practice "business ethics" often refers to the internal practices of business governed by rules that apply only in that particular arena of activity. The field of "business ethics" commonly has little to do with the good for human beings as such, and much to do with practices that promote "good business."

Thus every human practice comes to have its own "virtues" instrumental to the practice concerned. But what happens when a practice becomes so powerful that it begins to dominate the human world: when, instead of being merely the combination of skills and activities involved in playing chess or football, painting portraits, or writing history (MacIntyre's examples), it becomes the practice or practices of organizing the world economically?

Global economic management clearly requires great knowledge and skill. It involves activities which qualify as practices in MacIntyre's terms: we deal here with historically ramified cooperative activities ranging from investing to currency trading to raising capital for ever new ventures. These practices in themselves may be thought to be morally neutral. One might say that it is the use to which they are put that makes the difference. But MacIntyre seems to suggest that the goods "internal" to such organized activities (e.g., investing *profitably*), as well as their "external" goods or consequences, are subject to moral judgment. But it is not clear how this is can be so apart from some sort of larger narrative of what human life is for. Absent such a *telos* (whether of the Spirit or of "natural law"), Aristotle, the philosopher of virtue gives way to Nietzsche, the philosopher of power. We learn then that there are "virtues" internal to totalitarian practice too—relentless surveillance, ruthlessness, a passion for order. Today, certain economic practices, with the "virtues" internal to them, could become instruments of a will to power so overwhelming as to threaten human well-being on this planet.

The systematic ordering of power in various globalized realms of practice is not happening in the way Nietzsche expected (although Rupert Murdoch may indeed think of himself as an *Übermensch*), but it is happening in a way that impacts all human life. It is said, for example, that a major share of the earth's capabilities for public communication and information is now controlled by five or so giant transnational corporations. And the stronger of these will no doubt soon swallow up the weaker in further acquisitions and mergers of the sort that have built these empires, these visions of *oikoumene*, in the first instance.

It is not hard to see why, in such a world as this, traditional moral codes are breaking down in the public world and are under siege in the private realm as well. Here the organized powers of the state, of the market, and of the systems they represent, are invading and "colonizing"[11] the human life-world—families, schools, churches, and such. There is no longer much space left in which the traditional sorts of personal morality can flourish. And Aristotelian virtues are not the only ones in trouble. So are the virtues of liberalism from which have been derived the principles of autonomous citizenship and human rights. Each colonizing world system today imposes on us its own teleology: whether that be a teleology of economic growth, or of profit maximization, or of technological progress. What really shapes our human behavior is the human *practice* we are part of, and what shapes the practice is its secular "ecumenical" intentionality, whether that be a world of human beings fully entertained, fully exploited, or fully controlled by whatever ideology serves the interests in power.

ECONOMICS AS MASTER METAPHOR

It is already apparent in this description that an economic interpretation of the *oikoumene* has become the master metaphorical context for understanding human behavior in our times.[12] The global economic system is the system in which all other systems operate. And the market proceeds by a kind of blind logic of its own. The vectors that result from hundreds of thousands of economic decisions each hour of the day or night are unpredictable, imponderable. We see the paradox: the market is that which we cannot today do *without*, and yet we do not know what to do *with* it either. What, after all, is the goal of all this money-making activity?

On the one hand, the wealth-generating engine of the "new world economic order" has accomplished many good things for humankind. It is hard to imagine the world without it. Economic competition is better than warfare, and in some cases can replace it. An example is instructive. Israeli citizens today are finding that the pursuit of prosperity limits the allure of militarism. The acquisition of wealth and the desire to keep it is a powerful restraining force on territorially based fanaticism. A Middle Eastern co-prosperity sphere involving both Israelis and Arabs *could* be within reach, provided the peace process can be revived (the moment of writing finds it all but dead) and sustained long enough to achieve stable results.

But the pursuit of prosperity inevitably involves one in a system of global intercommunication in which the money nexus replaces any conceivable spiritual nexus, giving support to the vision of the Chicago economist Gary Becker who won the Nobel Prize for a book[13] arguing that the most fundamental and ubiquitous form of human reasoning is the cost-benefit analysis. For Becker the new human being is an embodied calculator. The rational universalism of the Enlightenment *philosophes* is thus replaced by computerized networks over which members of an economic elite pursue incredibly large, and often esoteric, financial transactions. For the Enlightenment, every human being at least possessed the potential to join the kingdom of reason. But the new international economic order is such that a few tycoons and international corporations control the new monetary rationality, in principle reducing all others to being producers or consumers, bureaucrats or therapists.

Consider what the global money nexus can do. Capital is well-nigh infinitely mobile by means of electronic transfer across the surface of the earth. Whole industries can be moved to regions with lower employment costs. But the people who earn their livelihoods from these industries are not similarly mobile. The movement of jobs and capital from one place to another at the stroke of an executive's pen or computer key often has disastrous consequences for the livelihood of workers.

International economics now dominate the policies of governments across the globe. A salient example: the economics of the unification of Europe seem to compete at the moment with the economics of welfare within particular European countries. The election of Lionel Jospin as prime minister of France in 1997 on a platform promising the protection of generous French social services threatened for a time to compromise France's ability to qualify economically to participate in the proposed Euro-currency. Very similar internal economic requirements are imposed on nations by international bankers or the International Monetary Fund as conditions for development loans. Qualifying for such loans, and then paying the interest on them year after year (often amounting to many times the original loan amount), has led many nations, especially in the southern hemisphere, to internal economic measures that have devastated the lives of the poor. Now, with the threatened collapse of economies across Asia, the cycle of borrowing bail-out funds begins again.

Furthermore, it is plain that decisions, once purely political or military in character, now must bow before economic considerations. Economic embargoes are safer than military operations, but the capacity of a nation like the United States to use such tactics against, say, Iraq, depends on the economic cooperation—which may not be forthcoming—of other countries that trade with that nation. The government of the United States can be frustrated in its political objectives by its international trading partners or by decisions of the central bankers of a number of countries. The effort to move China toward greater recognition of human rights (including religious liberty for dissident house-church Christians) is frustrated by the desire of American and other corporations to keep the trading door open. Or consider the apparent willingness of many citizens of Hong Kong, now returned to Chinese control, to accept an abrogation of their political rights so long as economic freedom is maintained.

Furthermore, all the resulting production and international trade means nothing unless there are customers for the products concerned. Workers need to be turned into good consumers. They are being exploited by advertising designed to create demand, and not always for products that are really needed. The artificially created demand for infant formula (often unavoidably prepared with tainted water) in the face of findings that breast-feeding is in most cases better for the child's health is a scandal that apparently continues. The impact of such products and the advertising that goes with them is an assault upon cultural values in almost every part of the world. Consider this TV ad for athletic shoes on a Hong Kong channel seen late at night in a Korean hotel room in January 1996. A teenage boy races out of school toward the basketball court. A rock beat plays in the background. The boy gets off a jump shot, the camera moving in to freeze-frame upon on his brand-new shoes in mid-air. The voice-over, in English, breathlessly proclaims: "Your grandmother won't approve, but you've got to keep up!"

The international merchandiser makes no attempt to hide this attack on traditional culture, this willingness to set the generations at odds in the name of profit. Artificially raising the demand for ever-new pairs of basketball shoes is bad enough, but there are even more destructive commodities: tobacco in the civilian sector, and armaments in the public sector. But all this goes back to a form of the profit motive, which, on analysis, can be seen to be a morally unchallenged extension of the liberally sanctioned autonomy of the economic actor armed with new technology and information-handling techniques, served up on a bed of platitudinous pragmatism possessing no capacity to raise questions, to resist.

AN ARRAY OF POSSIBLE SCENARIOS
Attitudes of this sort could rapidly escalate to a point at which we will be faced with moral questions of a gravity and complexity that would have

been inconceivable to previous generations: questions having to do with the sheer survival of the human race, or at least of human civilization. Here, for example, is a possible scenario, one which could bring disaster to much of the human race. The global economic system (as George Soros has repeatedly suggested)[14] could begin to collapse from its own internal contradictions. Artificially induced consumer demand in the developing world could far exceed the capacity of southern-hemisphere economies to satisfy it. This could produce internal unrest, which could be fanned into violence by warlords and other ambitious politicians. Such development would undoubtedly cause intense immigration pressure on wealthier nations. Such conditions would certainly accelerate environmental degradation as communities and cultures struggled to survive in an increasingly anarchic human situation. The distinction between state-sponsored warfare and gang-type violence by members of religious and ethnic groups might then virtually disappear. The legal and economic structures of the world could begin to break down. Soon the globe could be plunged into a general conflict: for all intents and purposes "a war of all against all."[15]

So much for the worst-case scenario. At the very least, we late-twentieth-century people may be doing ourselves in less dramatically but with similar ultimate results simply by despoiling both the cultural and the physical environments in which we live. A culture of crime and violence has in different ways captured the commercial environments of the former Soviet Union, the crowded urban favelas of many third world nations, and the tribal territories being fought over in several African nations that gained their independence from Western colonial powers only a generation ago. Despite recently reported statistical improvements, a similar violent culture, born of the drug trade, still dominates the inner cities of the United States. A comparable culture of violence infects our relationships with the natural world. We seem unable to persuade third world nations not to repeat our environmental mistakes. Not only are our own examples unconvincing, but urging care in these matters often looks like a thinly disguised attempt to impede the industrial development to which these nations believe they have a right.

Issues and threats such as these transcend individual decision-making and they also transcend moral and ethical categories inherited from previous generations. They are of a dimension that can only be met by co-ordinated movements in many places to save human life on this planet, and the living planet itself, from a fate of humanity's own collective making. Such movements would need to find some way of overcoming the fragmentation of moral reflection and the competition of national and cultural allegiances observed in these pages and elsewhere.

Many non-governmental organizations, secular and religious alike, seek to address these questions. But the more comprehensive they are, the more they themselves become scenes for reenactments of the sorts of contention that divide us, and the more vulnerable they become to economic and ideological co-optation by establishment institutions. This seems to happen quite regularly. NGOs tend to begin their work full of idealism and then, out of necessity, accept money and other favors from corporations, or even (as has been the case recently, particularly in Latin America) from the World Bank.[16] This gradually incorporates them into the economic system whose assaults on human well-being they may have started out to resist.

Moral issues, formerly seen as having to do mainly with personal conduct within stable orders of value, have in these ways now become radicalized. They now have to do with the life, or the death, of the human race as such: indeed with the fate of the created order in which we live. The planetary scale of our human struggle presents challenges beyond any the churches have faced before.[17] Before we can even speak of a twenty-first-century "global civilization," life together on this planet will need shared visions and institutional expressions for which we have few really relevant precedents.

The tissue of human life-together has now become supremely vulnerable. It could make an *ultimate* difference whether or not we protect the environment, or succeed in avoiding nuclear war, or prevent the global economic order from becoming a gulag for the overwhelming majority of human beings who own no controlling interests in the globe's multinational corporations and media empires.

Early in this decade Jonathan Schell wrote a book[18] on the nuclear threat making the now-familiar point that today, for the first time in human history, we have the means for annihilating all human life, and perhaps all life of any kind, on earth. Schell so dramatized the point as to make it unforgettable. Make one mistake and there will be no more children, no more novels, no more poems, no more violin concertos, no more scientific discoveries, no more of *anything* that has made human life worth living. And, on top of that, there will be no more memory that these things *ever* existed.

The nuclear threat, as we all know, no longer arises from the confrontation of two global superpowers, but it is far from over. The threat of nuclear holocaust from miscalculation by any one of the existing nuclear powers caught up in regional conflicts, or by one or another rogue state desiring to blackmail the West, is still very real. And the danger of nuclear war is only one of several sorts of dangers that confront us. The sorts of global challenges we face today are not mere policy questions: they articulate "ultimate questions of human life"[19] with their inevitable religious dimensions, indeed *theological* issues concerning what we believe about the origin, meaning, and ending of human life on earth.

One way to dramatize the nature of these new moral challenges is to note how vastly amplified are the possible consequences of practical choices that seem relatively routine at the time they are made. The field of epidemiology, of all things, offers an insight that can be either troubling or inspiring, depending on one's point of view. It seems that for many diseases there is a threshold level of infection in a given population below which the process of person-to-person transmission of the disease will not escalate into an epidemic, and, conversely, above which it is likely to do so. The trouble is that for many diseases it is not known precisely what the crucial rate of infection is. Certain social scientists have argued that the same threshold phenomena also hold for social ills such as urban crime. A gradual increase in the crime level, passing a certain crucial point, can suddenly take off into an epidemic of criminal activity. But, conversely, a small decrease, passing the same crucial point, can start the crime statistics decisively downward. One is reminded of the slightly exaggerated application of fractal geometry which some science journalist has proposed for illuminating what causes the world's weather: extremely small inputs can have vast consequences in the system. A leaf falls, and the breezes stirred by its fluttering passage combine with other forces until they produce a hurricane. A minor mistake in diplomacy leads to resentments in a nuclearly armed nation-state that leads to global holocaust.

Of course, neither in producing the weather nor in the conduct of diplomacy does any single small *or* large input function alone. Many leaves fall, but, even so, their effect is undoubtedly overwhelmed by a few sunspots. Many diplomatic mistakes are made, but, even so, their effect is probably outweighed by perceptions of overriding national interests. But the point is that moral decisions are no longer *merely* personal in their consequences. The consequences of selfishness used to be limited to the persons concerned, a few families, or at most a small town. Moral failures used to be seen mainly as personal departures from a generally understood and stable order. In epidemiological terms, this means that in the past most instances of economic greed or mistreatment of workers led to infection rates below the epidemic level. They could usually (but not always) be contained. Even warfare used to be containable. But the systems implications of human behavior today means that societies are much nearer to an infection rate likely to break out into an epidemic, or even a pandemic. Now human actions, sufficiently multiplied, can threaten the very existence of order in human life-together, and therefore the very existence of human meaning.

But the reverse may also be true, and this should give us hope. A relatively modest improvement in conditions of social justice, a small amelioration in economic conditions among the poor, *could* start matters moving in the right direction. Our difficulty is that we do not know where our societies *are* along the scales of values concerned: whether we are near conditions that could in time lead to some sort of social salvation or near conditions likely to deteriorate toward some sort of social catastrophe, or, perhaps in different ways, close to *both* possibilities.

Such uncertainties boggle the mind. We citizens of the late-twentieth-century world cannot face them with any confidence, knowing that we live in an age in which the traditional foundations of moral vision—having to do with the very nature of the human being—are disappearing from view. It is no longer clear how we should proceed from things we think we know to the imponderable issues we face. Where in all this is the network of human beings *as* human beings? Is there a systemic logic of the human life-world waiting to be applied (e.g., Jürgen Habermas's "theory of communicative action"), or should past failures in this regard (e.g., Karl Marx's "dialectical materialism") warn us away? Who knows what the interests of humankind needing protection really are, or whether or not all human beings ultimately have the same interests? In the nature of the case there needs at least to be a community in which human beings can come together to *ask* such questions. Who makes space for that questioning? Who stands in for that possibility?

A New Interpretation of Christian Oikoumene?

I have been calling the different versions of global economic activity implicit interpretations of the *oikoumene*. This has not been a careless or
perverse use of a word rendered sacrosanct by years of Christian ecumenism. It has been a linguistic device for making an indispensable point.
There is need for another *oikoumene* based not on the economics of world
systems but on the "economics" of God.[20] It may seem a surprising move
now to propose the Christian *oikoumene* as a response—on the same playing field as it were—to the economic conundrums of human life on this
planet. But that is exactly what I want to do.

As Christians, we must prepare to play some responsible role in forming
a twenty-first-century civilization. Such a *global* civilization can in the
nature of the case have no precedents, no antecedents. This will be a
civilization in which systems and practices—the global market economy,
the system of nation-states, the media—go forward without any conscious
moral reason behind them (e.g., without the sort of moral principles Immanuel Kant thought intrinsic to rational agents) but only their own intrinsic momentum, their own *inner* logics.

These practices are now linked together in a nexus of activity, a complex world system, which threatens to strangle us. Precisely because the
postmodern practices of economy, state, media go forward blindly, inexorably, destructively, the globally interdependent civilization they create
needs, as a counterbalance, another kind of nexus: the sense of global
human solidarity I have spoken about. By this solidarity I mean at the
minimum a *pragmatic* sense of who we are together and how we live
together, even if it is not based on universally recognized first principles.
Perhaps the Christian church is better positioned to provide *that* sense of
relationship to the "other" than it is to wrestle with particular policy
questions in the public realm. We need a broader, more energetic, vision
of the human solidarity in which we must seek to live as active, distinctively traditioned, participants.

It is important to take note of how far ecumenism has already gone in
identifying the problem of damage to people's lives caused by the great
world systems, driven as they are by economic forces. The World Council
of Churches has taken much criticism for its preoccupation with political

and economic matters, especially from conservative interests in the West. The original North Atlantic ecumenical constituency, furthermore, has been slow to grasp the economic and political concerns of the newer membership constituency, churches of the third world, now increasingly simply called "the South." A preoccupation sometimes blamed on the Geneva staff of the WCC is in fact the direct result of the Council's expanding membership. Newer member churches have demanded the right to be heard. Where does ecumenism stand on the matter of global economic oppression now?

For a generation or more, ecumenical concern about the *oikoumene* in economic terms has been formulated as "liberation theology." That school has taught a solidarity of *resistance* to oppressive and dehumanizing forces. The enemy has been identifiable. Class concepts and Marxist analysis picture a world in which the capitalist system as such threatens to shut down human life. In some versions of this scheme the energy comes from a psychology of victimization and the resentments that flow from it. In other versions, notably Paulo Freire's *Pedagogy of the Oppressed*,[21] those who see themselves only as victims are urged to become the subjects of their own historical destiny.

What is to be said of such resistance solidarity now? Liberation theology is in at least its third, perhaps its fourth, stage of conceptual evolution. It has taught us an enormous amount about the lives of human beings in situations other than those of the prosperous West. It has generated a new form of the church, the "base community." The liberation theologies of different continents and human communities—Latin American, African, Asian, North American minorities, feminist—have linked up sufficiently to provide a cross-cultural agenda for a human solidarity coming to be. I think of Robert MacAfee Brown's book *Kairos: Three Prophetic Challenges to the Church*,[22] which seeks to derive precisely such a sense of common humanity emerging in opposition to oppression by showing the close parallels of vision and expression linking liberation documents from South Africa, Latin America, and Asia.[23]

It is only fair to say that the sort of economic analysis offered in the preceding section of this chapter is anticipated in the work of liberation theologians. Indeed, the nub of it can already be found in the writings of the young Karl Marx! But today a more comprehensive intellectual context is needed: one that substitutes the whole of humanity for Marx's

"proletariat," one that protects Christian faith from takeover by any ideology, one that decisively resists co-optation into the agenda of any
totalitarian regime.

Liberation theology itself is evolving into something new, in part along
these lines. This is so in at least three ways. First it has had to adapt to the
collapse of state socialist regimes in the former Soviet Union and Eastern
Europe, and therefore to the discrediting of socialism, if not in theory, at
least in what it has so far turned out to be in practice.[24] I believe that this
adaptation has by now been largely accomplished. Admiration of state
socialist regimes was never a large element in liberation theory. But some
form of chastened socialism as such still stands for many liberation theologians as a political ideal.

Second, liberation theology has lost what confidence it had in Marxist
economics as a foundation discipline. Here there is a clear parallel to the
postmodern deconstruction of democratic foundations in the capitalist
world. Liberation theology has become more simply a biblical theology
used directly to interpret the experience of the poor and gather them into
base communities for worship, study, and action for immediate ends.

Third, class analysis, so prominent in earlier liberationist works, is now
giving way to a new interest in the integrity of cultures, including the
cultures of ethnic minorities and of women, and especially the many cultures and situations of those so often patronizingly lumped together as
"the poor."[25]

A realization is growing that recognition of the multiplicity of human
cultures is more than a capitulation to pluralism or social fragmentation.
It is *also* a means of access to expressions of a more basic level of human
experience than mere economic theory or class analysis can reach, an
opening to "thick descriptions" of what it *is*—in many different situations—to be poor and powerless and afraid, and also to what it *is*—in
equally diverse circumstances—to live in hope. To give only one example:
the American slave narratives currently being studied at several theological
centers are a rich source of awareness not only of *other* humanity but also
of our own humanity. Paradoxically, attention to the many human cultures may make us aware both of what divides us and of what we have in
common.

It will no longer do, moreover, to treat consciousness-raised people in
the base communities, and even less ourselves, as totally alien to the col-

onizing economic forces of today. All of us, rich and poor—first world, second world, and third world, "north" or "south" alike—stand in some sense *within* the systems that at the same time threaten our humanity. Many (although of course not all) economically marginalized people seem just as eager to participate in the fruits of industrial capitalism as they are to resist its dehumanizing tendencies.

I do not mean to say that the gap between rich and poor is of no significance, or that the solidarity we seek can permit us to evade the demands of economic justice. Quite the contrary. But it is salutary to realize that the search for a solidarity of humanness against systemic oppression is now a widespread concern, not merely the concern of impoverished people far away. There is clearly a better chance of constructing a new morally focused ecumenism on a basis less dependent on a presumption of class warfare, yet without blunting the cutting edge of realization of what our self-devised systems are doing to us as human beings.

Continuing the Dialogue: New Settings and Possibilities

Issues like these have urged forward the attempt to understand what it might mean for the church to be a communion of moral communities. The three-year WCC "ecclesiology and ethics" study has sought to lay groundwork for a vision capable of meeting the challenges posed by the great world systems. The interpretation of that study in these pages has also added the dimension of the *missio Dei*, God's mission to humankind.

But whether a genuinely fresh vision of this sort *can* be grafted onto fifty years and more of ecumenism's programmatic history remains a question. I argue that, while the preparation has been inevitably insufficient for the challenges that lie ahead, no better groundwork is, or has been, available for the attempt. Behind the ecclesiology and ethics study lie the rich, parallel histories of Faith and Order and Life and Work: on the one hand, a long-term effort to articulate the church's essential being and unity; on the other, an equally long-term attempt to clarify what the church and its members must do in the world in consequence of the gospel. Without such background, any attempt to address the contemporary world as *oikoumene* would have been bound to be far more shallow than it can be now. Yet the fact that the two ecumenical traditions have proceeded independently has reduced their potential. It has always been acknowledged that their concerns are interrelated. But circumstances, both theological and institutional, have tended to keep them in separate compartments of concern.[26]

The WCC itself has addressed this bifurcation of effort several times. At least from the Fourth Assembly of the WCC at Uppsala (1968) onward there have been attempts to formulate the implications of ecclesiological thinking for moral witness in the world, and vice versa. The formula found in *Lumen Gentium* (Second Vatican Council, 1964)—which speaks of the church as "sign," "sacrament," and "instrument" of the unity of humankind—was influential in that assembly and has received much ecumenical attention since.[27]

And Faith and Order and Life and Work have from time to time reached out toward one another. On the Faith and Order side, from the 1953 Montreal Conference onward, the ecclesiology and ethics theme has been present in such themes as "The Unity of the Church and the Renewal of Human Community" and its several variants.[28] The most recent Faith and Order attempt to see the Christian community and the human community as deeply interrelated has been the study entitled *Church and World: The Unity of the Church and the Renewal of Human Community*.[29] This document says, "Where churches are involved in common witness and joint action in matters of justice this should have implications for the communion of these churches with each other."[30] The ecclesial-ethical implication in all this has been clear. It has only needed further development and spelling out.

On the other hand, there have also been implications for a new ecumenism in the insights of Life and Work. The World Conference on Church and Society, held in Geneva in 1966, already sounded an ecclesiological-ethical note. Witness this paragraph:

> The Church is called, in the world, to be that part of the world which responds to God's love for all men, and to become therefore the community in which God's relation to man is known and realized. The Church is in one sense the center and fulfillment of the world. In another it is the servant of the world and the witness to it of the hope of its future. It is called to be the community in

which the world can discover itself as it may become in the future.[31]

Most recently, Life and Work impulses have been behind several formulations central to the work of the Council, culminating in the program for "Justice, Peace, and the Integrity of Creation" or "JPIC." At a conference in Seoul in 1990, a challenge was issued to make ten moral "affirmations" based on these themes part of the very substance of the communion, or *koinonia*, the churches seek to articulate together.

Despite these overlapping concerns and even converging language, the traditions, research methods, and terminologies of these two streams of ecumenical effort have not until now met often enough in an interaction that could help the ecumenical future become clearer. The volume recording the reults of the three joint "ecclesiology and ethics" consultations[32] is the high-water mark so far of this attempt. But it is only fair to say that even this effort has from the start been accompanied by misgivings that are not laid to rest even with the latest publication. Some misgivings have had to do with a fear of moralism, of losing the force of the gospel of grace. Others have grown out of worry about losing each movement's traditions, achievements, and critical focus. At least one critic, formerly prominent in Faith and Order and never a supporter of this joint venture, argues in effect that we have now *had* our fling with "ecclesiology and ethics" and should go back to parallel lines of business as usual.

But what would happen then? Every advance in theological or moral discernment needs *some* sort of social-cultural-institutional vehicle if it is to shape events significantly. The institutional configurations of a study—its formulations of issues, its patterns of participation, its modes of publication—have much to do with the sorts of insights that emerge. The shape of the ecclesiology and ethics study as a discussion between the traditions of Faith and Order and Life and Work has surely been fruitful. But it is not likely to be continued in the same way. The search for a new ecumenical vision may need to find a vehicle superior to this one, and perhaps a new way of formulating the question altogether.

Perhaps the matter now needs to be pursued for a while primarily in the field. The most important criticism of the sort of ecclesial ethic propounded here concerns precisely its possibility as a way of life for congregations in a world of global economic injustice such as ours. Critics claim that not enough is said about how the needed moral community might look and how it could concretely work. Max Stackhouse, for example, argues that it does not "help to appeal for more communitarian values unless one can specify the sources, shape, nature, and sustainability of the values and the community.[33] The next two chapters of this book seek to meet this criticism at least part way by describing the process of moral formation at the level of the congregation. It may of course be that only specific, focused, local description of *each* congregation in all its particularity can suffice to paint the full picture. But perhaps the pages that follow will suggest some things to look for.

Whatever is done, realism is indispensable. Distinctive, different moral communities, even when well conceived and well planned, are exceedingly difficult to sustain. Self-deluding rhetoric is easy. Turning inspiration into coherent action is hard. Holding these admonitions in mind, chapter 3 studies how congregations living among today's multiple and fragmented values can generate moral *capacities*. Chapter 4 then shows how the congregation is also shaped by its ways of dealing with moral *opportunities*. Together these moves constitute a dialectic of formation that determines the kind of moral community a congregation turns out to be. It is not too much to say that the future of ecumenism depends on what happens among people who actually try to follow such paths.

THREE

Formation:
Generating Moral Capacities

However persuasive the ecumenical prospect just presented may be, little of that vision can be fulfilled unless faith communities can enact some sort of principled moral coherence in today's pragmatic and system-dominated world. This chapter begins to ask how that can happen. It pursues this inquiry through an attempt to depict such principled communities both in theological and in human-science terms. In their theological and moral depth, congregations need to distinguish themselves from the world of pragmatic, cost-benefit values. Yet they need to live concretely and visibly *in* that world: with a determinate membership, location, structure, practices, and beliefs. And, if they are to be more than merely ethical debating societies, they need to hold their moral principles in a very *primary* way, at the level of what is increasingly called "formation." A formed, or nurtured, moral awareness needs to be part of what the congregation *is*, incorporating all that has from the beginning shaped its being.

To be sure, the notion of Christian morality as being grounded in some sort of deliberate formation has been more consciously operative in some parts of the church than in others. The term as such is more familiar to people in the Catholic traditions where it is used to describe spiritual and moral training within the process of theological education, or the preparation of novices for full membership in monastic communities. But the word is coming increasingly into use in Protestant contexts as well, not only to mean specific soul-shaping activities pursued by individuals but also the comprehensive configuring of shared Christian life in the midst of the world. In both of these senses, formation shapes what Protestants are also learning from Catholics to call "spirituality."

Any community tends to orient its members to the world in a certain way, encouraging certain kinds of behavior and discouraging others. This is a nurturing process in which a certain sense of identity, a certain recognition of mutual responsibility, and a certain pattern of motivation eventually evolve. Formation can be the gradual work of culture and upbringing, or it may be self-conscious and intentional. A focus on formation points toward an emphasis on actual communities with their cultures: toward what anthropologists call the complex "thickness" of lives actually lived.[1]

Such an understanding of formation can lead to useful insights. It can, for example, direct attention away from purely inferential, or rule-based, models of ethical *reasoning* toward nurturing models of moral *upbringing*. It can also point away from excessive focus on casuistry—the discussion of hard cases or what you do if confronted by this or that impossible dilemma—and toward the elements of training, character, virtue, and all the rest of what lies behind the actual arguments one finds plausible. James Nelson emphasizes these *unconscious* formational elements that shape ethical positions, which, on the surface at least, purport to be reached on a purely rational basis.[2]

Moral formation in the church seeks to generate communities in touch with the world and all its problems yet shaped in a daily telling and retelling of the Christian story. Such formation makes generation after generation of disciples. Discipleship in turn finds resources in many complexly interacting elements of ecclesial life: religious education, the preparation of pastors, moral discourse in family and congregation, the experience of seeking to serve the wider community. The sacraments of baptism and the Lord's Supper are fundamental to all other kinds of formation. The nurture of children (and others) becomes sacramental in the context of the promises for upbringing made at baptism. Care for the earth is given profound meaning in the eucharist. The management of the planet as a human household takes on new sense within a theology of stewardship. The congregation is shaped as a community by the assumptions and practices embedded in the ethos and form of government of the communion in which it holds standing. This chapter draws on all these formative activities and others to try to understand how local congregations can come sacramentally to represent the moral *oikoumene* of God.

Formation among and by
the Powers of the World

But there is another kind of formation that is still more pervasive and powerful in the contemporary world. As the context in which congregations live, it needs to be considered first. Chapter 2 has described a world of global systems—the market system being the most important—with which human beings today are trying to deal by means of practical, fact-based styles of reasoning much too shallow to cope with such principalities and powers. The values of this market world powerfully shape the lives of all human beings. Unless one is brought up in a wholly isolated Christian community (and there are few of these left), it is fair to say that from nursery school to adulthood a *secular* formation reinforced by peer groups at every age, reflected in the media, and needed simply to function in an advanced industrial society, functions far more forcefully than anything congregations can provide. This worldly formation needs to be discussed at the outset. It is the only way to be realistic about the situation churches face in trying to form their people in a different way of seeing the world.

MORAL IMAGINATION

What sort of analysis will best bring out what is going on? I think it will be most helpful to begin with the grounding of all moral practice—economic, congregational, or otherwise—in one or another imaginatively framed and maintained view of the world. One has *bred* into one, by environment and upbringing, a tendency to see the world in a certain way, to picture other human beings and empathize—or not—with their condition. Mark Johnson has written a book entitled *Moral Imagination*[3] which makes the point vividly. He writes:

> We human beings are imaginative creatures, from our most mundane, automatic acts of perception all the way up to our most abstract conceptualization and reasoning. Consequently, our moral understanding depends in large measure on various structures of imagination such as images, image schemas, metaphors, narratives, and so forth.[4]

And all this is grounded in the kinds of communities that have nurtured us. Johnson continues: "the few moral principles we actually have should be understood as summaries of the collective experience of a people."[5]

Yes. But there is something more to be said. Imagination always takes form in a context of power.[6] The great world systems are gigantic works of the collective imagination, which in turn shape the effective action-worlds of all who are involved with them. I mean by this that they result from construals in the mind's eye of different complex action-possibilities, and they stay in power only as long as these particular ways of construing the world of possibilities remain dominant. One cannot do otherwise than respond in some way to whatever meaning-construct for human life prevails in one's context.

Often these imaginatively constructed action-worlds are projected from paradigmatic narratives. Roger Betsworth,[7] for example, describes several narratives that shape human lives and activities in America: Benjamin Franklin's narrative of the self-made man, "manifest destiny" in subduing and populating the continent, Andrew Carnegie's "gospel of wealth," social Darwinism, psychotherapeutic well-being in the consumer culture, the global anticommunist crusade, and many others. Each of these is a narrative construct that has shaped the application of human capacities to generate power structures which in turn have extended and empowered the fundamental narratives, giving them the appearance in many cases of being simple descriptions of reality.

Clearly today's global market system is a complex network of interacting power-centers whose activities fit into a still more elaborate master narrative. This economic narrative is unprecedented in many ways, among them the fact that it exists simultaneously in multiple cultural settings. Americans entertain a form of it, Germans another, and Japanese a third. China is in the midst of getting its own, unique, economic narrative together. Yet the different national forms of the economic success story cooperate pragmatically across the globe today to a degree that holders of the different confessional or denominational forms of the Christian narrative may well envy. The resulting shared picture of an economically integrated world has enormous cachet. The pragmatic usefulness of this picture, for those able to see themselves in it, is undeniable.

For many of this present generation, life has become basically a matter of calculating costs and benefits in enormously technically elaborated transactions guided by a dominating, acquisitive, expansionist, narrative picture of what human existence on this planet is all about. The mythology controlling these activities and goals is obscured behind a facade of economic rationality deemed self-evident where goods and services need to be exchanged. It is as if the market system as we know it were an inevitable, self-positing mechanism rather than a political–cultural construct.

CO-OPTABLE MORAL IDEALS

But the contemporary human world is not altogether devoid of moral ideals. Despite the plurality and thinness of its philosophical reasoning, despite its rough pragmatism, the late-twentieth-century age entertains a remarkable set of secular moral assumptions that enjoy broad support. There exists a significant, seemingly cross-cultural agreement about "human rights." Many see Amnesty International as an "exercise of the conscience of the human race." There seems to be growing agreement that the welfare of persons *as such* deserves protection. This broad accord plays itself out in the well-nigh universal condemnation (if not yet the elimination) of slavery, child labor, torture, and the like. These assumptions are connected with the notions of civil rights for racial–ethic minorities and of the political and economic rights of women.[8]

Yet, precisely because of their thinness and "ironic"[9] qualities, these significant moral insights can be co-opted (and often significantly distorted) by spokespersons for the international economic order. Increasingly, the principle of human rights is defended not in itself but because it is better for international trade. Indeed the independent philosophical foundation for the notion of human rights, which might help defend the idea against misuse, is more precarious than we think. While rights are *thought* by many secularists to have a rational basis independent of any and all doctrines held by traditioned communities, little agreement exists about what that rational basis *is*, and none appears to be in sight. Meanwhile pragmatic economic assumptions invade, colonize, and take up residence *within* the rights agenda.[10] The result is that, for many, maintaining *political* freedoms seems incomprehensible as a serious concern if people are free to make money. If there is economic freedom, citizens of Hong Kong ask, what other significant freedom can there be?[11]

SPHERES AND SKILLS

Economic forms of moral imagination play out differently in the different *spheres* of social life: home, office, school, business, politics, and so on. While the rights agenda provides clues as to what distributive justice entails in general terms, the actual enactment of justice has a different texture in each of these cases, and each case serves repeatedly to test the adequacy of the general conception.[12] Likewise, economically oriented formation goes on in the characteristic *practices* of the social world. Various performance standards, assumptions, ideas of "good practice," are embedded in the ethos of what it means to be a lawyer, physician, stockbroker, truck driver, homemaker, or politician. Each *practice* requires certain skills, but also a certain imaginatively held orientation to life.

The practice of law, for example, bows to the power of money as much as any other profession. Among lawyers and their clients, money is a commodity thought capable of compensating people for every conceivable misfortune, "wrongful death" included. Even medical ethics, in these days of business-oriented "managed care," becomes a *form* of economic ethics. Certain societies in the capitalist world teeter on the brink of seeing medical services as a commodity whose distribution should be based not on rights and obligations we share as human beings but on market forces: supply and demand, the ability to pay.

The skills and orientations needed to succeed in each particular calling form human beings as much as does the general ethos of modernity, and indeed contribute strongly to that ethos. Such occupational "goods" are not necessarily parts of any transcending moral awareness or of any horizonal assumptions of what it is to be human. They are embedded pragmatically in what we do, and in how we live. These different spheres of life and practices of the contemporary world are interrelated to produce a complex whole: the material civilization that covers the entire earth and exists in one form or another in all human cultures.

Christians as well as everyone else are significantly formed by these contemporary agendas. Indeed, in most Western nations, Christians are welcome to interpret the world's agendas in relation to a larger theological conception of life so long as this larger conception is not imposed on others and supports behavior that bolsters the broader community's purposes.[13] But this book argues that congregations should do more than interpret and support the communities they live in. It argues that they should strive to engender formation of quite another kind: a formation in the kinds of moral awareness required by the vision of a Christian *oikoumene*. That awareness is one that sees humanity drawn by Jesus Christ toward a "beloved community" (Josiah Royce's phrase) living in the power of the Holy Spirit. What might be involved in doing this?

Formation of and by the Congregation

Whatever else they do, churches nurture distinctive forms of moral awareness and behavior.[14] In some ways these formations reinforce the secular agendas just described, and in other ways they compete with them. Effectively or not, with better or worse outcomes, congregations engender certain ways of seeing life just by being the kinds of communities they are. Indeed it is evident that the historical Christian polities themselves—Catholic, Orthodox, Protestant, and their many variants—play out in certain forms of life, certain ways of living, which shape the way church members comport themselves in the world. There is no way of talking about "Christian ethics" *without* asking how congregations function in moral formation, without probing the actual imagination-shaping that goes on in worshiping communities.

Congregational formation can be understood in two distinct senses, easy enough to distinguish in thought but always interrelated on the ground. There is, first, the formation *of* the congregation: that is, the process by which this gathering of believers itself takes on the shape it has in the society around it. A communion and its congregations may be deeply involved in legitimating the public order (Troeltsch's "church type") or they may be separatist in spirit, critical of the public order and aloof from it (Troeltsch's "sect type"). The circumstances of history, the convictions of leaders, the outworking of events, all conspire to give communions of Christians such distinctive stances toward the world around them.

But then, secondly, there is formation *by* the congregation: that is, the moral forming of individual members through the congregation's instructional practice and example. Here the congregation shapes the lives of its people. But clearly, in doing so, it *also* forms itself for the future. The moral education of members in one generation *is* the formation of the congregation itself for the next generation. These differences of meaning need to be kept in mind, even though they are hardly separable in practice.

THE CONGREGATION IN ITS SOCIAL ENVIRONMENT

How does the congregation come into being? Some influential writers today seem to presuppose that effective congregations can be willed into being in the modern world by a rhetorically forceful analysis of what is wrong with our *understanding* of the church's relation to the culture around it. Recall, for example, Loren Mead's argument (following Yoder, Hauerwas, and others) that churches in the Western world are captive to a "Christendom" conception that makes them innocuous chaplains to whatever cultural and political forces may be in power at a given time. As chapter 1 shows, many today stress that the church needs to be radically "different." It needs to recover its traditions of formation, worship, and moral witness in all their integrity to prepare a people of God who can see through the pretensions of our time.

I am sympathetic to this analysis and to the movement based on it. But this sort of prescription may not work well in the kinds of human community we know. The trouble is that we are not invited to think about such congregational formation with enough sociological realism. It appears that for Stanley Hauerwas and his school, Christian community offers "its own self-authenticating reason for being, apart from a civil or social justification." Indeed it is urged to see itself as "the shape of a more real social order than that in which it resides."[15] But how is this supposed to work?

Much of the Hauerwasian literature of congregational life *sounds* as if the congregation were a total cultural environment, as if it were *possible* to transform the world's story entirely within the Christian story. But total cultural environments scarcely exist in the contemporary world. A devout member of the Knights of Columbus may *also* be an avid baseball fan *and* a member of the Teamster's Union![16] Readers from other cultures can readily supply their own examples. Most of us citizens of the late twentieth century exist in a multiplicity of cultural environments, and engage in several different occupational and familial practices, each with its own symbolism, logic, customs, and the like. Pluralism enters our personhood. We are literally multiple selves, formed in different, and perhaps divergent, ways by our lives in the church, in our families, in our secular occupations, and perhaps in political, recreational, or other activities as well. Each of these spheres of life is a distinct *culture* in its own right. The relation of the community called church to all of these other cultural situations varies from place to place, but the problem is unavoidable. "Ecclesiology" maps only part of the setting for faithful life.

I agree with Robert Bellah, who writes of the Hauerwasian proposal as follows:

> My problem is that I do not think [Hauerwas and his colleagues] have really explained to us how we get there from here. None of us educated in modern Western culture, and that includes almost all educated people anywhere in the world today, can simply jump out of their skins, deny that culture, and by a sheer act of will, imagine that we are radically resident aliens within it.[17]

And Bellah argues further that the analogy of the early Christians battling the pagan Roman world is profoundly misleading because it misunderstands the extent to which modern Western culture is suffused with Christian elements:

> However secular our culture has become, it is still saturated in language and practice with elements of biblical religion, even if those elements are no longer coherently organized. That is, it is a false analogy to imagine ourselves living in something like the pagan culture of the classical world.[18]

To recover anything like the nearly exclusive forming role the church once had would have to mean restoration of the sorts of one-possibility religious communities that existed in premodern times. That is not likely to happen short of some disaster wiping out the structures of the modern world. Bellah tells of having studied a small Mormon village in New Mexico in 1953, "where it composed almost the entire social life of the community outside the immediate family."[19] This village came close to being a genuine one-possibility culture in its isolation and lack of knowledge of the outside world. To contrast this situation with our own is to make the point vividly.

Still, religious communities exhibit different degrees of isolation and participation in contemporary society. Martin Marty somewhere makes a distinction between "thick" and "thin" traditions that puts the question in perspective at least for North America. On the one hand there are "thick" religious communities, such as the Amish, for whom the faith tradition controls nearly all aspects of life. Some Missouri Synod Lutheran communities may also come close to this holistic envelopment of life in faith. Groups such as these already are "resident aliens" of the sort Hauerwas talks about, although they hardly have the broad social impact he desires to see.

On the other hand, most of the "mainline" Protestant churches such as Presbyterians, Methodists, Disciples, Episcopalians, and the like are "thin" traditions. This means that for most of their members church life is only one area of activity alongside others. Faith may influence much that members of these churches do, but it is mixed with many other motivations and concerns.

So it seems that the "thick" traditions have the formational density needed to enact the faith in its integrity, but in fact are self-defensive cultural enclaves in the larger society and therefore ineffective. The "thin" traditions, on the other hand, include many more people who occupy positions of influence in the secular world but, apart from their leadership groups, they have few distinctive religio-moral convictions and cannot be said to be effectively "formed" in the Christian sense at all. They, too, are ineffective, but for a different reason.

What people need and want, especially in the thinner traditions, is not a sectarian solution to the church/world problem but rather guidance in how to live authentically *both* within the church's reshaping of the moral imagination *and* among the corrosive pressures of political life and of the market, among the beguilements of many alternative life-styles. A way needs to be found to *integrate* personal moral issues with questions of social ethics and the public weal. It has not been made clear at the level of congregational life what a moral strategy for life both inside and outside the household of God would look like. Many persons of faith simply do not recognize public moral engagement as a vocation for themselves. Conversely, many of the most morally effective Christians in the world's struggles have difficulty relating their moral and political convictions to the faith they are being taught in church.

The question, then, is this. How can congregations—especially in sophisticated Western cultural settings—be shaped in practices that in turn are capable of offering significant moral formation to the persons in them? Before there can be strategy for formation, there needs to be description of how formation can happen in multipossibility situations when members of congregations do not want to cut themselves off from significant lives in their worldly occupations or indeed suffer a division of consciousness such that Christian life in the congregation and Christian life in the "world" are experienced as incommensurable or incompatible.

A FORMATIONAL PHENOMENOLOGY: LITURGY

Let us begin to meet this dilemma with a phenomenological description of congregational formation.[20] Congregations bring together—from the complex world just described—myriad elements of shared human life. Their members bring with them specific genetic inheritances, cultural idiosyncrasies, traits of character, educational backgrounds, habits of language, economic involvements, family ties, occupational perspectives, and so on. Through networks of relationship with others outside the congregation, they represent still wider ranges of human experience. None of these things can really be left behind. All are *ingredients* for the church community's moral construal, or imaginative metaphorical reconstruction, of the world.

A faith community cannot be adequately understood solely by consulting its formal polity. It can only be understood as a gathering of persons who bring with them all the kinds of life-substance mentioned and more: a community that aims at configuring all this so as to represent the identity of Jesus Christ and thereby to articulate the shapes of God's presence in the world through the work of the Holy Spirit.

These life-ingredients do not come into the life of the congregation so as to represent the identity of Jesus Christ without being transformed. Such transformation or trans-signification is the work of many specific congregational practices, above all the sacraments together with preaching, and indeed the whole form of life represented in the ecclesial community. I have argued in another place[21] that the sacraments represent a trans-signification[22] not only of the elements of bread and wine but of the community itself, as elements of the common human life-world are reconfigured to represent in the world the shape of Christ's bodily, historical presence.

Another word for such reconfiguring of the self-justifying structures of human power could well be "transfiguration."[23] A social transfiguration, as I see it, takes place as the sacramental community generates and makes present, within the world's ways of imagining and giving effect to power, a wholly new way of seeing the relations between imagination and power, consisting of ways of seeing and acting in the world not directed toward capital accumulation in the global market, or toward any other materialistic vision of life. The focus toward which the congregationally transfigured elements of social life must point is the final fulfillment of human life in God's household.

It is not well understood how profoundly *moral* are the implications of baptism and eucharist for this transfigured form of life. This moral valence of the sacraments is well brought out by Vigen Guroian. He writes:

> Many turn to the market economy, management, or the legal system for criteria to determine what is right or true. But Christians must remind themselves that their identity and morality are grounded elsewhere, in those distinctive practices of the church through which it constitutes itself and remembers, not only in word and thought but in action, the truth it confesses regarding the lordship of Jesus Christ. I am referring specifically here to the rites and liturgies of praise and dedication to the one God whom Christians hold to be the source of life and reason for doing good deeds.[24]

The heart of Christian moral formation thus lies in worship, through which the story of salvation is reenacted in the modes of prayer, proclamation, and sacrament. Worship together involves certain focal actions intrinsic to the shared life of faith, actions that center, sustain, and order that way of life. Ritual actions show the way. They are "rites that embody what is right." They are "the connective tissue in a shared way of life, the whole of which morally educates and forms."[25] Many Christian traditions refer to the prayerful, biblically informed, and ritually cogent enactment of the story of God's way with the human race as "liturgy" or *leitourgia*. This Greek word itself originally had a moral sense. It meant the public charge to perform a particular public service, or *diakonia*. The connection is still present in the Christian understanding of liturgy.[26]

Thus I believe that the liturgy leads to, indeed instigates, a *sacramental* transfiguration of everyday life. The sacraments engender a capacity among members of the body to *discern* how and where the Holy Spirit is at work in the world as they know it. Thereby they name those life-ingredients as capable of being configured together to articulate the readable pattern, or signature, of Christ's impact, the whole gestalt of his presence, in the nexus of society.

One could say that by their sacramental relation to Jesus Christ, Christian communities of faith are lived decipherments and expressive embodiments of the people-configuring work of the Holy Spirit in the social and cultural worlds from which they come.[27] Congregations discern Spirit-formed social realities in those worlds by bringing them into a christological frame of reference that makes them visible. Congregations thereby articulate the human communities around them *as* spaces in which the Spirit's people-gathering power is active. By proclaiming the gospel, celebrating the liturgy, and acting prophetically they signify that Jesus Christ is continually forming communities of people to be agents of God's *oikoumene*.

It will be important to remember this point for grasping the argument to be made in chapter 4. If the congregation is *already* a place where publicly unrecognized signs of the Spirit's work in the world are brought together as a recognizable gestalt that manifests the presence of Jesus Christ, then it can be hospitable to theologically tongue-tied but spiritually sensitive seekers who need a space in which their own agendas can be deepened and transformed. One does not have to *name* Jesus Christ as the author of a deeply desired form of life to represent *something*, at least, of that shape of existence in common human language and activity. Christian congregations are able to name Jesus Christ vicariously, on behalf of others who, for reasons of conscience, cannot do so themselves. The congregation can provide not only material hospitality to the stranger, but also spiritual hospitality: a sanctuary of *meaning* for those who, for many reasons—intellectual, religious, political—are unable to confess the source of this meaning.

A congregational transformation of ways of seeing the world, capable of giving spiritual sanctuary to others, can only take place through some kind of renewal of the moral imagination, and along with that, an enablement of the capacity to discern what is going on in the human community. As Paul wrote, "Do not be conformed to this world, but be transformed by the renewal of your mind, that you may prove what is the will of God, what is good and acceptable and perfect" (I Corinthians 12:2). I suggest that these words refer to precisely such an imaginative transformation of orientation in the face of the forms of imagination in worldly power.[28] Proving "what is the will of God . . ." means more than testing one's own experience for evidence that God's will is being enacted there. This proving or testing may also mean discerning configurations of the Spirit in society itself.

In practice, of course, such discernment is far from easy. It may be difficult, if not impossible, to find the Spirit's people-shaping work in the public world.[29] The effort to discern and signify the reality of a people of

God often finds the world of human action to be ambiguous, murky, or worse. Our best efforts may be short-circuited by misperception. Yet traces of a people-forming Spirit are sometimes discovered in seemingly unpromising situations of personal, economic, cultural, or political life. This can happen when events are found to have some inherent reconciling power, or when participation in them, often entirely outside the bounds of the congregation or its formal theological language, can be seen as acts of witness to the reign of God. The Truth and Reconciliation Commission, at work in South Africa as these words are written, may well be the context for such events.

Out of some such discerning process as this, the congregation takes form as moral community. Its members bring to it elements of culture and society that, in the power of the Spirit, form a kind of mosaic of the face of Jesus Christ: not the appearance of the historical personage, but the recognizable pattern of Jesus' presence in history understood as sign and sacrament of the fulfillment of God's intention for humankind.

THE LINK TO SPIRITUALITY

This discussion brings congregational formation close to what many today mean by the term *spirituality*. This term no longer refers only, as it once did, to specific meditations and practices explicitly focused on the self's relation to God, most often lived out by members of orders and a few other very special people. With modernity's characteristic "affirmation of everyday life,"[30] spirituality has also come to mean the depth dimension of daily existence cultivated by both meditative and moral practices. The meditative and the moral, indeed, cannot be separated. They are part of one whole cloth. Spirituality can now mean the whole shape, the shared fabric, of human lives in God.

The fact that spirituality is today a growing interest in certain Protestant traditions that did not know they had such a thing is all to the good. It can mean quite simply the practices of worship and work that shape fundamental attitudes to life, a sense of what is real, and indeed the ways people understand what is ultimate in existence. The "protestant ethic" is certainly formational in its own way, with the central notion that one's worldly work can be as much a Christian "vocation" as any more ecclesiastical calling. Therefore it needs to be understood and pursued in a way worthy of the gospel.

There are many specific traditions of Christian spiritual practice, each with its characteristic practices and exercises, each with its characteristic understandings of the link to moral life. There exists an extensive and growing body of literature on spiritual formation—both in its earlier, narrower meaning and in its contemporary, broader meaning.[31] This literature has been, up to the present time, largely distinct from the literature of "ethics." I am not sure that this separation needs to be maintained so long as care is taken not to *absorb* the ethical into the "spiritual." The sacramental spirituality of the congregation is the foundation for Christian moral reflection, but it is not a substitute for it. There needs to be continued critical reflection on what any given spiritual tradition means for the conduct of those devoted to it.

The Moral Architecture of Congregational Life

Thus spirituality, even understood as a transignification of social life into sacramental substance, does not suffice as the whole story. One has to unpack the moral implications of each spiritual-sacramental form of life. I will begin to do this first by distinguishing the elements of specific moral content that are found *within* the community's spiritual life. Then, in the next section, I will explore the moral, and indeed sacramental, significance of the faith community's *public* life.

Moral reflection begins and is carried on within the life of the congregation itself. One could say that certain moral principles or materials—both from Christian tradition and from the worlds in which church members live—are drawn into congregational life and used to help build the sacramental household. These perspectives begin to participate in the moral substance of the body. They combine to produce the assumptions and principles that go into actual formation. I will identify four of these elements and describe the way they interact.

First there is a world of communally maintained dispositions, habits, and patterns of actual conduct: what have earlier been called *practices*. Here formation—from whatever source—has been so effective that it has produced dispositions below the level of conscious awareness that nevertheless powerfully shape conduct. Persons raised up or acculturated in particular religious communities normally feel that certain patterns of action are appropriate or fitting, and that others are not, without being able to say exactly why. This sense of the fitting is engendered by culture, liturgy, the telling of stories, the fabric of associations. It exists before conscious moral reasoning begins. Such primordial convictions constitute a certain moral "character," a certain array of "virtues." In their application such virtues may not reach very far beyond the private sphere. But they sustain a shared world of community, identity, and motivation. The resulting deeply held identity sense comes to expression in primordial moral intuitions. "It was the only thing I could do," we say. Or "It just didn't seem right." Here one has the core of personal moral *being:* that which determines what it is *possible* for a person, being who he or she is, to do.

But there is another layer in the congregation's moral repertoire. Within a given community certain leaders, scholars, or sages will often carry on processes of conscious reasoning about matters of conduct. Such reasoning interprets the community's traditions and its members' gut feelings to meet new problems. It wrestles with issues and leads to the thoughtful formulation of rules for the community to follow in maintaining its identity. The Torah, later voluminously interpreted in the rabbinic literature, is a vast panoply of such communal reasoning. It is definitive of what the Jewish community understands itself to be. The Christian community has likewise produced a vast literature of in-house moral reflection, or practical religious ethics. Over history every human tradition of life, whether distinctively religious or not, becomes, as Alasdair MacIntyre has written, a prolonged *argument* about what the tradition is and means. Such argument is indispensable to the tradition's continuation through time. It is not enough for custom and culture to define, implicitly, what is "fitting" for members of a particular community to think and do. The sages and scholars of a tradition need to help the community in question to reason out what their customs mean: to bring to bear a critical sense that distinguishes between the tradition's fundamentals, and cultural accretions that inevitably confuse and distort it.

And then, thirdly, there are the sorts of moral thinking that go on outside the faith community in the surrounding culture, as these are internalized by the congregation and its members. A great variety of things can be included in this category: from what the society or culture in question regards as "fitting" in matters of everyday life to the sophisticated work of ethicists in the academic or professional realms. "Ethics" in the last-named contexts sense means systematic reflection on the issues that confront human beings as such. Practitioners of the ethical disciplines in this sense seek conceptual models for reasoning about the perennial moral questions, as well as dilemmas emerging in the late twentieth century for the first time. Urgent issues arise that need for practical purposes to be resolved. The typical work of a hospital "ethics committee" is a case in point. The committee may need to determine whether life support for a particular patient shall be terminated or not. Or, shall this patient receive a heart transplant ahead of that one? Ethicists deal with such questions by seeking to establish principles for "postconventional," and therefore potentially universal, forms of moral discourse. To such ends ethicists explore the implications of various theoretical models: utilitarian, deontological, contractual, or work to establish principles for the various professions. Moralists who function mainly within some tradition or faith-community—i.e., those representing the second category above—cannot allow themselves to be wholly cut off from those who think about human well-being as such. Members of faith communities are likely also to be citizens, employees, professional persons, public servants, and the like who struggle with moral issues in their own personal and occupational lives, and inevitably bring assumptions from those worlds into the church. Members of congregations may not easily distinguish, indeed, between such assumptions and the results of congregational formation as such, seeing the latter as support for the former, or conceivably the reverse. Often it is not clear which assumptions come from secular moral sources and which come from the tradition of faith. If both are present, how are they to be related?

And finally, there is often in congregational life some master metaphor of faith—perhaps a particular historical event or tract of human experience—which serves as an organizing principle for the people's interpretation of their tradition. This may be something biblical: the exodus, the giving of the Law, the exile. Or it may be something more recent: Luther's nailing his "ninety-five theses," the Pilgrim fathers landing in Plymouth. Some Northern Ireland Presbyterians (unfortunately) cannot forget their victory over Roman Catholics at the battle of the Boyne. Then there are paradigmatic roles or persons. Whole historical periods (it is said) have had their characteristic vocational models: in the Middle Ages the monk, in classical Protestantism the wise father of the family or the entrepreneur, in liberation theology the oppressed sufferer, the *campesino*. Or the paradigm may rest on the experience of a certain group: women, African-Americans, gays and lesbians. Sometimes the argument for a master model claims a great deal: say, that in this or that particular sphere of human experience the conscience of the human race comes particularly to focus, or that here one sees the truth with unique clarity. But even where no particular sphere of human experience is taken as a conscious paradigm, I suspect that every synthesis of moral reasoning in the congregation has some such element in it. It is important to know what it is.

Those who think about Christian moral life need to be in touch with all four of these realms of meaning: with the sense of what is fitting in the community of formation or upbringing, with the tradition's own habits of discourse and argument, with characteristic forms of moral reasoning in the public realm, and with whatever sphere of human life suggests the most powerful current paradigm of religious meaning. No one of these moral ingredients *ever* exists alone in actual lived experience. Taking them apart for analysis in the mind's eye is more a matter of shining the searchlight first at one element, then at another. What is self-consciously thought out in one era can become second nature in the next.

When one thinks about it, every aspect of the primary communal formation in which one participates to the point of basic identity and motivation is *itself* the product of a history in which the other elements have played a role. What is taken for granted by a primary community today, what is so basic that it is just part of "who we are," is likely at one time to have been the subject of deliberation directed within but informed by worldly categories and strongly shaped by the particular life histories and outlooks of the deliberators. What was salient and self-conscious as an issue at one time is taken for granted at another. Slavery was a deeply controverted issue in America between the late eighteenth century and the close of the Civil War. Today an abhorrence of slavery is part of our basic makeup: we are formed by every influence in our upbringing to reject it. This does not mean that, given enough time, all moral problems will have been solved so that the right answer becomes second nature. Often such settlement, as Americans learned from 1861 to 1865, does not happen without a fight. Sometimes, even with a fight, the issue still isn't settled, or comes back in other forms to haunt future generations.

It is probably true that each age in the history of Christianity, and indeed each human situation, calls forth a different *kind* of synthesis of the elements of congregational moral consciousness. In some situations one aspect may be more important than others, as when primary moral formation dominates the scene in an essentially one-possibility culture. Or two elements may virtually merge, as when the church is so dominant in a situation that ethics in the public realm is not distinguishable from moral reasoning in the faith community. Or one may imagine a situation in which traditions of primary formation and their characteristic styles of reasoning are so suppressed, so privatized, as not to surface at all in public discourse. In the last-named circumstance the public and the private are so sharply separated as to constitute two worlds, each with its own forms of moral reasoning.

It is wise for Christian moralists to be aware of the situations they are living in. That is to say, it is important not only to dissect the different kinds of moral presuppositions and examine their interrelationships, but also to have a critical overview of what is going on as one does so. And this leads to a whole new challenge: namely, to be aware of what the congregation, with all its *internal* moral languages, looks like *externally* as a moral paradigm in the public world. This observation leads the argument to the final section of this chapter on critical consciousness in ethics, engendered by the use of the human sciences.

The Spiritual Appropriation
of Critical Disciplines

Theological ethics needs not only the formational experience of faith and church participation told in familiar in-house terms, but also some awareness of the way one's faith community looks to independent observers, or of the way that community might figure in a secular social analysis or history of the period in question. The observational language of the public world is in fact indispensable for understanding what the in-house formational experience is all about. No matter how well-formed religious communicants may be, no matter how thoroughly the various forms of public social imagination they bring to church are transformed in baptism and eucharist, and stewardship and polity, members of the religious community necessarily live in both worlds. And in "thin" traditions such as those of mainline Protestantism, public ways of thinking are likely to pre-dominate to the point of making the terminology of religious formation largely ritualistic and perfunctory.

FIRST AND SECOND LANGUAGES:
SOCIAL SACRAMENTALITY

In his celebrated book *Habits of the Heart* Robert Bellah makes just this distinction. In describing the responses received from his interviewees, Bellah speaks of "first languages" and "second languages."[32] The typical "first language" is that of characteristic contemporary Western individu-alist careerism or self-cultivation. In this language the cost-benefit analysis predominates. The "second language," where there is one, is that of re-spondents' deeper values—the values of intentional formation in family, school, and church—the values they will identify under questioning as *really* giving direction to life. Few, if any, of the persons interviewed by the Bellah team were able to make much intelligible connection between their second languages and their first.[33]

Part of the problem is that in modern Western societies the "second" language of faith-formation is generally so poorly articulated that it oc-cupies little space in the consciousness. It does not press its claims in the so-called real world. What is the answer, then? Is it to raise people's consciousness of the church's capacity for moral formation to the point that the question of the interaction of the two languages and the realities they represent becomes unavoidable? Believers would then presumably begin to see that their presence in the midst of the public world as a distinctive community could make a difference—for good or for ill—in that world. They would begin to participate consciously and critically in the public history of their faith community. The practice of personal mo-rality as shaped by communal formation would then become *also* a matter of public witness.

It begins to become clear that what is formed in the congregation is not merely ecclesial practice as such, but the whole array of public social activity—occupational, educational, economic, political—represented by the active lives of the congregation's members. Every private moral issue *also* has a public meaning. The line between public and private becomes increasingly hard to draw. The reality of the faith community *is* the en-semble of the devotional and the worldly practices of all its members. It is all that these believers are in the private *and* public activities and relationships of their lives. Taken together, these practices should constitute a field of social trans-signification articulating a form of the real presence of Jesus Christ in the world.

Seen in such a perspective, the space of human life-together becomes open to sacramental transformation. And social philosophy of one kind or another replaces metaphysical realism (Aristotelian or otherwise) as the appropriate explanatory discipline. A social sacramentality of this kind necessarily seeks expression in various sorts of civic participation and action. It supports resistance in the public world to the powers of evil and solidarity with the forces of hope. Other human beings, unbelievers for example, may at least be partially drawn into this network of sacramental moral practice, which represents God's purposes for the human future in present time and space.

Grasping the nature of this social sacramentality, I claim, calls for a judicious use of social science categories and techniques. Some, of course, will prefer a purely theological and traditional account from start to finish, saying that the community called church takes form in a process not detectable, let alone measurable, in socialscience categories at all. These colleagues will prefer to speak of the work of Jesus Christ in the power of the Holy Spirit, gathering those called by God into ecclesial community. I am far from wanting to deny the theological explanation, as the second part of this chapter makes abundantly clear. But I share with many others the view that the Spirit is a power whose inherent push is toward worldly concretion. When one is seeking such concreteness, one wants to know as well as possible how and where to find it.

Such an objectifying standpoint, some will say, misses the inner reality, not to say the spontaneity and integrity, of the sacramental sociality being studied. I say that it need not. To be in dialogue with social theory for purposes of communal self-understanding is not for the church to adopt the theory concerned as the *only* valid frame of reference for this purpose. Nor is it to become captive to whatever metaphysical presuppositions the theory in question may entertain. It is to help the community of believers become self-critical about the kind of social reality they constitute in living out their communal and public practices.

CRITICAL PERSPECTIVES:
FORMATION AND MALFORMATION

What human science disciplines might lend themselves to churches as discussion partners for this purpose? Each theory of society provides a different social map, offers a different analysis of what is going on in the social world. Social location and social reality are not absolute facts. They always involve a positioning (of the church or other community) on a theoretical grid placed over the recalcitrant reality of common human life. So one needs to choose a heuristic language that maps social reality and location in ways sensitive to the values one wants to maintain. To map the human world in such a way that the faith community can be properly self-conscious about what it says by what it is, is *not* the same thing as accepting the location this particular map gives to the category of "religion." Those living particular religious practices may employ social theory to help them discern the social location they want to occupy precisely in order to achieve the outward identity their faith tradition inspires them to seek. Typically, the religious tradition itself does not have the resources for such objective self-understanding.

The specific choice of social analysis depends on what the religious community wants to know about itself in any particular situation. The needed movement in thought may well be one that begins with Hans-Georg Gadamer,[34] and moves to Jürgen Habermas.[35] Gadamer is the man of tradition: he thinks there is no other way of knowing the truth than being formed in the fulness of what one's community has handed down. He is suspicious of all that comes under the heading of social-scientific "method." Habermas, however, supplies the critical outside view. What happens, he asks, when the community of tradition participates in social interaction with other communities, other points of view? What happens when the traditioned community is judged by the moral standards of a broadly educated secular public?

Without attention to objective description (in Habermas's sense) the congregation's inner, liturgical, moral formation (in Gadamer's sense) may turn out to be *mal*formation. The liturgy may seemingly be faithfully celebrated, and the Word to all appearances be truly preached, and yet what the church *is* as moral community may be a denial of the gospel. Liturgy and worship uncritically or blindly practiced may well perpetuate or legitimate unjust arrangements both within and outside ecclesial boundaries.

Single-minded devotion to the liturgy can lead to irresponsible social isolation, countenance unjust social arrangements, or even lead to ethnic-
religious violence. Churches liberated from the constraints of totalitarian
regimes may quickly embrace movements of recrudescent nationalism.
Worship has sometimes been a rehearsal ground for violent repression of
ethnic and religious minorities.[36] It may well turn out, in this more objective perspective, that a community whose tradition talks grandly about
"freedom" turns out to be oppressive toward its own members and perhaps toward others as well.

An ability to discern *mal*formation, whatever the analytical instruments
used, needs to be part and parcel of any truly ecclesial, formational, Christian ethic. The task of discernment *can* be relatively easy. Malformation
can be something like the theological defense of apartheid by the orthodox, conventional, white churches of South Africa before the collapse of
the regime that invented it.[37] But what if one is dealing with something
not so obvious? What if one is wrestling with the dilemmas of "thin"
traditions—such as those of North American "mainline" Protestantism—
in situations that present so many moral issues that no single issue (except
for "single issue" people, a special breed) stands out as the question of the
moment? The public reality of the church as moral community is then
much more difficult to discern. The reality of the mainline churches as
dispersed moral communities in the complex circumstances of North
America may indeed be all but undetectable.

Nothing that the sociologist, or for that matter the ethicist, can see
really distinguishes the behavior or insight of this population from that of
the people around them and interacting with them. One looks for some
distinctive characteristic that could distinguish this particular social tissue.
Or, to put the matter in other terms, one looks for an analytical technique
that might detect trace elements of a *different* moral formation in the
worldly lives of these Christians. Yet, in complex modern societies, the
church's being in sacramental-moral dispersion remains stubbornly invisible. This invisibility is malformation of another kind. It is ironic that
asking such a question produces a new meaning for the term *invisible church*.
The invisible church in this new sense is the moral community one cannot
find on the sociological map. How would one know it if one saw it?

Some will argue that this is as it should be. They will say that the change
effected by grace and received in faith is an inner one, invisible by defi-

nition. The grace of God produces a depth of authenticity in human beings that is simply not visible on the street. One is reminded of Kierkegaard's "knight of faith." The morality concerned is that of the reign of God, a morality not graspable in terms of the kingdoms of this world. Insofar as Christians are citizens of this world they appear to be like everybody else. Maybe they will behave differently in extreme situations because they have deeper inner resources. But under ordinary circumstances, the true meaning of the church as a moral community will not be visible to the outside observer.

Something in me—no doubt my preference for the Reformed tradition—rejects this position. The community of faith needs somehow to be a *visible* moral presence in the world of ordinary human affairs. It needs to evince a pattern of practices in everyday life such that common human life is *sacramentally* transformed. This common life—not merely the bread and the wine—then becomes a manifestation of Christ's body, that is, the total gestalt of Christ's presence in the form of a visibly active community. I am not sure that any social theory is capable of explaining how this can be so, any more than any philosophical theory, such as Aristotle's, can explain the real presence of Christ's body in the sacramental elements. Yet it is social theory that helps us *ask the question*, remembering how important it is to ask questions well.

Against Romantic Expectations

This chapter needs to end with some cautionary observations concerning the claim that the church as moral community can transform the moral imagination of the world. This is clearly what needs to happen. But it will not do to be unduly romantic about the possibilities for success. In the first place, for most pastors, to speak of "formation" in the congregation is more challenge than accomplishment. They are not doing it very well. Most Christian congregations today, especially in the West, are in fact not very effective communities of moral nurture. Under the fragmenting pressures of modern life, they are not transmitting tradition from one generation to the next. They are suffering a grievous loss of biblical literacy. The present generation may be far less "formed" by the churches in scripture and apostolic tradition than at any time in the recent past.

Secondly, by taking seriously the duty of pastors and congregations to bring people to serious moral awareness, the churches are tying themselves to whatever proves to be possible in this regard. Attention to formation within communions and congregations sometimes reveals just those regions of entrenched habit—spirituality of a sort—that are most resistant to fresh theological or moral thinking. Is it possible to base a socially engaged Christian practice, say in opposition to apartheid or in favor of justice, peace, and the integrity of creation, upon the formation that most congregations in our time are likely to receive? In the present state of the church in many places is not what we do malformation, or simply non-formation, rather than genuine training in the faith?

And finally, an emphasis on moral formation is likely to disclose, or exacerbate, potentially church-dividing differences among the communions, as well as divisive tensions within particular churches, that have not previously surfaced in ecumenical discussion. On the one hand, to the extent that these disagreements underlie more public ecclesiological differences, the study of formation may illumine the ecumenical enterprise. But on the other hand, it may turn out that these entrenched, often unspoken, assumptions pose more severe challenges to the unity of the church than familiar kinds of ecclesiological or confessional diversity. The churches are still ill-prepared, with their present methods of ecumenical discourse, to deal with such issues.

I conclude that the churches—at least those of American mainline Protestantism whose situation I know best—are not doing a very good job. Yet admitting this does not get to the bottom of the matter, as if merely trying harder were the answer. The challenge is one that will not yield to trying harder, if that is all that can be done. Needed is an altogether different way of *thinking* about what needs to be done. This is the task of chapter 4. It deals with the way congregational moral *capacities*, as they have been described here, are activated and energized by *possibilities* discerned in encounters with the public world.

FOUR

Formation:
Discerning Moral Possibilities

The preceding chapter has shown how communities of faith—
through their educational, liturgical, and spiritual practices—can generate
certain moral capacities. These capacities include dispositions below the
level of reflection as well as life-habits, attitudes, and practices subject to
conscious thought. Above all they include the congregation's capacity to
see itself as one moral community intersected by and relating to many
others. Such insight, transcending simple institutional self-concern and
aided by judicious employment of human science perspectives, helps believers to correlate the requirements of participation in multiple communal
settings with their various life-dynamics.[1] In all these relationships the
congregation, with all its own communal complexities and inevitable
shortcomings, can become a kind of moral sacrament.

Now it is time to begin to analyze this public sacramental role. Well-
formed congregational capabilities need to include the ability to discern
situational possibilities. Grasping moral opportunities can make the congregation aware—sometimes for the first time—just what its capabilities
are. The theme of formation continues virtually seamlessly throughout
this interaction. Congregations are formed, and in turn form their members, not only by what they do to transmit their traditions of faith and
practice. Formation continues as possibilities of public witness are acted
out. A congregation is formed as much by what it goes through in relation
to other human communities as it is by its own distinctive formative activities.

Ourselves and Others:
Communication across Shifting Boundaries

A recent ecumenical document begins to get at the implications of this insight in the following passage:

> The boundaries of moral formation in church and world are fluid. The Church has its own moral substance. This can be seen in the moral deposit of the ecumenical struggles of recent decades: reverence for the dignity of all persons as creatures of God, affirmation of the fundamental equality of women and men, the option for the poor, the rejection of all racial barriers, a strong "no" to nuclear armament, pursuit of non-violent strategies of conflict resolution, the responsible stewardship of the environment, etc. Yet even this has been drawn out by moral struggles in society in which the church has had to learn at least as much as it has taught. In this way the efforts of moral formation in society have carried their own ecclesial significance: the church has often learned how better to *be* church through these efforts.
>
> There is something crucial here: moral struggle, discernment and formation are not simply to be "annexed" to our understandings and ways of being church and used to draw out the genuine treasures of our traditions. They also challenge those deeply and teach us to learn from the world (which is, after all, God's) how better to recognize and "be" church as a faithful way of life. The kind of *koinonia*[2] born in the cooperation of people of good will around specific struggles for a peaceful, just, and sustainable world may not be ecclesial *per se*. But it has ecclesial consequences in that it, too, is part of the spiritual and moral formation of the church itself as mediated by others in God's world.[3]

There are two broad points to be taken from these paragraphs. Ecumenical relationships and efforts have brought the churches to broad agreement on a certain "moral substance" in which, as churches, they are called to form their members.[4] But they have reached that point partly by learning from the moral achievements, as well as the moral failures, of other human communities, which have at certain times helped them *be* the church in more authentic ways.

Clearly, there is an inherent dialectic at work here. On the one hand, the kind of churchly formation believers have received determines the character and the limits of the moral witness they are able, or have the vision, to live out. Their upbringing both extends and limits what they are able to *see*, and thus what they are able to *do*. But the actual circumstances of each congregation's social environment shape the possibilities for witness that exist in any given case.

The precise combination of capacities in the church and possibilities in the public world is bound to be different in different situations. Still, in relationships with the world beyond the institutional church one can learn more about the meaning of the gospel itself. What a congregation experiences in the effort to bear public witness can be just as formative as its practiced interpretations of the content of its own faith tradition. That tradition was no doubt shaped by costly attempts to bear public witness in the past. Congregations and communions thus need to look at the complex ways in which they both form their members and are formed themselves in the process of being public moral communities. I will try, as the academics say, to "unpack" the dialectic implied in these complex relationships. My argument proceeds in three steps: (1) an analysis of the ways—sometimes equivocal—in which moral substance can be inherited from the past; (2) a look at what moral substance can mean in the practice of citizenship; and (3) reflections on resistance to some forces at work in the world, and cautious, critical solidarity with others.

INHERITED "MORAL SUBSTANCE"
The World Council of Churches document uses language that depicts the sacramental substance of the church largely—although certainly not exclusively—in moral terms. Whether or not it is legitimate to understand "moral substance" sacramentally, the church has taken on this substance partly through formational self-definition and partly through relationships with others lived out in complex historical processes. A dialectical interchange between different communal contexts has been going on throughout the history of the church, and has left its legacy both in formed moral capacities and in the ability to discern moral possibilities. The WCC statement focuses on this interaction as it has been described in recent ecumenical conversations. The meanings of the terms and values named are best understood from inside the ecumenical "struggle."

What happens if this story of interactions with others in the moral sphere is generalized as a way of looking at church history as a whole? They suggest the need for careful discernment where mutual learnings between "church" and "world" are involved. Western societies—and no doubt others—have from time to time adopted (or even legally enacted) standards of conduct which the churches—beforehand, at the time, or later—saw to be consistent with the Christian message. I say "beforehand, at the time, or later" because it has not always been clear where the initiative lay. Did the churches, seeing issues earlier and more clearly than others, successfully push for the outlawry of slavery and child labor or for the establishment of civil rights? Or did they belatedly learn something about the implications of their faith from the energy and witness of re-formers belonging to other social communities? The paths of influence and response have run both ways. Often they have run both ways simultaneously with respect to the same issue.

And the complexity has not ended there. The broader social success of church-instigated, or eventually church-backed, policies has often set processes in motion that in time left the churches marginalized in the very worlds of value they helped to create. Schools, hospitals, human rights laws, and the like often gained independent momentum and backing, abandoning their original ecclesial and moral roots. Finding themselves shunted aside by such secularizing processes, the churches sought other ways to remain socially involved. Sometimes they began to reflect in their own lives the institutionally secularized forms of their original theological insights. They relearned their own messages from the world: but in thinned-out and distorted forms. They became captives to the social consequences of their forebears' influence on the public world.

This is still happening. Many American congregations seem today to suppose that a message of personal freedom, once learned in church as the freedom conferred by the gospel but now lived out in an individualistic, consumerist culture, is still a tolerable translation of what the faith is about. This assumption is, in fact, a form of captivity. It limits, if it does not negate, the potential witness of a Christian moral formation. In a generation or less, the distinctive outlines of the gospel have begun to disappear largely because it has been so successful in influencing a society bent on using it for its own purposes.

It is little wonder, as we have seen, that ethicists such as Stanley Hauerwas have for some time been calling for a clean break from such well-meaning captivity to a "Christian" culture that is not Christian at all, and a return to the sort of ecclesial-moral formation that stresses the special story of the community of faith in the midst of a world that has forgotten its spiritual origins. As usual, Hauerwas expresses himself in terms intended to shock: "How [is] the church to behave if freedom, justice, and a Christian nation are bad ideas?"[5] But he makes an essential point. If churches become chaplains to the established political order, they accept for themselves whatever notion of the nature and function of "religion" that order may take for granted. Churches too easily accept the "freedom of religion" that goes with the assumption that "religion" is something that can be trusted to be politically innocuous. As Hauerwas says:

> We live in a time where Christians in the name of being socially responsible try to save appearances by supplying epistemological and moral justifications for societal arrangements that made, and continue to make, the church politically irrelevant."[6]

Is there a way of being socially responsible that does *not* simply justify societal arrangements that offer "freedom of religion" in return for guaranteed irrelevancy? The best way, I think, is not to count on strategies of confrontation to change society, but, as differently formed people, to enter the fray with a knowledge of the complexity of the interactions that have made us what we are and continue to do so.

CITIZENSHIP AS SPIRITUAL PRACTICE
Short of a radically sectarian withdrawal from society, which even Stanley Hauerwas does not advocate, Christians necessarily live out *some* form of citizenship, responsible or otherwise. Why not treat active, responsible citizenship as itself a spiritual practice: one of those in which believers are formed in the community of faith? Such a return to genuinely distinctive formation may well be prerequisite to any genuine practice of seeking "the well-being of the city" (Jer. 29:7). Once this is accomplished (no easy task), and once we understand the *conditions* (circumstances, limitations, dangers) imposed by the way history has formed the complex of communal relationships involving churches in each particular situation, there is the possibility of grasping what citizenship entails.

One must understand that everyone else one meets in the public arena is trying to do more or less the same thing. There are as many personal and communal histories of moral formation being interpreted in public terms as there are people to meet on the street. But public discourse needs so far as possible to be conducted in a language simultaneously understandable to persons of all these formational backgrounds as well as to the worlds of government, medicine, law, business, and so on. Above all, the public language must be understandable to, and in turn is partially shaped by, the media. If a citizen of any one of the Western democracies expects explicit religious teachings to have some special privilege in public discussion, he or she is considered out of order. Yet religious formations are nonetheless present in the public square and have some influence on how the discussion goes. How so? I will propose three theorems about public discourse in this pluralistic world which together throw light on what goes on in democratic discourse among people representing different moral, cultural, and occupational formations.

First, no question of common human life can be settled purely by logical argument. "Reason" alone isn't good enough. There is an *essential* incoherence in public reasoning apart from unspoken value-assumptions of some kind. The economic philosopher Kenneth Arrow has argued that the nature of public discussion is such that logically *consistent* (as opposed to complexly pragmatic and many-factored) solutions to social problems are not possible when many independent minds and viewpoints are involved. Not, that is, unless all minds happen to agree with one mind, in which case the solution is as good as dictatorially imposed. Decisions reached in other ways, by majority vote let us say, are always *to some degree* arbitrary: filled with practical inconsistencies and anomalies. Perfect consistency in policy planning is possible only if we submit to the "dictator."[7]

It seems consistent with Arrow's insight, although certainly not derived from it, that perspectives from many sources founded on root metaphors of various kinds tend to rule the contributions of different participants in a policy discussion, determining for them—as it were behind the scenes— which arguments appear to be plausible and which do not. And in a radically pluralistic society such assumptions, basic metaphors, or faith commitments may well be so diverse in their import that pragmatic decisions, even internally inconsistent ones, are hard to come by.

Second, there is no way, even for the believer who wants very much to do so, of arguing directly from his or her faith tradition to *particular*, detailed determinations in the realm of public policy. Some things, like murder or rape, are always wrong. And one wants to promote justice and peace and environmental integrity where possible. But to reflect these convictions in *specific* public policy decisions emerging out of political processes is supremely difficult. Christians cannot begin with a Bible story or parable, with a view of the person of Jesus Christ, with the teachings of their particular communion, or even with the results of a lifetime of moral formation, and say that this datum, this "given" that has authority for her or him, leads inexorably to some *unique* resolution of a public question: say the question of how best to finance the county hospital, or whether a proposed change in zoning a residential area is appropriate.

A person of faith may say that he or she personally favors a certain general *direction* to be followed or *value* to be maintained. But moving from this to the choice of particular means—firing the hospital manager, dealing with the physicians' corporation in a certain way, bringing in a managed care firm—is usually not a moral but a technical question. The dilemma as stated typically concerns not exalted moral principle but what, specifically, to *do* about this or that particular problem. And often there is not one single issue but many interconnected issues. The decision to be made typically involves a whole *set* of moves whose consistency with one another in practice and likely overall impact may be hard to predict.

Yet moral questions often hide behind the technical questions. How can they come to expression? It is often hard for moral considerations even to surface amid the many specific questions dealt with in public debate. Technical expertise and political pragmatism tend to rule the day. Yes, it is possible for citizens with deep moral roots to make "here I stand" speeches on particular policy issues: say on abortion, or euthanasia, or taxing tobacco products. But seldom does the public agenda formulate questions in such a way that they offer pure alternatives between sin and righteousness as understood in religious traditions. In the heat of debate, certain questions may *appear* to do so. But the "here I stand" speech is more likely to represent a *political* reality, say the capacity to deliver a hundred thousand votes in the next election, than a contribution to solving the specific technical problem at hand.

Third, although there is no direct route from the content of any faith-tradition to any single publicly plausible line of policy argument, once the public case for a policy is made—on broadly acceptable and understandable grounds and without privileged appeals to traditions of faith held by some but not others—*then* one's religious (or secular) formation will have much to do with how one responds to it. One can *then* say, "I voted for this because I am a Christian, and therefore can give you deeper reasons for my support of this policy than those we discussed in the city council." One can even say, "I voted for this, not because I think that it is so transparently right that it raises no questions of conscience, but rather because my Christian faith allows me to live with the inevitable ambiguity of decisions that simply have to be made. This decision is imperfect—inconsistent in its impact on different persons and groups—but it is *better* than inaction and better than the alternative possibilities."

Given that kind of conclusion, there is obvious room for second and deeper thoughts outside the public arena about the debate going on within it. Perhaps such thinking belongs in the city's churches, temples, and synagogues, as well as in political study groups of various kinds. While practical decisions are being made in the public realm it is legitimate to ask how prior religious or philosophical commitments have influenced the seeming *plausibility* of technical or political decisions in the public realm.

Here, again, one sees the relevance of Bryan Hehir's point about issues needing to be well, rather than poorly, stated. I think Hehir means that issues should first be stated in terms of ultimate warrants and commitments such as those articulated *only* within long-standing traditions of faith and not available in publicly accessible terms.[8] Churches may well prod political discussants, both in the process of making public decisions and afterward, to explore the commitments *underlying* what seem to them to be plausible answers to practical questions.

For example, Christians may be able to agree with others about the shortcomings of the relationship between patients and physicians in our culture.[9] They may further agree that technology, and even the struggle against death itself, "should be subordinated to a relational approach that overcomes disrespect and inhumanity and seeks a genuine human bond with those who suffer." They may then be able to say what faith assumptions, what assumptions about the nature and destiny of the human, support this view, which in turn has led them, and perhaps others, to vote a certain way. In this secondary debate *about* the public debate they may contribute their conviction that "a covenant, and a very particular sort of covenant, is the basis of creation." They may bear testimony that the inner meaning of the physical universe is found in "relationships of covenantal fidelity through which God becomes present in space/time."[10]

Eventually it may be determined whether or not the worldview seemingly implicit in a particular political proposal sufficiently coincides with an underlying biblical vision to win support from people of biblical faith. Perhaps, from the standpoint of Christian moral formation, a given public decision finds in the Bible its most adequate and indeed profound grounding. It is certainly in order for Christians who have carefully used "public language" in the city council to propose, outside that context, their own vision as the best account of what lies behind the agreements reached.[11] A Christian participant in dialogue *about* public dialogue can offer "an anthropology of cohumanity, which presents human creatures as fulfilled in covenants of mutual assistance, which in turn reflect the work of the triune and covenanting God."[12] Presuppositions held by traditioned communities may even lend greater *coherence* to decisions made on a purely pragmatic basis in the public realm. This may be true even if there are other belief systems competing to offer clarifying presuppositions.

The downside, of course, is that too much religious interpretation of public political dialogue can undermine agreements that might otherwise go forward on a happily pragmatic basis. A Jewish city council person says to a Presbyterian colleague: "If I had *known* that *that* was what you thought you were doing when you voted for this, I might have had second thoughts. We are using the same words, but we mean different things by them." One can understand the wisdom of neopragmatists like Richard Rorty who want to keep deep religious or metaphysical convictions out of public debate, either by denying that they are meaningful or by just "changing the subject" when such things come up. But thereby Rorty deprives human decision-making of convictions that make certain principles stick, even in the face of strong opposition.

It need only be added that the kind of first-principles discussion of what lies behind public decisions *need* not undermine confidence in those decisions. On the contrary, Christians who think deeply about what is going on, offering better reasons than the public ones for supporting certain policies, and knowing that on some matters only forgiveness and absolution are sufficient to maintain one's humanity, may turn out to be better citizens than those who content themselves with merely pragmatic levels of involvement.

RESISTANCE AND SOLIDARITY

It would be wrong, however, to leave this subject without saying that Christians must sometimes take very partisan stands. Even though articles of faith are never abstractly translatable into specific public policy decisions, there are circumstances in which faith requires Christians to stand resolutely against, or—as the case may be—resolutely alongside, some policy or movement in the public world.

In many ways standing–against is the easier position to describe. Confronted by radical evil, one does not enter a policy debate. One resists. The possibility of declaring a *status confessionis*, by which one's attitude to some issue is made a question of the integrity of the faith itself, is always available. Things like Nazism, apartheid, or child molestation are evils simply to be resisted, not to be negotiated. Above all, one must resist any attempt to defend, or compromise with, such things *theologically*, as the "German Christians" under Hitler and several white South African churches in the apartheid era did.

There are other evils that should likewise be resisted but in which the target is more difficult to describe, as is the exact nature of the amelioration desired. I would place the impact on many human beings of the current global market economy in this second category, where declaration of a *status confessionis* is probably not appropriate because of the great complexity of the issue. Resistance to evil applies here too, but something more than a simple no is required. Needed, rather, is energetic analysis of the issue and a determination to take steps to do something about it as possibilities for such steps appear in the course of events.

Solidarity with what is strongly approved is on the whole a more complex matter than resistance to evil. This is so because solidarity involves some degree of identification between the movement in question and the substance of the faith: enough at least to justify "standing alongside" in practice if not with full theological conviction. There certainly appear to be initiatives, movements, events in the world with which those who participate in Christian moral formation will feel enough kinship to justify a stance of solidarity. I would argue that such a stance is justified if there is reason to think that the Holy Spirit is at work in the matter concerned, or, what is the same thing, that the movement anticipates the rule of God. But how does one distinguish between genuine secular anticipations of the rule of God, and political movements we just happen to like? Can one look at worldly initiatives and determine with certainty that the Spirit of God is at work there?[13]

This question cannot be answered by constructing plausible theological arguments. Only the actual experience of engagement can tell. And here the capacity most needed is another term from the vocabulary of spiritual formation: discernment (the Greek verb is *diakrino*). The word means to make penetrating judgments, to find particular meanings, qualities, or possibilities in persons or situations. But it also means to make appropriate distinctions. Discernment itself is a gift of the Spirit. But one can only be truly discerning about that which one knows at first hand, by personal experience. That is why knowing the human world thoroughly is the first step on the way to discovering how the Spirit may be at work there in ecclesiologically significant ways.

From taking a stance alongside, or within, such specific struggles one may gain insight—available in no other way—into what is going on in the world. If the community of faith identifies with what Michel Foucault called "subjugated knowledges,"[14] it may well learn something transforming of its own ecclesial self-understanding. Still, one cannot be certain that any social movement, even one from which one gains significant self-knowledge, is worth supporting unreservedly. Solidarity needs always to be critical in the sense of asking how far this or that cause anticipates the reign of God. It needs to be critical also in the sense that one asks what the stance of the visible church in the world alongside such a movement, given the church's own social role, might mean. A stance in solidarity with some social movement opposed to the organized church may in some instances convey the needed message better.

Bert Hoedemaker suggests that many Christians today feel a deeper and more challenging *koinonia*, or communion, with non-Christians whom they believe see the world as it truly is and are doing something about it than with members of their own churches who lack such insight and courage.[15] Indeed Hoedemaker describes what it might mean to reconceive the nature of the church itself around this insight. In this perspective (it is not clear how far Hoedemaker himself shares it) Christians seek *koinonia* with persons who genuinely confront the radical moral challenges this contemporary world poses to the human race, and *then* search out whatever relevant resources the Christian tradition may possess. Such a program, consistently pursued, would in time sociologically relocate and politically reposition the church in relation to its human surroundings. It would tend to hand over stewardship of the tradition to people other than those who exercise this stewardship now. Such a community of the

morally serious might, or might not, come to interpret the biblical tradition as it has customarily been understood in conventional church circles.
One wonders whether this might in the end mean a loss of the substance
of the tradition, and therefore a loss of capacity to pass on significant moral
formation to others? Or might the reverse happen? Might such develop-
ments lead to such a rejuvenation of faith as would empower a deeper and
more relevant moral witness?

I suspect that the most likely outcome might be a transformation of
congregational self-understandings within a still recognizably faithful frame
of reference. A search for deeper *koinonia* beyond the church's traditional
boundaries would be bound to change believers' perceptions of the faith's
center, as well as of its edges, but not an abandonment of fundamental
Christian convictions. The search for *koinonia* "outside the camp" (Heb.
13: 13) could help articulate deeper theological justifications for, or criticisms of, public policies than can usually be expressed in the public arena
as such. It could help us see what Bryan Hehir, after Georges Bernanos,
meant by calling for "theological convictions that can illuminate contemporary questions that are being poorly stated." Movements most amenable
to being better articulated in this way are precisely the sorts of initiatives
with which churches can thoughtfully and critically make common cause.
But not by a kind of takeover strategy. It is important to respect the secular
convictions, if secular they are, of those whose goals we find ourselves
able to share.

In the end it is the Christian community, gathered around a story of
God's generosity to humankind, that can make sense of moments when
human beings are better, more "decent" in Avishai Margalit's terms,[16]
than they are able be on their own. The same story of God's generosity—
now taken to the point of enduring crucifixion—also makes sense of situations in which there *is* no being-better but only radical evil. Christians
are formed in a metanarrative which society, for both better and worse,
needs for the very possibility of understanding itself.

If this is so, the congregation, living in this narrative, can *decode* the
signs of God's reign, become involved in aspects of society that seem to
represent this reign appearing, and live a story more adequate for the
history of humanity than the secular myths, powerful as they are. The
congregation, whose members are formed by their "worldly" occupations
in attitudes and forms of life characteristic of secular society, is a place
where *this society* is re-formed in ways which bring out how God is at

work, which lift up the potential of *this society* for being a place where the reign of God is present and to come.

When such potential is discerned, the time comes to speak and act: to ally oneself with the works of the Spirit and resist those of the Evil One. The congregation earns the right to be heard when it has critically understood the society around it and has also participated in building that society so as to have gained a genuine stake in its life.

Offering Moral Hospitality

The preceding pages have offered an account of the process by which congregations continue to be formed—beyond the internal formation that generates moral capabilities—in and through the possibilities they grasp for interactions with the other communities of the human world. But may morally capable congregations have something still more profound to offer to others? May they be able to do something more than argue particular positions in that world, positions that ultimately may reflect only their own institutional interests rather than the world's true good? Can they offer spiritual *gifts* to humankind?

One such gift could be the offering of a kind of *space* for deeper reflection to fellow human beings of all sorts. And among these fellow human beings might be the serious secular ethicists of our time. In a certain sense the church earns the right to be morally present in the world by understanding what is going on in that world. Christians often believe, and behave, as if no one besides themselves had a moral perspective. That is not the case. I will argue that the congregation's sacramental moral household can offer a gift of *hospitality* to ideas and movements that, without changing their secular character, places them in a larger reflective setting, perhaps changing their import in the process.

The public world, whether it knows it or not, needs something like this. Reinhold Niebuhr himself acknowledged that the gulf between "moral man" and "immoral society" is not absolute. Churches can provide the secular world space for a deepening and broadening of its thought. Niebuhr's words are worth remembering:

> The most perfect justice cannot be established if the moral imagination of the individual does not seek to comprehend the needs

and interests of his fellows. Any justice which is only justice soon degenerates into something less than justice. It must be saved by something which is more than justice. The realistic wisdom of the statesman is reduced to foolishness if it is not under the influence of the foolishness of the moral seer.[17]

The churches have still not grasped the opportunity that these words suggest. That opportunity is for the churches to be communities that offer dialogical space in which the secular institutions of the world can raise—in their own ways—questions beyond those they would otherwise be likely to ask. In the next few pages I try to explore what this idea might entail.

SECULAR ATTITUDES: SUSPICION AND EXPECTATION

It is important to be realistic. Suspicion of religious institutions and ideas is still the order of the day for many secular thinkers. The great "masters of suspicion"—Marx, Nietzsche, and Freud—remain influential. Many continue to think that "religion" is merely a projection, or a form of ideology for justifying class interests, or a superego illusion. I believe such suspicion may also have something to do with attitudes to the social roles of churches. A rejection of implicit claims to religious authority may make it impossible to hear what congregations are saying by their social presence. The religious, or worse, the churchly origin of any moral insight can make it taboo to those who wish to keep their secular credentials pure.

This seems to have been the case with the response to the recent feature film *Spitfire Grill*.[18] Here was a script which dealt profoundly with the theme of atonement—making things right through personal sacrifice—in a way theological viewers could recognize. Yet it did not place this theme in any explicit doctrinal or ecclesiastical context, and secular viewers at first missed the "religious" meaning, if, indeed, that is the right word for what was offered here. *Spitfire Grill* won favorable reviews, and film festival awards. Or, it did so until it was discovered to have been produced by an organization connected with the Roman Catholic Church. At that moment the ready reception for a tale about making things right turned to rejection. From being seen as carrying a message concerning the depths of meaning possible to autonomous human experience, *Spitfire Grill* came to be viewed as an instrument of propaganda, a thinly disguised plot to proselytize. The content of the film had not changed but attitudes toward it had, to the point at which there was talk about false pretenses and even withdrawal of awards the film had earned. Even the most secular observer might be persuaded to see the irrationality of this response. But the suspicion of religious motives is a factor that needs to be dealt with.

Still, there are indications that important intellectual figures in Western thought are beginning to change their minds, if not about the Catholic Church at least about the need for some transcendent dimension in human social life. Many might now agree with Reinhold Niebuhr about justice needing to be saved by something more than justice, even if they would not put the matter in Niebuhr's terms. One senses, for example, in the work of certain social philosophers a desire to articulate the "something more" that human society strives to express, without having adequate words for doing so. The University of California political philosopher Philip Selznick, for example, has written, "A person who rejects traditional religious imagery, yet tries to articulate an ultimate concern, is likely to be tongue-tied. I count myself among the tongue-tied."[19] How might a community of faith grant a Philip Selznick the rhetorical space, in his *own* way, to cease to be tongue-tied?

At a University of Santa Clara colloquy in the spring of 1996 honoring John Rawls on the twenty-fifth anniversary of his book *A Theory of Justice*, six out of the seven major speakers—all of them moral or political philosophers of repute[20]—spoke in one way or another of the need for input from religious scholars or theologians.[21] Since the Santa Clara meeting one of the speakers there, the legal philosopher Ronald Dworkin, has enlarged on his desire to build a bridge to religious values at a series of lectures at Auburn Theological Seminary.

I think that this desire stems from two sources. First, the collapse of confidence in the Enlightenment notion of universal human reason (already noted in chapter 1) has undermined the foundations of an independent secular morality. Philosophers today are living in a world of "modest pragmatism" in which many opinions jostle and any piece of useful conceptual material can be added to the bricolage. So long as Christian thinkers contribute without special pleading, so long as they understand that what they have to offer is shorn of its metaphysical warrants the minute it enters the public sphere, they are presumably welcome to take their chances in the fray.

Second, it has become clear to many who welcome theological input that postconventional moral arguments are often not tradition-independent at all. Rather, they covertly interpret values embedded in the cultures to which the thinkers in question belong. Even for ethicists who proclaim their allegiance to a purely secular rationality, it seems that worldly moral formation of one sort or another plays an indispensable storytelling, symbol-making, and motivating role.[22]

And there may be something else happening, too. The Cambridge theologian John Milbank explains a new openness to the religious by arguing that cultural change has overtaken the secular assumptions of social philosophy itself. Such philosophy (not, perhaps, the sort of political philosophy pursued in the Santa Clara conference) is now in a postmodern and post-Nietzschian situation. Milbank writes:

> While the Nietzschian tracing of cultural formations to the will-to-power still results in a "suspicion" of religion, it also tends to assert the inevitably religious or mythic-ritual shape these formations must take. In this mode of suspicion, therefore, there ceases to be any social or economic reality that is permanently more "basic" than the religious. Theology accepts secularization and the autonomy of secular reason; social theory increasingly finds secularization paradoxical, and implies that the mythic-religious can never be left behind. Political theology is intellectually atheistic; post-Nietzschian social theory suggests the practical inescapability of worship.[23]

But one has to ask *in what form* the dimension of the "religious" is expected by the philosophers to assert itself in political and economic argument. The style of questioning one finds tends still to relegate religious traditions and the bodies that maintain them to the private sphere. Safely insulated from the public world, these traditions—provided they are "reasonable" in Rawls's sense—can then be recognized as useful in forming people who will turn out to be good citizens.[24] But traditional understandings of life are not, or at least not explicitly, considered appropriate points of reference for settling questions that these citizens will face in the public realm.

One gathers that such secular thinkers are hoping that their theories will gain practical support, and are willing to accept it whatever its source. They favor religious bodies that will behave rationally, bringing perspectives from "reasonable comprehensive doctrines" held in the private sphere to bear on public argument without seeking to impose religious warrants. They are, secondly, looking for ideas and concepts that can be separated from explicit religious connections and employed to enrich secular thought. The idea of forgiveness (or its secular counterpart, "amnesty") for example may, as the French say, be *disponible* (i.e., available for use) in the field of jurisprudence.[25]

Even with such limitations in mind, many look to the churches and are disappointed. Secular thinkers are heard to complain that "Christian ethicists" who concern themselves with public issues have little to add to what one hears from the general run of thinkers indebted to the long tradition of liberal thought in Western modernity.[26] Some are now saying they long to hear a distinctive note from Christian colleagues, something fundamentally different, something that could *make* a difference.

STRATEGIES OF CHRISTIAN RESPONSE

In response to invitations such as these, Christian ethicists need *both* to participate with others in the effort to articulate the public good *and* to find ways of speaking and acting publicly out of the riches of a distinctively Christian moral formation.

Whatever the attitude taken to theologians in these circles, significant issues of human well-being are at stake, and therefore Christian thinkers need to be involved. Indeed some Christian ethicists today work mainly in this frame of reference, understanding it as a Christian duty to participate fully in humanity's search for the meaning of goodness, or principles for living together in peace on this planet with respect for the dignity of all persons.

I therefore believe that it was a mistake on the part of John Paul II in *Veritatis Splendor* to excoriate certain unnamed Catholic ethicists for departing from natural law theory to work in frames of reference such as moral "proportionalism" or "consequentialism." It is important for at least some Christian thinkers to earn the right to be full participants in the moral reflection of today's secular world. The 1994 Cairo conference on world population growth offers a useful illustration of the range of modes of thought with which it is important to be conversant.

At this meeting, as Peter Steinfels has pointed out,[27] at least three groups of languages were being spoken: the languages of the different religious traditions (Roman Catholic, Protestant, Jewish, Islamic, and others), the languages of human science and public policy (sociology, anthropology, demography, public health, the discourse of governmental and nongovernmental organizations), and languages vividly descriptive of specific human situations (feminists, representatives of oppressed groups, religious dissenters, and so on). All of these modes of discourse were, and are, being commented upon by those who are trying to think in postconventional terms about the human condition as such (secular moralists, political philosophers, and the like). A list of moral projects like this hammers home the point that the church's effective, witnessing, being as moral community means participation in, without capitulation to, many different levels and types of moral discourse.

At the Cairo conference the Vatican strategy apparently was to attempt to block support for abortion rights or birth control from being approved rather than to get into the ongoing argument about the human condition and try to enlarge it, or at least give it room to move, toward transcendental concerns. I believe that this was, and is, shortsighted.

Churches can and should offer a sort of metaphorical space in the world for those, believers and otherwise, who believe that human society can overcome its violent origins, its continuing resentment and mistrust, and come to realize its true calling to become the beloved community envisioned in the biblical story. The churches exist to *hold open* a social space in which society's existing structures and practices can be seen for what they are and in which human community can be articulated in a new way, a space in which the metaphors of common life can be exposed to their transcendental ground.

Can the faith community embrace secular discourses in such a way as to deconstruct their claims to be autonomous? Can theological participation provide space for a re-construction of secular moral discourse by giving it a language for ceasing to be "tongue-tied" about its ultimate concerns? Can the practice of the *ekklesia* speak persuasively about the grounds for a trust in one's fellow human beings that is required for the workability of the discourse itself? Participants in the household may well find in *all* these discourses elements of the gospel in forms alienated from means of explicit expression. By providing a *different* sort of dialogical space in the midst of the civic debate, churches may help the secular discourse to come to itself and thus join them in a household of life. In that event, it may cease to be alienated. Faith and human solidarity are not identical, but they come closer to one another than before.

As already indicated, the essence of the space held open resides not only in deep formation around the symbols of faith but in a certain kind of reconciling, forgiving *practice*.[28] By coming within, or even near, that realm of practice, human beings are led to extend the meanings of their own ordinary-life activities to fulfill the potential that exists in them without the limitations imposed by ideological, positivist, or merely pragmatic understandings of what such occupations mean. Brought into a social space kept open to transcendence because it permits the articulation and sharing of basic trust or faith, the virtues connected with ordinary human practices both deepen and ramify to become what they were meant to be.

Duncan Forrester illustrates this point by showing how the virtue of justice deepens and extends itself in the vicinity of Christian practice to become *generosity*.[29] One could likewise say that the virtue of *prudence* deepens and extends itself to become *wisdom*. Legal correctness becomes the *righteousness* that flows down from heaven "like a mighty stream" (Amos 5:24). Such transformations of finite, worldly virtues into qualities of character that exceed all reasonable expectation happen when human beings are drawn into a space of discourse in which moral practice mediates the reality of grace.[30]

I do not propose that, as guests within the Christian "household," social movements should be expected to find new, explicit foundations for their work in the gospel of Jesus Christ (although that could happen) but rather that such movements might "come to themselves" in their finitude, shed their claims to self-sufficiency, and begin to see that instead of having reasoned out their visions of the world in purest intellectual autonomy they have actually *interpreted* certain kinds of moral formation in presuming which they "overlap" (perhaps in Rawlsian fashion) both with Christian tradition and with the presumptions of other walks of life. They may come to realize that they have turned these things into abstractions that seem to stand on their own feet, but cannot. And in discovering that different sorts of secular self-understanding that seemed bitterly opposed politically, or logically incompatible philosophically, really can coexist within a larger moral household, they may be able to reconcile their differences and give themselves to deeper, more universal, human concerns.[31]

I am saying, then, that the "household of life" is a larger human community, with specific religious communities at its core, where such realizations happen and energy is released for serving the still-larger human community.[32] The common theme of the household is "life" itself. Is it possible that many a political argument that separates human beings from one another is really resolvable, given sufficient mutual trust (no easy achievement) into different interpretations of some common moral concern?

The legal philosopher Ronald Dworkin mounts just such an argument in his book on abortion and euthanasia in suggesting that the opposed sides in these cases represent different interpretations of a prior, deeper, principle shared by both: the principle of life's *sanctity*.[33] Sanctity is another word for *holiness*. The notion of life as a holy gift opens up rich veins of moral tradition. I suspect that Dworkin's suggestion does not work if merely advanced as an argument for the negotiating table. It might well work, over time, in the context of a community able to live out the implications of Jesus' word "I came that you might have life, and have it more abundantly."

The "household" strategy does not suggest that Christians should try to tell the world how to think.[34] Rather it offers the world a context in which *it may do its own thinking* free of the shallow alternatives the world gives. It offers a context for thinking of a sort that may not be permitted by one's own self-image or by one's colleagues in business because it is not quantitative and goal-oriented, yet thinking that Christians and these other human beings deeply want to do together.

One of the best illustrations I know of the need for such common thinking has to do with the relation between caring and economics in modern medicine. There is need here for love, compassion, forgiveness to counter the iron laws of economics in order to produce simple justice. But in North America, at least, health care is being "managed" to its detriment by profit-making corporations, among other things eagerly watching (although they dare not say so) the progress of the movement toward the legalization of "physician-assisted suicide." Public debate on this topic has been much too narrow, focusing mainly on what is being called the "Kevorkian moment," that is, the moment when a "terminal" patient—in great pain or deep despair—asks for medical assistance in ending his or her life. Shall this be allowed or not? But the narrowly focused question is not always the real question. Settling the question in favor of physician assisted suicide—presumably on grounds of the patient's moral autonomy—could gravely upset the whole balance and setting of human life-together in ways that seldom enter the debate today.

Discussants fail to see that the availability of such an option could tear holes in the whole network of caring, in family, church, and the larger society, to which people are accustomed and on which they depend. This network of caring has clear religious implications. The question is whether we human beings are part of a household of life that cares for us simply because we are members of the household, or whether we are mere pawns in cost-benefit calculations. The minute that sanctioned suicide becomes an option, the door is open for pressure on sick people to go that way: to save money for another generation to inherit, to save families from years of caring responsibilities, to save profits for health maintenance organizations, and so on. By focusing on only one question—shall physicians be authorized to respond to a patient's request at a given moment—the larger import of the matter is ignored. Is not the whole idea an aspect of the economically conscious management of care, in fact a way of rationing care by urging persons to refuse to continue consuming economic resources when their cases become hopeless?

The real issue, as so often, is what kind of a human community we want to be. Do we want to be unconditionally compassionate and caring, or is there to be a moment at which the option of disposal rather than care comes into play? This is a case in which openness to a larger household of meaning can transform the terms of the argument by adding factors that do not appear when attention is focused only on the moment of decision about a particular action.

It is conceivable, too, that the community of faith could bring together in a larger moral context both religious and secular discussants on the different sides of the "Kevorkian" question because of its sensitivity to the meaning of an underlying issue: the issue of suffering. The distinctive Christian language of scripture, theology, and liturgy could take on the task of building bridges between diverse human beings—without imposing itself on them—because it speaks of the most elemental issues of human life. It speaks of suffering and it speaks of hope. There is something here which is prior to moral discourse altogether: what Jean-Jacques Rousseau, building on the Christian story, thought of as a prearticulate *sentiment* that the suffering of others is also our suffering.

Emmanuel Levinas has offered a luminous treatment of this understanding in *Totality and Infinity*.[35] It is not by accident that the images of our common humanity today involve the gaze of suffering. Think, for example, of photographs of the Holocaust in the 1940s, or of Biafra in the 1960s. The sense of common life in a household offers us the opportunity for awareness that the other suffers just like me.[36] Rebecca Chopp has shown that suffering simply *interrupts* the continuities of our moral thinking, simply short-circuits the usual sorts of reflection about obligation, autonomy, and all the rest.[37] Conventional meanings are radically displaced. The sense that we have rational control of our lives is undermined. We *need* the support and reassurance a household of life can give.

As for hope, the whole content of this chapter seeks to locate the grounds for it. Hope cannot be entertained *without* a realistic appreciation of the suffering in the midst of which it arises. I believe that this Christian hospitality to human suffering and hope can be sensed by persons and movements having little or nothing to do with the church, but much concern for what happens to human beings in our time. The Christian household offers a sensitivity to the kinds of suffering that lie *behind* the confident secularity of so many people. It offers a willingness *not* to give advice, or to argue positions, but to be *with* other persons in their individual and communal identities, prayerfully including all in the larger context of God's purposes for humankind.

Such hospitality could be especially meaningful to thinkers—secular and religious alike—who deeply *feel* the human issues with which they deal and who know that some of these issues cannot be resolved within the limits of this life. The community of faith offers a space for those who know that in human terms they have no answers to issues of human suffering, who know that in making decisions they cannot avoid a deep sense of guilt, who sense the enormity of the questions that face us human beings, and who know that in face of intractable moral mysteries there need still to be grounds for hope.

MORAL HOSPITALITY IN ACTION

It is a mistake, I think, to have any one fixed idea of how the church should encourage the emergence of a household of life in the world including both those who act by faith and those whose secularly grounded actions move into rhetorical space provided them by the faithful. All depends on the actual circumstances. In my own experience, people who actually had the faith (mostly traditional in form, often supported by their congregations) to go on freedom rides through the American south in the late 1950s and early 1960s opened space for many with less courage or more secular bent to expand *their* horizons and hence engage in new political practices that moved the cause of civil rights forward across the nation.

Or consider a more recent example. Among the many roles played by the churches of East Germany before the wall came down, and of South Africa before apartheid was abolished, was to keep open sanctuaries, both literal and metaphorical, in which these two democratic revolutions began to take form strategically in the minds of their founders. In the former East Germany, participation by the churches in the peace movement launched in opposition to the 1975 Warsaw Pact decision to deploy nuclear weapons on that territory in turn gave the churches the chance to link international peace issues with internal civil rights questions. This linkage made it possible for the churches "to provide a protective space in which other issues concerning human rights and the environment could be discussed."[38] These and other moves gave secular leaders a "household" space to begin asking questions in the right way, and thereby to become at least guests in that household: perhaps in the mode of temporary foster care![39]

In South Africa, declarations by black church leaders before the fall of apartheid gave many, including at least a few staunch Africaaners, space to think, still within their own cultures, thoughts other than officially sanctioned ones: again to ask questions in the right way.[40] At this stage of the struggle the churches became political representatives of the oppressed, making space in the society for *them*, whether Christians or not, to be heard. Following the fall of apartheid, the adoption of a constitution, and the election of Nelson Mandela, the role of the churches shifted. The oppressed now had their own *political* representatives. Church leadership as such became less publicly prominent. The churches saw that they needed, among many other things, to participate in the reconstruction of society "on the basis of values determined by the Kingdom of God and in solidarity with others committed to those values."[41] One way in which they have done this has been to provide leadership, as well as the indispensable notion of a forgiveness that is not a condoning or forgetting of the past,[42] to the Truth and Reconciliation Commission. By hearing confessions from both sides and considering pleas for amnesty, this body, chaired by retired Archbishop Tutu, has been performing a kind of national exorcism. Here a whole nation is being liberated into a space in which questions can be asked in a way that should make for peace.

It will be said by skeptics that the churches in many of these cases at most have offered acceptable ideological cover under which politicians and other leaders, themselves indifferent to theological claims, could act. Certainly this has been true often enough. But I think that the churches have sometimes succeeded in supplying space in which politicians, on their own terms, could dream fruitful dreams. The theological utterances of Desmond Tutu, for example, generated a kind of moral clearing in the tangled thickets of South African public opinion that could then be filled with the political vision of Nelson Mandela. A certain imaginative, re-sourceful *boldness* becomes possible when one stands in space maintained by a theological vision, even when one cannot accept the traditional language in which the vision is expressed. In these and other such cases the churches have offered a "household of life" in which questions could be asked in a deeper way than the political situation in any given case made possible. Is it not then possible to regard members of other human communities who feel drawn toward such depth as at least guests in the household, from whom the household's regular inhabitants may also have something to learn? I argue that this line of thought is not only possible but necessary in our time.

And, if so, might it be possible to establish some sort of intercommunal *linkage* between householding moments of this sort in all their variety and sometimes evanescent character? Many now begin to see the building of such a larger household as a primary aim of all the many ecumenical processes, meetings, consultations, and relationships. In part through the very presence of Christian faith communities constituting sacramental social spaces within and among them, human cultures might be liberated to move toward justice, peace, and integrity in their relationships with the created order. Might there come to be a globally extended family, an *oikoumene* indeed, of such gatherings of the people of God? The pages that follow begin to explore that question.

An Oikoumene *of Moral Practices?*

The patterns of practice by which Christian faith communities make their moral witness in today's world turn out to be shaped in a variety of distinctive ways. These configurations differ in content and emphasis, but also seem to be acting out various thematic readings of the gospel story. Particular historic patterns, taking their rise in particularly formative situations of the past (for example, Henry VIII's maneuvers to divorce several of his wives and the role of his tactics in the emergence of Anglicanism, or the problem of defining and maintaining the community of communicants in Puritan Massachusetts Bay Colony and its implications for subsequent American Protestant ecclesiological patterns) have now hardened into "communions" or "denominations." These, among other things, are contemporary bureaucratizations of ecclesiastical arrangements that arose in circumstances other than those we face today.

Escaping from Divisive Fixations

Can the Christian community be satisfied with this sort of fragmentation into divisive fixations? The churches are facing a global human community rapidly becoming more and more interconnected and interdependent, yet increasingly divided spiritually. The operational global nexus, as chapter 2 has made clear, is increasingly economic in character. Decisions and transactions by major players in the contest for economic advantage are often corrosive of broader human well-being. A shared concern about the impact of a global market economy on the human life-world is potentially a commitment to the world's people as opposed to the world's power structures. This in turn requires a commitment to those most likely to be left out of our moral dialogues altogether. These are the large majority of the human race who have a vivid, if inarticulate, sense of justice and injustice, but who do not participate in sophisticated moral arguments or try to articulate the ends of human life in academic terms.

There is something elementally universal in the experience of being powerless, put upon, exploited, excluded. The well-known "preferential option for the poor" is not only a commitment to aid and support the economically deprived. It is a strategy of solidarity with the insecurity that lies at the heart of each individual's existence: an insecurity most manifest in the experience of having no control over one's life or circumstances. It is also a strategy of solidarity with the *discourse* of the poor, a human language more subjugated and yet more inclusive, indeed potentially more ecumenical, than any other.

The point needs reiteration. The churches cannot live effectively in such solidarity with the suffering of the world while they themselves remain divided. The opportunity sacramentally to signify God's gathering of the people of earth into a blessed community is severely compromised by the inability of Christian communions to surmount the ecclesiastical barriers that separate them. They are squandering a great opportunity. The churches are already deeply rooted in diverse formative cultures. They can, if they will, demonstrate the capacity of the gospel to bring a more comprehensive unity into place, embracing many different cultural situations. They have the chance to help weave the many different *practices* of the world into a larger narrative that has room for myriad supporting story lines, yet leads to a common end at last in the reign of God.[1]

Councils of churches, and the World Council of Churches in particular, should be the churches' instruments for discerning the signs of the coming-to-be of that universal moral community of humankind, the realm of God's reign. If councils of churches have an ecclesiological task of their own—which is not to say that they are churches as such—it could be to work out the practical meaning of that vision of the *oikoumene*, of the "household of God" or "household of life," and to help their member churches move toward being genuine signs, sacraments, and instruments of that reality in the world.

The great question, then, is this. Participating inescapably in a global nexus increasingly defined in economic terms—terms that constitute in their own way a pragmatic understanding of what human life is all about—can the churches begin to think their ways toward realizing a nexus of relationships within which they can weave the fabric of a Christian moral culture? Has such a Christian moral culture existed in the past? Might the vanished fabric of "Christendom"—at its best—have been something like this? What might such a Christian moral nexus look like under the totally different conditions of today? Clearly the ecumenical movement should now seek to foster, for the sake of humankind, a network of just, peaceful, sustainable, and nonexploitative relationships. One might almost say that today such a Christian moral-ecclesial culture-in-the-making is potentially ecumenism's most tangible substance, and perhaps the basis of its most important gift to the world.

Resources for Moral Sharing

Given such a goal, what resources do the churches and the ecumenical organizations they support have to work with? And, in view of available resources, what should such a project involve conceptually, institutionally, strategically, tactically? It is plain now that the real discussion partners in the effort to realize Christian faith in terms of a global ecclesio-moral community may not be the organized denominations and communions as such, but, rather, different contemporary visions of ecclesio-moral practice in the world that exist within and among them. The appropriate strategy is to try to penetrate behind the facades presented by our existing communions, to realize that they each represent fixations of church-world interactions from the past, and yet that they today harbor many contemporary styles of interaction with other human communities, many centers and forms of creative spiritual energy.

The fixated forms of ecclesio-moral life could now be gradually breaking up—rather as ice floes crack, melt, and float loose in the spring—precisely over moral issues. The break-up of these patterns could turn out to be very damaging if they *only* represent polarization over sexual taboos.

Yet the disintegration of old patterns could also make room for energetic new alignments focused on moral issues we have scarcely begun to discern and define. The need today could be to reconstruct different visions of church-in-world not as new "denominations" but as varieties of spiritual-moral practice lifting up different concerns within the communion of one church.

Bringing with them many configurations of lived practice—some focused on issues of personal integrity, some seeking justice and peace in the public world—churches come together to try to articulate, find language and structure for, the *oikoumene* they imply. We ask, what is the whole (or "catholic") purpose of God of which these formational experiences are partial appearings? How do we put *together* these lived clues to what it might mean for humanity to realize its calling to *be* God's "image" in the universe?

At this moment in the ecumenical journey, the Greek word *koinonia* offers itself as a key term for grasping what such an *oikoumene* of moral-spiritual practices might mean. For present purposes it is worth noting that *koinonia* has strong formational and practical connotations. The term denotes a living-together that shares a certain spiritual *substance*, a common rootage in some particular religio-cultural "thickness." Formation in the things of God, indeed, enables disciples to participate in God's very being, as humanity is sacramentally incorporated into the life of the Trinity.[2]

The ecumenical challenge lies in the fact that the comprehensive *oikoumene* of God, to which these existing forms of *koinonia* point, remains a prophetic vision expressed in theological concepts, in various common activities, in more or less bureaucratic ecumenical institutions. These ideas, activities, and institutions *represent* the ecumenical vision in the world. So to speak, they mark it, hold a place open for it. But they are not yet the *substance* of it. The comprehensive *oikoumene* of God does not yet exist in the world with the kind of tradition and substance and "thickness" that can truly form people ecclesially and morally.

Yet there are anticipations of this ecumenical *koinonia*. The nearness of the comprehensive, inclusive communion that is God's will has been palpable during many ecumenical events.[3] There are also places of ecumenical culture, of ecumenical spirituality, in which many persons (but few in relation to the churches' total memberships) have been "formed." One thinks of the formation that used to go on in ecumenical work camps, in many national Student Christian Movements, in the World Student Christian Federation, and even now among staff members, committees, and adherents of councils of churches. The Ecumenical Institute at Bossey, near Geneva, has been especially distinguished in fostering formation of this kind. But such ecumenical formation has not yet been sufficiently comprehensive, continuing, or deep. It has been for a privileged few. It has seldom involved the whole of people's lives. It has not yet produced a profound spiritual tradition of its own. It has always tended to represent *some* of the existing ecclesial traditions of formation better than others, sometimes leaving whole communions and confessions feeling effectively excluded.

Articulating the visible form or forms of a truly comprehensive *koinonia* remains the problem: a problem theological and institutional at the same time. At the practical level we borrow institutional concepts from the many secular "*oikoumenes*" existing all around us. The World Council of Churches, as already noted, somewhat resembles many other nongovernmental international organizations. Ecumenical efforts also borrow the "movement" model from a variety of secular initiatives, as well as Western parliamentary models for running assemblies and meetings of all kinds. The Roman Catholic version of the *oikoumene* still manifests aspects of the imperial model learned from ancient Rome. Most importantly, we all seek to discern the meaning for our time of the *conciliar* model based on the ancient "councils" of the church, speaking of a "conciliar" unity far deeper than what is meant by "council" in such a title such as World Council of Churches.[4] How far, and in what way, do these various conceptual and organizational models serve as vehicles for the central conviction that we are being formed in a comprehensive *koinonia* of the moral-sacramental practices of Christian faith?

A Need for New Language

Given the long-term importance of this attempt to find the moral-ecclesial *oikoumene* toward which different Christian faith practices point, the familiar patterns of ecumenical conversation could well be refreshed by taking into consideration the different lived traditions of spiritual and moral witness in which people are formed. To accomplish this, new ecumenical languages will need to be invented and placed alongside already well-known vocabularies.

This task will require full appropriation of the achievements of inter-church dialogue as historically organized in the Faith and Order and Life and Work movements (not forgetting bilateral dialogues and union negotiations). But needed, too, is some way of breaking free of the fragmentation of consciousness and effort these multiple enterprises have represented.[5] Such a goal cannot be reached by simply pasting together in the same paragraphs sentences in each of the different "languages" involved, seeking to say the same thing first in one ecumenical vocabulary and then in another. Given vocabularies always reflect specific institutional histories. They carry codes that insiders recognize. They tie the "native speakers" of the enterprise to those codes. The point is not to forget where the movement was before it got to where it now is, but to find a vocabulary that can take its achievements up into a new synthesis.

In the nature of the case, the needed new vocabulary will not spring full blown from any individual's attempt to produce one. It will be the product of shared ecumenical experience. Those who learn to live together in a morally engaged global community of faith will eventually find the words to talk about it. The time may be ripe, in fact, for this to happen. In some situations the church is still captive to long-standing cultural expectations that restrain fresh thinking and innovation. But increasingly, these cultural expectations are disappearing as secularized societies cease to have much notion of, or indeed to care much about, what the church may claim to be its role in the world. In some parts of the world there have never been any such expectations. But even in historically "Christian" lands, more and more young people grow up without religious education. For them there is a tabula rasa so far as religious institutions are concerned. On the one hand, these conditions call for a massive educational effort to restore biblical and theological literacy. But, on the other hand, the churches are also freer than they have been in centuries to be what they believe God wants them to be.

Not that finding the way will be easy. In some situations circumstances give the church few strategic options. Overthrowing injustice or oppression, or a sheer struggle for survival, may be the unavoidable agenda. But more often, and especially in the West, it is hard for Christians to find their way, not because the territory is trackless but because there are too many possible paths, too many ways of seeing the world, too many signposts, too many competing visions, which they are invited to consider as if they were spiritual consumers. The watchword is "choice," as if choice were the same thing as freedom.

Many in the West share the conviction that in this vertigo of possibilities many traditional forms of ecclesial life and thought are failing to work very well. Some are manifestly dysfunctional. Yet there are signs of the future in present patterns of practice, if only they can be identified for what they are. Can the churches break away from formulas of the past that prevent them from seeing the opportunities that exist for this generation? One way to do so is to see that living the Christian story and bearing moral witness to it in the world are inextricably inter-related. Eucharistic worship, rightly understood, renders ecclesial and moral reality one.

Chapters 3 and 4 have sought to show what this means, in terms both of thought and practice. It means, among other things, recovery of the very substance of the faith as confessed and lived. This means, above all, a return to the sources, a deep revisiting and renewal of shared connections to the story of salvation through its repetition in worship, where the en-acted narrative manifests its transcendent dimension of mystery and be-comes more than just another beguiling story. Such formation leads disciples to a bodily form of witness, a moral positioning, an engagement intrinsic to the persons they have become in the community of faith. It likewise shapes the community itself to take an intrinsically moral role in relation to events around it. All this is one reality, one process, one jour-ney, one experience. Not first a theological moment and then a practical moment, but one single, integral, way of life, seeing, hearing, thinking, doing.

Of necessity, the life of faith understood this way focuses on the im-mediate necessities of each local situation, whatever that may be. Larger visions of history, even when they purport to translate biblical eschatology, may actually blind believers to the needs of neighbors next door. The reading of the signs of the times needs first to open disciples' eyes to immediate opportunities for moral witness that can be grasped even when they cannot see very far or explore the larger ramifications of their actions. There are moments when the right action is apparent, when it is faithless not to act even though one cannot see all the consequences.

In many such cases moral actions are the result of formation that simply makes certain moves intuitive. People so formed are not greatly helped by chains of abstract ethical reasoning. They confront challenges in terms of communal relationships, customs, kinship patterns, deep-seated convictions about what is fitting. They do their practical reasoning in terms analogous to the shapes of life lived in conversation with the scriptures and shaped by participation in the liturgy. Such formation provides the preparation, the conditioning, the equipment, and the companionship to face the unknowable future that confronts us every day. In such circumstances, not to move to the side of a neighbor in need, across the street or across the world, would be a betrayal of the integrity intrinsic to Christian identity.

Yet not all moral challenges are so unambiguous as these. Acting out of a scripturally and liturgically formed integrity may not solve all moral dilemmas, or be without objective risk. There can be no guarantee that in the larger scheme of things intuitive steps will turn out to have been the right ones.

Vaclav Havel somewhere makes a distinction between optimism and hope. Optimism is the expectation of success. Hope, on the other hand, does not require belief that things will necessarily turn out as expected, or turn out well for ourselves in particular. Hope says there is ultimate meaning in faithful action however immediately ensuing events unfold. Indeed we human beings can only see "through a glass, darkly" (I Cor 13:12 KJV). Many of the issues we face involve existential issues of the most fundamental sort: issues of the quality of life, issues of justice, issues of survival. It is legitimate to stand back and reflect on these things. When we do that, moral formation provides narrative, liturgical, and conceptual materials for reflection. But formational conditioning will not necessarily provide immediate answers to specific problems. It may do more to help faith communities live with human dilemmas in hope.

It is important to remember that thinking in terms of formation means that when individuals act, the church is acting in them. Therefore they have a responsibility to act as witnesses in and for a community of faith, that is, with the support and pastoral care of a worshiping congregation. But further it means that they act in the context of the whole ecumenical church, in ways that are in touch with the experiences of others who have passed this way before.

In certain circumstances, as chapter 4 makes clear, an action that seeks to body forth the integrity of a formed identity is also one that takes believers into critical solidarity with some other movement in which the faith community discerns the Spirit at work, or the reign of God antici-pated. Of course, it can be dangerous to think that the Spirit's presence can be objectively identified. Still, there is an enormous attraction in find-ing in the company of others more of that sense of *koinonia* of which Christian formation has already provided a taste. We want more, and sometimes find it in relationships beyond the visible church.

But this is surely a principle to be applied cautiously. What feels like *koinonia* may be no more than a very human sense of companionship in facing danger or even seeking adventure together. Yet if the church is intrinsically a moral community acting in the power of the Holy Spirit, then it follows that living out its witness where the Spirit is also at work should extend to others the sense of *koinonia* that is intrinsic to the eu-charistic community as such.

Communion among Diverse Practicing Communities: Resonance and Recognition

The description just given almost sounds as if the local were all. Does the diversity of particular situations make it impossible to generalize about them? Are there no concepts of broad application that can grasp the many forms of "thick" particularity that mark the way traditioned, formed peo-ple exercise their responsibility for moral integrity?

Not, it seems, if one is searching for abstract moral propositions pur-porting to be universal in themselves. Rather, what congregations do is share among themselves the experience of the larger church, whose "lo-cality" *is* the *oikoumene*. This is why the life of each congregation requires an ecumenical dimension. Theological concepts do not define the catholic or universal church. Shared life experiences do. Every local moral chal-lenge has implications for other human communities. Every moral issue of broad human concern has local applications waiting to be articulated.[6]

Are there issues involving so many communities and situations on earth today that they deserve to be called "global" or "universal"? Can such comprehensive notions be persuasively articulated at all? We face post-modernism's penchant for the deconstruction of all large systems of thought, as well as the power structures legitimated by them. On the one hand, such deconstruction very properly attacks the pride of certain great syntheses of the Western academic world: syntheses that assume, for example, that objectivizing human sciences are forms of discourse superior to the "subjugated languages" of the poor and dispossessed. But on the other hand, such attitudes can be seen as demolishing, or at least undermining, the very notion of an ecumenical vision as itself a kind of global synthesis. Just at the moment theologians and ethicists are trying to give ecumenism a new comprehensive meaning they find themselves living in an age whose thinkers have set out to dismantle all such large ideas. The emphasis on formation, with its preferential option for the immediate and the local, seems in tune with the prevailing philosophical temper. But the very word *oikoumene* seems to violate this postmodern preference for particularity, evoking as it does a notion of the essential unity or solidarity of the human race. Can ecumenists still convincingly speak an "ecumenical" language?

Yes, provided it is done with humility and attention to the phenomenon of difference. Whatever postmodern philosophers may say, it is still possible to recognize what certain words mean across gulfs separating radically dissimilar cultures. The defense of human rights in many different contexts is an example. But unless filled out in the "thickness" of specific local application, all such general ideas as democracy, justice, peace, the integrity of creation are likely to remain abstract, no matter how compelling their sound. And such is the fragmentation of contemporary cultural existence, that some of these words are in fact beginning to lose the broadly applicable meanings we thought they had. Is this happening also to the notion of a Christian *oikoumene*?

It is important to recognize that purportedly universal ideas or concepts have often in fact been instruments of (largely Western-based) power structures. Ecumenism needs instead to seek more inclusive and organic ways of thinking: ways capable of hearing and interpreting humanity's "subjugated languages."[7] The culturally shaped communications of the poor may be radically diverse. But they have a certain common resonance recognizable, for those who have ears to hear, in and through the Spirit of Jesus Christ.

The key insight is that the Holy Spirit generates a kind of resonant energy field among those who recognize Christ's presence in the world (Matthew 25:31-46; Luke 24:28-43). This identifiable resonance *connects* biblical and postbiblical instances of hospitality to Jesus. God's incarnate presence in history indeed can be seen as articulated in the *ensemble* of the many perspectives in which the spiritual, moral resonance implicit in Christ's presence has been, and continues to be, known and appropriated by those who follow him. Each particular form of discipleship generates a community distinguishable from, yet recognizable to, other such communities. The Holy Spirit instigates an energy field of resonance *among* these diverse responses to Jesus.[8]

Thus the *oikoumene* is not to be understood as a globalizing, imperial, concept appropriated from the ancient world as an instrument of subjugation by powerful churches of the West. It is rather to be seen as an intentional field of *mutual* recognition by those representing different, yet resonating, patterns and configurations of activity that follow from the Spirit's working. Before there can be an articulable *oikoumene* there is the resonance in which diverse local communities of faith recognize and share the forming, energizing power of the Holy Spirit.

The metaphors of resonance and recognition recall an image found in the Johannine literature. The sheep know the shepherd's voice (John 10:3, see Rev. 3:20). Voice includes the notions of timbre, tone, pattern, texture, characteristic turns of speech: the very factors that enable personal recognition. The voice of the shepherd is heard by the disciples and lived out in patterns of practice that communicate that characteristic "sound" (as an orchestra conveys the composer's musical intention) even when the original voice cannot literally be heard.

These resonant moral life-patterns are expressed above all as liturgy, where the rhythms of discipleship are constantly incorporated into the rhythms of *perichoresis*, the divine dance (see chapter 6). The liturgy gives the Spirit's resonance a tangible, recognizable form. Discipleship means hearing, being drawn, being formed, by this pattern: not just its sound but also its content, the authentic note of a way of speaking by which we are shaped, attesting to an identifiable way of being in the world, yet a way of being that has many different expressions. It is this action-pattern-recognition that is celebrated, acted, and co-risked in ecumenical relationships.

Ecumenical recognition means that the other community's liturgically and morally acted-out pattern of commitment is received as analogous to one's own, and one's own commitment is received as analogous to the other. The analogy exists because of the shared recognition-pattern of moral practice in the Spirit. People formed by the liturgical—that is, worshiping—enactment of the story such that life in the world con-forms with that formation are able to *ascertain* that others are doing the same: recognize that others "have the same spirit." Spirit is always something that realizes itself in concrete life-practice. One knows it by how it looks and how it sounds. Such recognition is something holistic, never *merely* doctrinal or jurisdictional but nevertheless including both doctrinal and jurisdictional elements. It is mutual recognition of the lived reality: a sense of moral and sacramental communion. This is what *oikoumene* means.[9]

Inevitably, of course, certain markers or indicators of the presence of moral and liturgical recognition emerge, if only to make conversation easier. These function like pointers or signposts that say someone has been this way before. They resemble what the Scots call *cairns* on the hillside. Someone has been here and, placing stone on stone, has named the goal of a process of costly and risky involvement on behalf of neighbors "justice." Such contextual naming gives justice a thick network of meanings that cannot be conveyed until someone walks this way again. Or some community has again placed stone on stone, naming a painfully worked-out and costly concord among combatants "peace." The word *peace* thereby takes on a carefully constructed meaning for those who were part of this history. Terms such as *justice* and *peace* function in the ecumenical movement to help persons with analogous experiences find one another, and thus support, enable, encourage, and empower one another.[10]

The traditional "marks" of the church—unity, apostolicity, holiness, catholicity—function in exactly this contextual way. Their meanings depend on the wholeness of experience in which they are grounded, but they also function as pointers that create a certain presumption that we, and all others who claim them, are grounded in the same resonating and recognizable community-forming work of the Spirit. The problem sometimes is that the signs have taken over as substitutes for the lived realities to which they refer. Yet often there is little to go on but these marks, expressed as they are in jurisdictional, confessional, or doctrinal agreement, or in willingness to participate in conciliar relationships. Today the churches need to share more deeply the liturgical and moral substance to which the traditional marks refer. One basis for such sharing lies in the nearly universal recognition of a common baptism which itself has clear moral implications (see chapter 3). What may it take for this existing baptismal-moral sharing to become communion?

To be in communion means to be in a network of relationships such that the Spirit's resonance is shared and recognizable messages are given and received. Communion means a recognition by ecclesial communities that they are living the same stories in ways, both liturgical and moral, that manifest the mystery, the transcending ground, of what is historically manifest. This recognition is expressed as willingness to share the liturgy in both its senses: as worship and as work. Communion is a readiness to celebrate the same liturgy, with the same moral implications, together. Outside the network of mutual recognition, no particular local expression of church can be authentic. It is of the essence of the church universal to exist in this web of relationships, in which the local is all-important but the ecumenical nexus of recognition is equally indispensable.

All creation of new ecumenical language is driven by the need to test whether a common fund of discourse can be conceived within which differing experiences can meet. The ecumenical encounter itself can generate still more new language whose connection with the classical stream of tradition is evident to all its "native speakers."[11] The degree of recognition achieved up to now among the different confessions and denominations through use of this new traditional-ecumenical language amounts to a "real" but still "imperfect" communion.[12]

The terms commonly used to describe or test such communion are themselves imperfectly or incompletely realized. As commonly interpreted, ecumenical language does not yet catch the moral fulness, the plentitude of witnessing presence in history, which completeness of communion requires. It is important not to drain the fulness from this language by defining its terms purely conceptually, juridically, or ecclesiastically, and not also morally. Nor must some particular structural aspect of the church's life (such as "the historic episcopate") be considered the sole fulfillment of what this language means.[13] All language related to communion points to the life, obedience, and liturgical-moral integrity of the community of faith in such a way that its world-relationships, solidarities, and ways of being prophetic are part of that wholeness.

The WCC as Space-Maker for
a Global Household of Life: "Ten Affirmations"

How can room be made on earth for this *oikoumene* of mutually recognized resonance among our ways of concrete moral-ecclesial being-in-the-world? The moral communion just described has as yet no obvious seat in space. No ecclesiastical jurisdiction exists as a place where the universal church in this moral sense comes to expression. Existing church polities, in their separateness, are at best partial realizations of the moral communion they have it in them to signify through their ways of life.

Even so, a *degree* of moral communion already exists among Christian communities of faith. If this reality is to be nurtured toward fulfillment it needs visible expression. It needs a movement that marks its possibility, that makes space for it in the world. The World Council of Churches may well come closer than any other entity to being that mark and offering that space. It *is* not the moral communion of which we have spoken, but it *is* a community of churches praying to receive the spiritual gifts that such communion in moral witnessing will require.

Current discussion of the nature of the Council runs between seeing it as a purely programmatic instrument of the churches (thereby denying it ecclesial status) and seeing it as the reality of churches-in-relation (thus suggesting that it has a real, though undefined, ecclesial character). But may not the choice between these alternatives be confusing, and in the end false? Programmatic initiatives can interpret and express the ecclesio-moral realities of WCC member churches. And churches-in-relation may fail to realize the ecclesial intentionality inherent in their relationships. But programmatic and ecclesial categories are not the only ones. There is also the notion that the institutional structures of the ecumenical movement can make space for things to happen that are neither simply programmatic nor formally ecclesiastical but spiritual and moral.

The WCC needs to mark, maintain, indeed *be* a space where a global communion of Christian moral practices can come to expression. The Council needs to offer hospitality to a search for language that can express such a communion's reality ever more adequately, to actions that embody this communion's moral witness, and to an appropriate process of mutual admonition and formation.

But here a question arises needing careful, not to say delicate, treatment.

In chapters 3 and 4 moral formation has, rightly, been closely tied to the sacraments. That, indeed, is the basis for calling the goal of this enterprise a moral *communion.* But many churches, despite cordial relationships, are not yet in formal sacramental communion with one another. Can there then be such a thing as an "ecclesio-moral" dimension of communion that avoids, or transcends, the churches' dividedness in the sacramental foundations of moral formation? Do not such deep divisions call in question, at least for now, the very idea of a moral communion as much as they do the idea of sacramental communion? Is it not plausible to say that fulfillment of the moral dimension of communion needs to wait until divisions at the level of ministry and sacraments have been overcome? And, if no moral communion considered as intrinsic to ministry and sacraments is as yet possible, it makes no sense to suggest that the WCC should mark or offer space for such a thing, much less claim some sort of sacramental moral character itself.

Responses to questions like these depend largely on the respondents' ecclesiological commitments. For some there is no doubt a deep dilemma. The more closely moral formation is tied to the sacraments, the less easy it becomes to argue that churches can be united in the moral dimension of *koinonia* while sacramental communion is not yet attained. Yet it is also possible to argue that the notion of moral communion, despite its indispensable sacramental nature, need not stand or fall with the churches' degree of unity in the eucharist. There is enough moral substance lodged in the reality of a common baptism (see chapter 3) to justify some sort of ecumenical space-making at this present time for that spiritual gift.

It can also be argued that the moral dimension of *koinonia* is distinguishable from the eucharistic aspect in another important way. Communion in its moral dimension involves shared wrestling with worldly issues. Such issues today, I have argued, are both radical in their import and global in their character. There is a commonality in the human questions that can only be addressed through an equally common Christian witness. Only an organization like the World Council of Churches can help its member bodies discern and act out the *comprehensive* moral implications of their particular sacramental-moral-formational processes. The effort to do this can itself generate a *koinonia* of thoughtful, daring, costly witnessing. A moral aspect of *koinonia* can come to realization in and through this grace-enabled work itself.[14]

There is a difference between seeing the Council as a eucharistic community in its own right, which few want to do, and seeing it as a place for such a *koinonia*-generating response to the grace already received in baptism, such an effort to think through what different morally formed communions, acting together, can mean to the world. And if, in fact, the member churches of the Council commit themselves to this effort, the Council's very existence then marks or locates a field of growing mutual recognition in the spiritual resonance of shared discipleship.

Some will wish to say even more. Some will argue that an organization making space for such a communion in moral formation for worldly ethical engagement cannot stand entirely outside the reality it enables to exist. For those who take this view it follows that the Council participates somehow in the communion it helps to foster. The Council becomes an instance of that communion in a peculiarly comprehensive and communicative mode. It is a mark of the ecumenical community it gathers, and therefore in some sense is *of* the church, even if not churchly in the fullest sense.[15]

It is not possible to settle, as a matter of principle, the question of the Council's ecclesial status. For purposes of this argument it is not necessary. The status of the Council as marker of a growing moral communion has a practical side that overtakes the ecclesiological arguments. Can the WCC do what needs to be done? The whole matter of communion in moral witness is moot if enough agreement cannot be found about the content of that witness to make the question relevant. Here a deeply ecclesiological question becomes in one respect a programmatic question as well. What happens when the attempt is made to give moral communion a specific ethical content? What can be learned from the history of attempts to do so? It is worthwhile to look briefly at the history of the "ten affirmations" produced by the WCC's 1990 Seoul Conference on "Justice, Peace, and the Integrity of Creation," affirmations now carried over as points of entry for the Theology of Life project.

The Seoul occasion was intended by its organizers to help build a stronger conciliar fellowship in the ecumenical community around shared moral principles. Indeed, for some, the intention was to give such principles status as marks of the mutual commitment implied in WCC membership.[16] The meeting was presented at the outset with an analytical document dealing with the challenges facing the people of our planet: a document thought by many to propose overly ambitious global reality-definitions couched in Western academic language too abstract to make contact with local experience in all its variety and profusion. The conference instead produced a set of affirmations reflecting the contextual and ecumenical experience of the people present, drafted in the course of the meeting and considerably modifying the preliminary documents.

The "ten affirmations" with their accompanying explanatory texts are too long to quote in full. A list of topic sentences or phrases will give the flavor. "We affirm," the document says, "that all exercise of power is accountable to God, God's option for the poor, the equal value of all races and peoples, that male and female are created in the image of God, that truth is at the foundation of a community of free people, the peace of Jesus Christ, the creation as beloved of God, that the earth is the Lord's, the dignity and commitment of the younger generation, that human rights are given by God."

Each clause is elaborated in three stages: the affirmation itself, and then two statements: one of resistance and the other of commitment. This structure implies that in each area of concern one is either on principle deeply opposed to something or strongly identified with it, with little in between. What seems missing is the notion of citizenship—that is, living constructively in hope in the midst of a social order that is imperfect but nevertheless not demonic: seeking, as Jeremiah put it, "the well-being of the city" (Jer. 29:7). There are times both for resistance and for solidarity, but also times for the affirmation of a kind of pragmatic "decency," which, in Avishai Margalit's[17] persuasive terms, means a civic order in which people, at least, are not humiliated. Surely it is meaningful, on the way to the demanding goals of "justice, peace, and the integrity of creation," to seek social values that can benefit human beings living in an imperfect world along the way.

The Seoul affirmations are of course vulnerable to criticism. Considering the conditions under which they were drafted, lacunae and weaknesses are inevitable. Slavery and torture, which still exist in our world, are not specifically mentioned. Presumably these issues fall under the heading of human rights, and perhaps of other affirmations as well. But perhaps the most important questions are theological. Where are the elements of grace and forgiveness? Where is the evangelical witness to the saving work of God in human society? And where, one may ask, is there continuity with the ecumenical tradition in social ethics that runs from Oxford (1937) to Geneva (1966) to the MIT Conference (1979)?[18]

Still, the primary values expressed in the "ten affirmations" are worthy of close attention. They are broadly consistent with the moral understandings mentioned in chapter 4 as generally held in the ecumenical movement, even if not precisely the same in content. Should these affirmations be seen as a first attempt to declare the moral substance of a universal church? Wisely, the WCC is not seeking as it were to promulgate any such list of affirmations from Geneva. Rather it is seeking what the affirmations mean in a process of interaction with persons representing the specificity and "thickness" of many local situations. These affirmations are the *beginning* of a global dialogue rather than the end of one.

In fact, the effort made after Seoul to persuade the churches to enter a covenant based on the affirmations did not wholly succeed. A feeling arose that the language adopted, grounded in actual experience as it was, could not be given clear (that is, unequivocal) meanings across a variety of contexts. In different cultural and confessional situations their implications could not be foreseen. This is likely to be a common problem. Once affirmations of this sort are taken home from ecumenical meetings, every proposition, even every preposition, connects or disconnects with local issues, both churchly and secular, and therefore with the power interests tied up in those issues. However subtle our reports from the ecumenical front, the defense back home of affirmations grandly adopted at world conferences can make returned delegates seem to be taking sides on matters never envisioned when the affirmations were drafted. They find themselves battling on one side or the other of dominant local dichotomies, opting for this or that alternative with all its ecclesiastical or worldly political consequences. This may well be the last thing they want to do and in fact may distort the intention of the original affirmations. Here may be a hazard impossible to avoid completely. It may be part of the cost of obedient witnessing. But the experience needs to be understood. It is an aspect of the *koinonia*-generating struggle that the search for moral communion can involve.

Do lists of moral affirmations nonetheless have a positive role to play in the journey toward a moral *oikoumene*? At their best, such affirmations have a sort of heuristic power. They help communions and congregations find the concreteness of actually shared moral commitments in facing the most characteristic problems of our time. Lists of principles can help believers discover the kinds of moral commitment that are present among serious formational communities at any given moment. They can help instigate the forming of more such communities and help deepen the communion among them. They can be carefully designed to encourage creative local readings of what they mean.

Skillfully interpreted by leadership, such affirmations can help churches at a distance from serious moral encounters concretize their solidarity with fellow Christians around specific acts of witness, for example the German women's boycott of South African products during the period of apartheid. But experience in this area has taught us to proceed with caution. Any such list of moral generalizations or affirmations must be guarded against being merely a list, merely a talisman to be repeated by those who pride themselves on being alert to the world's ills and possibilities. Furthermore, moral catechisms can get out of date even faster than theological ones. There is always the danger of overgeneralizing certain historical moments and analytical paradigms. This has happened, for example, in certain cases of subsequent use of the Barmen Declaration. Not every situation that seems to call for Barthian truculence is really analogous to that in Germany in 1934. The differences between one situation and another may easily be overlooked. Indeed historical paradigms, as well as moral principles, can be used covertly to defend and protect certain power centers or programmatic interests in the church rather than to illumine our moral paths. Even to make normative the transition to democracy in South Africa could be dangerous if used as a paradigm where it does not fit.

Finally, the impulse to issue lists of moral principles designed to address the signs of the times raises a question about the eschatology they imply. What, in the long term, do we think is happening in the world? How is God's mission to and with humankind to be understood in these days? Where, if anywhere, are there signs that the reign of God has come nearer? Are there indications in extensions of the principle of human rights, or in the apparent advance of democracy, or in successes claimed by peacemakers, or in the dire warnings of environmentalists? Indeed, it is not easy to discern, from this ambiguous moment in history, whether the household of life is anywhere taking form, or the holy city of God described in Revelation 21 is in any way drawing nearer. Yet these images of the household and the city can stand as eschatological metaphors or regulative ideas to guide the churches as they try to find their way.

The "ten affirmations" do live up to their affirmative name. They are profoundly hopeful because they presuppose that by God's grace something can be done about the state of creation and of the human condition. They are valuable indications of the content that ought to be found in a moral communion of ethical engagement with the world. But, above all, they themselves help create the kind of space needed for an effort to think out and live out what such a communion could require. As entry points for the wide range of local case studies in the WCC Theology of Life Program, they "serve as a preliminary definition of the framework and space in which people can build up confidence and trust."[19] If "space" has any meaning in this argument, it is a territory in which believers count on one another and have confidence that by God's grace something will come of their efforts. In this powerful sense, the "ten affirmations" and other affirmations like them help create moral space for the "mutual up-building" or *oikodomé* toward a common witness that now becomes a primary calling for the Christian churches of the world.[20]

If the World Council of Churches is to become a genuine instrument for the emergence of such an ecumenical moral community, it needs to enlarge its scope beyond present conceptual and practical boundaries, and find relationships with more of the centers of moral and spiritual energy at work in our time. For this purpose the "Common Understanding and Vision" proposals already received and modified by the Central Committee and scheduled to be voted on at the forthcoming Eighth Assembly in Harare, Zimbabwe, in December 1998, are much to the point.

The key proposal, however, will not be acted on constitutionally, remaining only a programmatic possibility. It is that the WCC should use its good offices to bring into being a body that might be called something like "The Forum of the Ecumenical Movement." This would be a gathering conceived and organized so as to make possible the widest possible membership, including such diverse groups as the Roman Catholic Church, the Christian world communions, the Lausanne Conference, and Pentecostal groups across the globe.[21] The whole ecumenical "household" is larger and more diverse than any one organization can represent. The WCC is an organization of "churches," and not all existing churches at that. There are other kinds of organizations in the household.

As proposed, each member body of a "Forum of the Ecumenical Movement" would hold its own world-level meetings in conjunction with meetings of the forum. And there would also be ample room for plenary sessions in which all the churches and organizations would meet together to share common concerns. Such a forum could promote the mutual upbuilding of a visible *moral* communion, if not a sacramental communion, toward a vision of the church universal as moral household of life.[22] Needed for this purpose is a much-enhanced system of communications among churches, congregations, and persons—whatever their organizational affiliations—committed to this vision.

Christians are challenged by the world economic system's ability to send and receive virtually instantaneous messages concerning financial transactions across the globe. They face the obsolete yet still powerful system of nation-states. A nexus of another kind needs to have its place in the world. A network of moral communication among churches and other Christian bodies could begin to function as a setting for the enactment of an alternative vision of human solidarity: one resisting the hegemony of purely economic and political energies. The initiative to create such a moral solidarity could include critical, provisional alliances with others who seek compatible goals.

The emergence of the very idea of such an inclusive ecclesio-moral community could give the ecumenical movement a new energy and substance. At stake here is not merely the future of a particular ecumenical organization. At stake is the future of the church and, even more important, the future of humankind. The final chapter has to do with that question.

SIX

Horizons of Meaning
and the Household of Life

The vision of a global network of Christian congregations understanding themselves—often in creative relationships with other human
communities—as participating in a "household of life" may or may not
be realizable through the efforts of today's ecumenical organizations. But
suppose the churches were to plant their hopes imaginatively in a position
both to receive the spiritual gift of membership in such a household and
to accept the accompanying moral responsibilities. What horizons of
meaning and possibility might be discernable from the perspective of that
sort of commitment?

Unlike the moral philosopher John Rawls, who locates his imagination
in a community of justice-seeking reasoners gathered behind a "veil of
ignorance" that denies them knowledge of their actual identities and values, churches are invited to locate their imaginations in a household where
fully realized human identities and values, far from being forgotten, meet
in search of a graciously shared abundance of life.[1] This household wel-
comes all the different human cultures, identities, and interests, including
our own. It seeks to live out a shared realization of the human good:
something like the "ten affirmations" or some still more theologically
adequate formulation. What hope for humankind as a whole might an
active pursuit of this vision allow the churches to entertain?

History and Eschatology:
Pluralisms and Horizons

The gracious summons to enter a household of life calls special attention to two dimensions of the ecumenical vision. The first dimension is that of eschatology, the perspective that views history's movement toward its end or purpose.[2] How do we human beings orient ourselves in this uniquely human context of time? The second dimension is that of social space. The imaginative movement forward in time is simultaneously a movement outward from ourselves toward others. Who is included in our vision of the human future? What is our relationship with others who also live on this planet at this moment in its history?[3]

The approach to such questions—temporal and spatial, human and cosmic—raises the question of *horizons*. These by definition mark the limits of what one can see from any particular location in space or at any particular moment in time. Each person's horizon is unique, and so is the horizon of each faith community. There are thus at least three dimensions to deal with: time, space, and the plurality of standpoints from which one can view them. And not only is there a plurality of standpoints, there are also plural*isms* in the sense of different perspectives *on* pluralism itself. How can a Christian vision of the household of life deal with such a range of variables?

Richard Mouw and Sander Griffioen's book, *Pluralisms and Horizons*,[4] helps clarify the options. Their central point coincides with ours: that the pluralism of our world, which involves a radical diversity of enterprises, cultures, intentionalities, and faiths, needs to be understood in terms of the ultimate horizons of meaning in which both pluralism and plural*isms* are placed. Christians can, they say, share a household of warm cooperation with persons of diverse life-perspectives provided they do not accept a *finally* irreconcilable diversity of perspectives. Of all the forms of pluralism they discuss, Mouw and Griffioen find only one—"normative directional pluralism"—theologically unacceptable because it not only accepts but endorses an ultimate relativism. Relativism in this context means assent to the proposition that different views of the world are ultimately divergent and incompatible, and that in the end this is a state of affairs worthy of support, perhaps in the name of human liberty.

Mouw and Griffioen refuse the relativistic option because they believe that Christian faith involves an ultimate battle between truth and false-hood, between obedience to God and rebellion. Yet it does not follow that obedience to God means the triumph of our *present* understanding of the faith or our *present* theological terminology. It is God's truth that matters, not ours.

A perspective open to pluralism but resistant to ultimate relativism enables Christians to take a positive attitude to the public world. It allows them to struggle against the notion that the world needs to be merely a neutral arena, an "empty shrine,"[5] without values of its own. On the contrary, it matters very much what values are commonly held in the public arenas of our time. An allegedly "empty shrine" of neutral objectivity will only invite covert ideologies of all kinds to fill it. The human world should rather be envisioned as a global household whose values lead to life rather than death. The Christian lives *toward* this goal, neither resignedly nor triumphalistically but rather hopefully, seeking to live out practices that forecast the kind of public space God calls the human world to become.

But what might that ultimate goal look like? It is important to say that dealing with the notion of horizons in time and space does not mean that believers should think they know literally what the human future is to be and how the human race as a whole is to be fulfilled in it. The Book of Revelation is no more a literal description of events yet to come than the Book of Genesis is a literal description of the process of creation. Biblical images of the beginning and of the end of time (perhaps no more or less "mythical" than the cosmic images of natural science) serve for purposes of orientation within a humanly proportioned world. They give us an imaginatively regulative context for reasoning and acting in moral terms: a context not provided by the formulas of astrophysics, however much we acknowledge that in their own scientific territory such formulas are the best available at the present time.

What, then, *can* be seen from this limited human standpoint? Even the immediate future looks clouded. Max Stackhouse argues that the global civilization awaiting us in the twenty-first century is not only unprecedented—that is, not based on any historical experience previously shared by human beings—but also hostile to the historic traditions of life, religious and otherwise, with which we are familiar. He writes:

> We live in a matrix of particular societies that is being formed and transformed by an emergent global society. This emergent global

society is not rooted in common memory or in a common historical experience. Insofar as it is developing as a *novum*, it exists as an artifact based on certain widely-accepted abstract principles that disrupt and detract all who participate in it from the historic traditions that have informed life's meanings.[6]

How should representatives of historic traditions threatened by such universalizing abstractions react? Some see these new conditions of human life as supremely challenging, yet do not doubt for a moment that religious traditions, rightly interpreted, are up to it. The Harvard theologian Gordon Kaufman, for example, approaches the next century with full awareness of its serious demands[7] but still with confidence that the future *can* be one to which specific life-traditions may contribute as they try to survive. Kaufman writes:

> The various cultural streams of humanity seem to be converging rapidly into a single interconnected human history. At this portentous moment, perhaps more than ever before, we need conceptions of the human and visions of history which will facilitate our movement toward an ordering of life and history that is at once humane and universal, an ordering in which the integrity and significance of each tradition and each community are acknowledged and the rights of every individual are respected.[8]

Kaufman's admirable, beautifully crafted, ultimately optimistic book is one that, in the end, rests on his confidence in the triumph of tolerant, humane, liberal values. His confidence is buoyed by the flowing together of the once separate streams of human history on the basis of opportunities for travel, the communications revolution, the coming of a global economic order. Kaufman counts on support of those hopefully common values by contemporary, sophisticated human beings who are able to come to terms with their own religious traditions in the manner Kaufman comes to terms with his own Christianity. There is little sense in Kaufman that Christian faith as such is destined to play much of a role on the public stage. But he thinks that faith *can* deepen the liberal value scheme that he shares with other members of Western elite academic culture.

It is fascinating that such a convergence of cultures into a single interconnected history dominated by liberal values is just what Kaufman's Harvard colleague Samuel Huntington does *not* see. Or, rather, Huntington sees the convergence as ultimately conflictual: not pointing at all to "an ordering of life and history at once humane and universal." For Huntington the world of the twenty-first century will be dominated by a conflict of major civilizations, often fueled by powerful religious conviction. We are urged, not to seek common liberal values, but to reach practical accommodations among the world's religiously constructed civilizations in a maintainable balance of power.

For Huntington, the secular writer, religion as public phenomenon (rather than simply private faith) plays a larger role on the world scene than it does for Kaufman the theologian. For Huntington, the coming of technological and economic "modernization" to previously undeveloped traditional societies (Iran is an example), far from drawing such societies ever further into a liberally homogeneous world, tends, after a first liberalizing stage, to provoke traditionalist reactions. As such a country gains confidence, it becomes proud of itself, including its traditional culture. As its people experience anomie, they seek to rediscover traditional values. If local religious traditions cannot adapt themselves to these opportunities, other religious traditions will be borrowed. This, for Huntington, accounts on the one hand for the successful resurgence of Islam across the Middle East and for the recent successes of evangelical Christianity in Korea, Africa, and Latin America. Of the last-named areas Huntington writes:

> In these societies the most successful protagonists of Western culture are not neo-classical economists or crusading democrats or multinational corporation executives. They are and most likely will continue to be Christian missionaries. Neither Adam Smith nor Thomas Jefferson will meet the psychological, emotional, moral and social needs of urban migrants and first-generation secondary school graduates. Jesus Christ will not meet them either, but He is likely to have a better chance. In the long run, however, Mohammed wins out. Christianity spreads primarily by conversion. Islam by conversion and reproduction.[9]

Whichever picture of the world one chooses, there may well be threats to life today before which human beings, in their own power, are all but helpless. There may not *be* for very long a habitable human world in which either Kaufman's or Huntington's scenario could be lived out.

Nor is it justifiable for theologians to assume that God will not allow the worst to happen. The Swiss ecumenist Lukas Vischer argues that we are still employing the methods and assumptions of the optimistic 1960s in confronting what has become a global crisis: literally a crisis of human survival. For Vischer our sense of the urgency of the present crisis has been blunted by being seen, even by Christians, as only a *management* challenge: something they can *deal* with if they act intelligently before it is too late. So proportioned to our human capacities, threats to life are not allowed to undermine the optimistic theological assumptions to which the West has become accustomed. Perhaps, Vischer argues, such threats *should* shake up our religious certainties. Theologians and ethicists have been all too sure that "God will lead humanity to the kingdom; injustice, degradation and destruction will not have the last word; God is already acting in history; darkness will be overcome; the church's calling is to side with God's purpose of life in history."[10] Vischer remonstrates:

> Can this view be maintained? Is there any justification for the expectation of a gradual realization of God's purpose in history? Does not the Bible rather offer a contrary scenario? But above all, *how do we cope with the evidence of an increasing degradation in history?* Do we not have to admit that the historical future is radically hidden from our eyes? We must always be prepared for life *and* death."[11]

One has the impression that for many people the view taken on these matters may not go very deep. It may depend on their reading of current events. Much depends on whether one sees the interests of the kingdom faring well or poorly in one's time. Reactions can even change from one day to the next depending on the headlines in the morning's news. I sense that most people—even most moralists—have not yet fully faced the question of what kind of eschatology they *really* believe in. When they talk of a radical reconstruction of the field of ethics—so that a Christian response to the world is *both* based on a new formation in the household of life *and* faces analytically the realities of the human condition—they may well be naming a task totally beyond the known capabilities of this present generation of theologians and ecumenical leaders.

"Household of Life" as Eschatological Paradigm

Are challenges such as these addressed by the notion of human participation in God's household of life? This term has already been introduced several times in these pages, especially in reference to the work of Konrad Raiser and Geiko Müller-Fahrenholz.[12] This idea of an open moral covenant articulated by Christian churches on behalf of the human race has in it the potential of transforming the way believers see the opportunities and threats facing today's world. The household image is an attempt to mobilize the community of moral-eschatological imagination that must follow on the decision to "choose life" (Deut. 30:19).

Recall that in chapter 3 the theme of imagination is brought together with the notion of moral formation. The point is that all morality, beginning with the level below conscious reasoning, is a way of seeing the world in which we are formed, a way of holding fellow human beings in an imaginative revisioning that gives rise to loving, forgiving—and also expectant and demanding—relationships with them. The eschatological passages in scripture are full of such imaginative revisionings of the world. They are, precisely, evidence that the communities from which their authors came put the world together in new ways, and thus found it fitting to behave in new ways as well.

The revisioning implied in the notion of a household of life is based on rich biblical foundations.[13] Strangely, this language does not appear before to have been brought together and employed in quite the way the authors named are now doing. Yet suddenly, now, the notion of "household" comes to life in the ecumenical movement whose very name is derived from the Greek term this English word translates. Chapter 2 has already explained that the root term *oikos* or "house" ramifies in several ways in New Testament Greek. In biblical usage it means, in fact, the "whole inhabited earth." But there is more. Paul, for example, reminds members of the fledgling Christian communities that they should behave toward one another in a spirit of *oikodomé* or mutual upbuilding (Rom. 14:19). Christians are urged to use their particular talents for the *oikodomé* of the body of Christ (Eph. 2:21). The community of faith is God's building (*oikodomé*), whose foundation is Jesus Christ (I Cor. 3:9-11). The *ekklesia* is God's temple (I Cor. 3:16).[14]

But the biblical evidence raises a question. How did the early church actually understand the household of which it was a part? Was the moral imagination fostered by membership in this community directed toward this world or to a heavenly commonwealth yet to come? In several passages members of the apostolic community refer to themselves as *paroikoi* or "aliens." The word, another derivative of *oikos*, means "living away from home." Müller-Fahrenholz writes:

> It is understandable that some of these small and persecuted Christian groups began to see themselves as communities of "aliens and exiles" in a hostile world, whose true homeland was in the heavens (cf. I Peter 2:11). Eventually each local Christian church came to be called *paroikia*, a home away from home as it were, a place of refuge. The "parochial system" became the organizing principle around which the church was set up. So the church was *in* the world, but not *of* the world. Obviously, this helped to foster a dualism which despised the earth and glorified the world beyond.[15]

How, it must have been asked by the early Christian community, can the mutual "upbuilding" of a household of life be practiced here and now when the real household of God is in the heavens and Christians are only visiting aliens on earth?

The idea of a household of life as covenantal community for humanity within the historical process involves connecting the notions of *paroikia* and *oikodomé*. It takes a further, creative, exegetical move to put them together. But there are biblical warrants for doing so. While we "sing the Lord's song in a foreign land" (Psalm 137:4), do we not also "seek the welfare of the city" (Jer. 29:7)? In the work of Raiser and of Müller-Fahrenholz the community of the "oikodomical covenant" is seen as a thoroughly practical reality, interacting with other mundane forces, very much *in* this world if not of it. Yet it is also part and parcel of God's future as the church hopes for it, believes in it, prays for it. It involves a commitment to the long-term future of the human race. In this picture we are not merely aliens *in* the world, but morally and eschatologically imaginative citizens *of* the world.

What does this in-the-world household of life look like? It is described[16] as a community in which God's Spirit is continually received in fresh ways, a community with its own "house rules" expressive of that Spirit. These rules call for the renunciation of violence, boasting, or self-justification. They imply a refusal to pass judgment upon or exclude those who think or live differently. They call for dialogue and a continual striving within the "spirit of truth," for communication that resolves differences peacefully. They sketch a logic of forgiveness, the exorcism of guilt, interpersonal solidarity, the sharing of burdens and mutual support, the promotion of justice and peace both within the household and beyond. They speak of a mutual hospitality that multiplies life's goods. Such solidarity and hospitality are acted out, above all, in the common meal we know as eucharist or Lord's Supper.

All these qualities of the "household" have to do with very basic, fundamental, human relationships and ties: precisely those in which we human beings experience primary "formation," the process of upbringing that leads us to a strong sense of identity, of what is "fitting" in and for our lives. The feel of this description is very specific, very local. It all comes *before* the community begins to construct moral arguments and derive ethical conclusions of wider application.

The development of the *oikos* idea, however, also requires an opening of the imagination toward a larger household, the household of the entire inhabited earth.[17] The point of the "ecumenical" movement is precisely to help convey the news that the *oikos* or household of life is a global reality, not merely a local reality, indeed a setting in which global issues are represented in the local, and the local in the global. The task is thus to share in a "mutual upbuilding" of this *larger* community in the Spirit. Ecumenism is a matter of ongoing learning through the experience of branches of the global household other than our own. We are called to a felt, experienced, and acted-out understanding of truth, righteousness, and peace in the global (and perhaps cosmic) context of life, and thereby to contribute to the world's becoming one community under God.[18]

Such a vision needs to be realistically evaluated. What could be its power in the present human situation? Is it indeed an imaginative place from which to see new horizons of meaning? It is helpful that the notion of a household of life is a work of contemporary moral imagination, not burdened by the past, not the property of any one Christian tradition, not as yet much fought over in theological controversy. One does not have to rid it of mistaken presuppositions before being able to appropriate it for theologically creative purposes. It has its own tonality and a rich set of overtones, open to the performative interpretations and realizations that interpreters may be led to give it.

Furthermore, it is capable, I think, of serving as a helpful point of entry to some of the more luxuriant imagery of the Apocalypse. The notion of a household of life can give Christian eschatology an *imaginable* point of reference in contemporary terms: a way of saying, for the late twentieth century, what ecumenists concretely hope for and believe might actually be possible. While the idea of a reign of God points to a horizon beyond human ability really to envision, a household of life based on something like Seoul's "Ten Affirmations" is thoroughly imaginable, even if not easily achievable.

This work of constructive theological imagination comes through most clearly as describing an alternative world: alternative above all to the interlocking economic, military, nation-state systems that bid fair today to dominate the whole human environment. Chapter 2 has pointed out that the root *oikos* (that versatile word) also underlies the term "economics." In a sense the household is an alternative economics just as it is an alternative politics. It marks a different way of looking at the world economic system which urges us to see it more like managing a household than as a matter of taking advantage of one another as nameless economic players in a totally competitive environment.

But in what ultimate horizon of understanding does this different political-economic metaphor function? There are two broad possibilities. The first sees the church rather than the world as the place of the true politics, thereby placing the fulfillment of the vision somewhere apart from or beyond the stream of history as generally understood. The second places the horizon of church-world interaction squarely within this world, its economics, its politics, its concrete potential. Each offers an alternative world to that of the economic and political powers that be: but the different visions give that alternative two very different senses.

Is the primary horizon of all that is meant by the Christian story a world of church and ecclesial discipleship, or is it the common world of human striving in all the various spheres of life? Some have called the difference one between an ecclesial, "pneumatological" eschatology and a worldly, "utopian" eschatology.[19] I believe, as I will show in what follows, that this terminology is misleading. "Utopian" eschatology is *also* pneumatological in a profound way. But let us look more closely at each possibility.

A SPIRITUAL-ECCLESIAL HORIZON

The first possibility is being elaborated by theologians who stress substantial use of the content of tradition and of moral formation within tradition. In doing so they are increasingly critical of modernity and its assumptions about reality, knowledge, and praxis. This theology is indeed "political," but it is the church that is said to embody, or at least anticipate, the "true politics."[20]

The proponents of this position are familiar names: Hans Frei, George Lindbeck, James McClendon, Stanley Hauerwas, John Howard Yoder, John Milbank, and others. Theirs is a strategy for a post-Westphalian church which cannot take for granted the "Christian" character of social institutions or even the kind of "religious liberty" many Western societies today allow to faith communities not expected to make trouble. For them the "true politics" is not the horizon of the secular city's historical development but rather a horizon visible only from the standpoint of the community of specifically Christian faith and practice.[21]

The word *politics* here takes on a distinctively theological meaning. The notion of a household of life, if grafted into this theological framework,[22] would mean not a utopian political and economic alternative to the present order of things, but rather a radically different, transcending alternative *ecclesial* community. In this vision, "Christian ethics" is in-house reflection on the array of moral practices that make the church the church.

The worldly presence of *this* sort of alternative politics makes a difference just because it does *not* become involved in the world's own formulations of its issues. The world's formulations are seen as self-defeating and needing to encounter a limit in something decisively *different*. The true politics, the politics that gives God "his" due,[23] constitutes a limit to the worldly political game, however ameliorative or even utopian may be its intent. On this view the message society needs to hear is not merely the word that there is out there yet another utopianized version of its own limited self, but rather the message that with its own resources it cannot save itself at all.

The church as *polis* on this model is thus not merely an example or model for the world. The character of the ecclesial community does indeed have some outward marks. It practices just relationships, refuses participation in all forms of violence, seeks forgiveness and reconciliation. But these practices are such as to convey the message that the true *politeuma* is not of this world at all. The members of this divine "commonwealth" are indeed "strangers and sojourners," or *paroikoi* within history. The presence of such a community of radically alternative practice challenges the self-sufficiency of worldly constructs and institutions, reminding them that they are not self-founding and self-authenticating. The mere presence of such *difference* might, it is thought, break the circle of self-generating violence. It could be taken to say that we need not be forever locked up in pride that breeds more pride, violence that breeds more violence.[24]

But one would not judge the "success" of a church conceived in this way even by the happy circumstances that violence decreased or wars were avoided owing to the witness of Christians in society. The "success" involved here, if the category is applicable at all, is visible only from the standpoint of the story of salvation. In the words of Stanley Hauerwas,

> The success of the church's faithful witness can be hidden either through the form of the cross or in the future of God's reign. What is crucial is to acknowledge that the church's "success" can never be made intelligible independent of Jesus Christ's crucifixion and resurrection and God's eschatological reality in the Holy Spirit."[25]

If life in the church is the true politics, the true well-being of the public world, its salvation in fact, becomes attached to the fate of the organized church, and also presumably to the fate of Christianity's theological patrimony and cultural content. Is this what theologians of this school want to say? The implication is that Christians already glimpse, if they do not yet grasp, what is beyond the eschatological horizon that limits the ultimacy of the pluralism and pluralisms all around us. They see the church as already possessing and living out a politics to be vindicated at the close of the historical process. But is it not possible that the church as an alternative politics has already failed, or will in the future fail? Resisting this thought, proponents of ecclesia-as-new-politics are content to live in a civil manner beside others who believe differently, seeking "the well-being of the city" where that is possible.

But behind this civility among neighbors with other convictions is there not bound to be an assumption that, since "normative directional pluralism"[26]—the acceptance of a final relativism—is unacceptable, the expected historical fulfillment must in some way involve a *cultural* Christianization of the world, however unlikely that seems from our present historical vantage point, however *un*civil such intentions might be thought by unbelievers to be? True, "cultural Christianization" is not a Hauerwasian or Milbankian category. But does it not come to this? What else could it mean to rest our hopes exclusively upon communities of Christian moral practice? Would it not mean to exclude the vast majority of humankind from the "true politics?"

While many secularists today can live with the prospect of being denied salvation in its traditional Christian meanings, because the category makes no sense to them, being denied participation in a "true politics" is serious. Especially so *if* this kind of politics has *anything* to do with politics in the ordinary sense of the word, which it must if this entire theological edifice is to make sense. But, then, it would appear that to be admitted to the *truly* political community one must also take on the whole panoply of Christian practice, liturgical, ecclesial, moral.[27]

One has to say, finally, that this position seems to claim the presence of a radical transcendence within history by means of rhetoric that does not address the complexities of the issue of how God is related to the world.[28] Hauerwas writes, "In the church's reality the eschaton becomes a history 'which becomes again and again transparent to God's eschatological reign by continuously expecting God's present reign in and through the churches' activities, procedures, and policies.' "[29] Consistently enough, the church's "success" is only intelligible within the circle of such theological language. Can we not speak of the Holy Spirit's presence in the world in terms that give *some* hint of the kind of visible historical gestalt or pattern, or resonance, we are being called upon to recognize *there*?

A "THIS-WORLDLY" HORIZON

The second possibility is to interpret the horizon of the "household of life" at least partly in this-worldly terms, thus placing it in the context of the political theology that arose in Europe through the work of J. B. Metz, Dorothee Sölle, and the younger Jürgen Moltmann, as well as of the earlier liberation theology of Latin America, Africa, and to some extent Asia. This vision is "utopian" in the sense that the church is seen as a kind of socio-political avant-garde for transformation of the whole society. To work for such social transformation is to participate in a worldly process *itself* seen as having a certain salvific power. God is understood to be at work in socially transformative processes. The "household" is understood as a tangible global community of human beings living out the alternative vision and thereby "unmasking and demythologizing the philosophy of the global system as a dangerous illusion, and in discovering the logic of life, i.e., the reality of relationships, a logic in accord with the practice of sharing and solidarity."[30]

This position seems to suggest *both* that the visible church as we know it is indispensable, *and* that, in the long scheme of things, it is a provisional institution. We work through the church for justice in the world in order that the church will be eventually supplanted by a global society bearing the marks of the reign of God. At best the church is a sort of conditional, temporary expression of that to which the world is moving by the power of God's Spirit. It follows that the church receives both its essential definition and its mission from *this* worldly process.[31] Konrad Raiser writes:

> The transformation of the whole human race, of the creation as a whole, into the "household of God" is the promise by which the church lives and the goal toward which its life is directed. Its task is not the christianization of the oikoumene. Rather the church is to live as salt of the earth, as light of the world, and through its life be a visible witness to the new community in the household of God (Matt. 5:13ff.). The church is to live for the world, is to change the world.[32]

Note Raiser's phrase: "Its task is not the christianization of the *oikoumene*." That is to say, in receiving and acting on the eschatological promise, we do not expect the fulfillment to be the cultural triumph of specifically Christian forms of life, worship, and thought. The human world is not to be fulfilled in, or as, the "church" in the common sense of that word, as an institution maintaining a certain tradition of language, customs, and the like. If the fulfillment of humankind were to be a triumph of the church, it might well be the triumph of an institution so transformed as no longer to be "Christian" in the sense of having recognizable continuity with a particular history and theological content. This confirms that "church" in the culturally Christian sense is, eschatologically considered, an interim reality. The household of life is a further, more humanly encompassing reality: not just an inviting synonym for the familiar institution, but a term, in Raiser's language, for "the whole human race" and "creation as a whole" under the rule of God.

Jürgen Moltmann says similar things. He credits secular forces and secular human science perspectives as authentic instruments in the fulfillment of the vision of the city of God. He gives theological endorsement to the growth of human freedom in the wake of the Enlightenment, interpreting history as a series of "freedom movements." For Moltmann, the human rights agenda in particular deserves attention and support. God's purposes for humankind include the church, but go beyond the church. Through its role in "the trinitarian history of God" the church fulfills its eschatological mission in critical solidarity with many historical "partner movements" on the way to realizing God's reign. In Moltmann's words, "The church has partners in history who are not the church and will never become the church."[33] These include Israel, other world religions, and the institutions and processes of secular life "which can neither be ecclesiasticized nor Christianized."[34] Thus for Moltmann the church is a provisional reality that will finally have fulfilled its purpose and be superseded by the kingdom. It is not by the inclusion of the whole world in the church that the universal kingdom will come.

Nowhere, perhaps, is this said more clearly than in the following passage:

> It is not the church that has a mission of salvation to fulfil to the world; it is the mission of the Son and the Spirit through the Father that includes the church, creating a church as it goes on its way. If the church understands itself, with all its tasks and powers, in the Spirit and against the horizon of the Spirit's history, then it also understands its particularity as one element in the power of the Spirit and has no need to maintain its special power and its special charges with absolute and self-destructive claims. It then has no need to look sideways in suspicion or jealousy at the saving efficacies of the Spirit outside the church; instead it can recognize them thankfully as signs that the Spirit is greater than the church and that God's purpose of salvation reaches beyond the church.[35]

It follows that churches, in the culturally "Christian" sense, will not find within themselves or their practices the political and economic structures needed for a household of life. They should not claim to represent the "true politics" merely in the forms of churchly life. Rather they should try to *induce* a true politics in the world, perhaps in cooperation with other religious bodies and new social movements. They should be interested in linking up with all that the Spirit of God is doing among human beings, and indeed in the cosmos itself, knowing that the household of life is a body politic which "gives God his due" without need for a separate religious establishment.

But if the goal is not the "Christianization" of the *oikoumene*, how far beyond recognizably Christian content can one go and still have a sense that there is something beyond *mere* politics, some horizon beyond the cut and thrust and compromise of ordinary political life? From where will come the critical sense that forbids identifying any particular political program with the reign of God? If this worldly-horizon formula is carried through, do the churches not, in a generation or two, risk losing the thickness of moral formation they were striving for at the outset?

Put this in another way. Is not the position just described what lies behind the vulnerability of many of its proponents to the charge that they sound just like good secular liberals, always opting for what is "politically correct," never speaking in a voice that is recognizably "different"? Think of the charges leveled by Princeton ethicist Jeffrey Stout at James Gustafson's *Ethics in a Christian Context*, and by John Milbank at those who allow this or that social theory to become a criterion for the cogency of the gospel message (chapter 1).

CAN THESE POSITIONS BE RECONCILED?

I want some kind of "both/and," as I feel sure do Raiser, Moltmann, and many others. The church needs to rediscover itself as a setting for moral formation in communities that embody the celebration of tradition and the life of the Spirit. But it also needs to continue its engagement with the world, recognizing that the Spirit is at work there too. Can the larger category of a household of life help bring these perspectives into a single vision?

I propose that the term "household of life" be seen as a kind of *vinculum* (i.e., tying-together)[36] concept for the whole new reality in the world that comes to be in virtue of the presence there of Jesus Christ. This new reality embraces all the complexity of the church-and-world interaction described at length in chapter 4. For analytical purposes one can describe the worldly and churchly elements in this whole separately: first one and then the other. But the tendency to settle on one or the other as the governing category is, I am convinced, a product of the contemporary tendency to reify the categories of "religious" and "secular," without realizing that each of these seemingly distinct worlds plays an indispensable part in the definition of the other. May the term "household of life" then serve as the needed *tertium quid*, neither the church as we know it nor the world as we know it, but the whole multifaceted impact of Jesus Christ, in the power of the Spirit, in the human world?[37]

In essence I am suggesting "household of life" as a term for the overall shaping of communal life through the total historical process brought about by the presence of Jesus Christ in the world. The visible church plays an indispensable *role* in this shaping process, but is not the whole of it. As Peter Hodgson writes, "God was 'incarnate,' not in the physical nature of Jesus as such but in the gestalt that coalesced both in and around his person."[38] On the one hand, this gestalt is not merely "church:" "This complex divine shape is not empirically observable or directly identifiable with any particular worldly structure since it is only fully embodied in the totality of the world."[39] But on the other hand, one cannot describe the specific quality of this configuration of practice in the world "abstractly or generically, but only in light of a specific vision of God as mediated by a determinate religious community—in my case the Christian community of faith and its vision of the triune God."[40]

Can the notion of "household" bear this much theological weight? I think so. First of all, the idea of a household of life provides a terminology that transcends—because it has not been implicated with—the categories over which the churches have been divided. Ecumenists may even come to bless these unresolved ecclesiastical disagreements, because they have prevented the movement from turning into a self-satisfied ecclesiastical power bloc. "Household of life" terminology also offers an arena in which one is not tempted to draw too many hard-edged distinctions and boundaries. It is well at this moment of time *not* to be asking the question who is "in" and who is not. On the contrary, "household" imagery suggests a region of kinship among family members joined in the variously resonating Spirit of Jesus Christ (see chapter 5).

It is also important to remember that in the Bible households are places of hospitality. They are open to visitors and sojourners and people needing sanctuary from all kinds of threats and misfortunes. In the presence of guests, one tends to suppress family disagreements. Members of the household may also learn from their guests that the Holy Spirit is at work in the world beyond the family, as well as within. With this may come a realization that the categories in which family arguments have been carried on—such as those articulating the eschatological horizons just discussed—are too narrow. A dialectic of "both-and" may begin to look like the only possible position. Different possibilities may come to be seen as complementary in a household that recognizes both ecclesial and transecclesial works of the Holy Spirit.

It is, in fact, as locus of the Spirit's action among human beings and therefore as the place where God "tents" or comes to "dwell" with us (Rev. 21:3), that the household gains much of its "vincular" capacity to bring disparate elements and powers together, as it were, under one roof. The household's "both/and" capacity is, in short, pneumatological in origin.

Michael Welker has written persuasively that the Spirit poured out from on high "points to a process of emergence and thus to a plurality of ways of being affected and to reciprocal interdependencies of life in its diversity, sprouting up and being strengthened in many contexts simultaneously."[41] Seemingly disparate realms—the church and other human communities for example—become "porous" to the Spirit and thus to one another. Isaiah 32:15-18 (RSV) connects the pouring out of the Spirit with justice, peace, and peaceful habitation upon the earth:

> *The Spirit is poured upon us from on high,*
> *and the wilderness becomes a fruitful field,*
> *and the fruitful field is deemed a forest.*
> *Then justice will dwell in the wilderness,*
> *and righteousness abide in the fruitful field.*
> *And the effect of righteousness will be peace,*
> *and the result of righteousness quietness and trust forever.*
> *My people will abide in a peaceful habitation,*
> *in secure dwellings, and in quiet resting places.*

Anna Marie Aagaard writes, "Where Christians experience life enlivened, connected, renewed, fulfilled, [they] dare to confess, 'Here the Spirit has come from on high.' " One senses that this power of the Spirit to join together multiple life-contexts under the one roof of God's "peaceful habitation" offers a powerful alternative to the "natural law" *vinculum* presupposed by ethicists in the Roman Catholic tradition. Both the Spirit-poured-out and "natural law" have the power to connect the language and experience of the church with the language and experience of other human communities. But the Spirit does so far more dynamically and resourcefully.[42]

Such thoughts furthermore suggest ways of describing the household in terms of the multiple, interconnecting charisms or vocations of its members. Instead of churchly and worldly eschatological horizons in conflict, may we not think of complementary callings within the body of Christ? Some members cultivate the community of resonance in the Spirit in all its traditional-liturgical-practical fullness; other members offer sanctuary and hospitality to persons, communities, and movements beyond the confessing community of faith in whom or in which the Spirit is apparently also at work.[43] In this perspective, the household of life can include the visible church as well as others who are at times, metaphorically speaking, guests in the sanctuary. Such guests may represent other recognizably resonating, if theologically tongue-tied, readings of the meaning of Jesus Christ for the world.

Imago Dei and City of God: An Eschatological Vision

Is this "both/and" view of the household of life at home in the larger context of biblical eschatology? It has been suggested[44] that speculations on the "economic," or historically unfolding Trinity from theologians of the ancient Eastern church—the Cappadocian fathers, John of Damascus, and possibly a few others—offer resources for interpreting the movement of history toward its fulfillment. These perspectives have seldom figured in the controversies of the West. Fortunately, Jürgen Moltmann has taken them up in ways that illuminate the entire eschatological thrust of scripture.

The heart of the story is this: as human beings *together* we are called to *become* the "image of God" (*imago Dei*) in the universe. This takes place in a historical process through which humanity is enabled by grace and by the Holy Spirit actually to *participate* in the divine life, not merely reflect it. Thus the Trinity itself proceeds to unfold through time and space in its "economic," or householding, character.[45] The triune God comes to encompass human life. Again a derivative of the term *oikos* appears. The human community, through participation in the life of the "economic" Trinity, is depicted as preparing itself to be a dwelling place for God on earth.

How is this worked out? Moltmann writes: "The one God, who is differentiated in himself and is at one with himself, then finds his correspondence in a community of human beings, female and male, who unite with one another and are one."[46] God created human beings *to be* his image in the world, that is to manifest God's social nature in the very character of human community. There is a crucial move here. The traditional translation of Genesis 1:26ff. says merely that God created us "in" God's image (implying a description of what we already are as creatures). Moltmann prefers the translation "to be" God's image (implying a *calling* toward that which we are in future to become). Jesus Christ then fulfills and exemplifies that which we are called "to be."[47] Christ is "son of man," or "second Adam" or "new human being."[48] In *his* "image" human beings are restored to their calling to be *God's* image in the sense of representing or reflecting on earth who God is. Sin is the refusal to accept and live out this calling, transforming it instead into something else we have devised ourselves. Righteousness is not something we once had, but have lost. It is something we are called to be by grace, but have thus far refused.

This new creation of humanity in the likeness of God is not an individual matter. It comes about in the fellowship of believers. It is God alone who can make this possible through justification—the forgiveness of sins and acceptance of our lives by God that we receive as a free gift in faith. Justification in turn leads to sanctification, which means "putting on the new human being, created after the likeness of God" (Eph 4:24).

But what in us constitutes our human potential for this likeness? Moltmann rejects the "psychological" or individualistic analogy typical of the Western theological tradition,[49] in favor of the vision of the great fourth-century Cappadocians—Gregory of Nyssa, Gregory of Nazianzus, Basil of Caesarea—who understand the Trinity as a social being whose "persons" relate to one another in *perichoresis*. The latter word is most often translated "coinherence," but *perichoresis* literally means "dancing around." This dancing God faces us not as a closed, monarchical entity but openly, as three persons in open, joyful interaction. Christ has gone to be part of this joyful life-together, and in him we are invited to *join* the wedding feast going on in God's heavenly household. We are addressed not as individuals, but as a community of women and men, brothers and sisters, parents and children. "The socially open companionship between people," Moltmann writes, "is the form of life which corresponds to God."[50] Moltmann elaborates:

> We have taken up these [Eastern] ideas as a basis for a pronouncedly social doctrine of human likeness to God as a theology of the open Trinity. Instead of starting from a closed and self-contained Trinity which manifests itself outwardly without differentiation, we have taken as our premise an open Trinity which manifests itself outwardly in differentiated form.[51]

And this means that Moltmann can take one further, theologically very striking, step. Human beings are not only restored from their sins, he writes:

> they are also gathered into the open Trinity. They become conformed to the image of the Son (Romans 8:29). This does not merely presuppose that the eternal Son of God becomes human and is one like themselves; it also means that as a result human beings become like the Son and, through the Holy Spirit, are gathered into his eternal fellowship with the Father. Christ is "the first-born among many brothers and sisters." This is to say that through the son the divine Trinity throws itself open for human beings.[52]

Eventually the wedding feast of the household of life becomes a *political*, not merely a domestic, event. In Revelation 21:2 the household metaphor of the wedding feast is contained *within* the larger political metaphor in which the realms of the great imperial "beasts," and finally the Roman Empire itself, are supplanted by the holy city of God. The *ekklesia* is joined in marriage to Christ in the divine household, but the vision of the bride descending out of heaven is *already* a figure for the advent of the *polis* in which God is to dwell with God's people. God's final word is not only "household." It is also "city."[53]

Early in his career Karl Barth saw this point clearly: "The hope in which the Christian community has its eternal goal consists not in an eternal church but in the *polis* built by God and coming down from heaven to earth."[54] And it is not that the church is to be *in* the eternal city, but rather that the church or household itself *becomes* the *polis* of God. Oliver

O'Donovan thinks Barth does not go far enough. The Barthian statement "fails to acknowledge the political character of the church itself, veiled and hidden in the time of its pilgrimage, yet always present in its witness to the Kingdom of God. The church never was, in its true character, merely the temple of the city; it was the promise of the city itself."[55]

Here is an apocalyptic promise grounded firmly in the realities of economic and political life on earth. The word *polis* indeed resonates richly through the practical political philosophies of the ancient Greek city-states. The biblical writer cannot have used this term without at least some awareness of its significance in those traditions and in the world of his time. In Aristotle, for example, the duty of those devoted to the public sphere is the proper care or management (*oikonomia*) of the city where human beings find their fulfillment as "political animals."[56] But the Book of Revelation is about the transformation of the *polis* toward being God's city, where human beings will live together in justice, peace, and praise.

Preparing us to understand this transformation, the apocalyptic writer draws devastating pictures of the Roman Empire, corrupt in both its political and economic dimensions.[57] Clearly, Rome has been a system devoted to concentrating wealth and power at its center and denying both to the vast numbers of provincials and slaves whose labor provides the basis for it. The emperor is not merely a great tribune or military hero. He is "Lord, God, Savior and Protector of the *oikoumene*." He heads a system in which conquered provinces have been plundered for the benefit of the capital city, much of the labor has been done by women who had no rights and by slaves. Exorbitant taxes have been levied to support armies to carry on incessant border warfare.

The description of Rome (code named "Babylon") in Revelation 18 is graphic. Notable is the way "nations," "kings of the earth," and "merchants of the earth" have *together* been drawn into the Roman system, profiting from it, but in doing so drinking "of the wine of the wrath of her fornication" (verse 3). This trio—nations, kings, and merchants—nicely sums up what the Roman system has been about. Within the "national" (i.e., vassal) structures of those days, political leaders and commercial leaders have been in league to enrich themselves on the backs of the people. When the fall comes these "kings" are going to have to distance themselves from the Roman cornucopia, to "stand far off in fear of her torment" (verses 9 and 10). The merchants will simply find that the markets for their goods have collapsed.

Then, in verse 11, comes a fascinating list of the goods exchanged in the international commerce of the day, from "gold, silver, jewels and pearls," to the final commodities mentioned: "sheep, horses, and chariots, slaves—and human lives." A few manuscripts have "chariots, and human bodies and souls." Whatever was originally written, the meaning is clear enough. In this system an unjust economy fueled the political system, which in turn was in league with the unjust economy. All of it is to be swept away, to be replaced by the city of God.

But the holy city of Revelation 21 is not just any city fulfilled, but "the New Jerusalem." There is no ground here for any triumphalism. As a symbol today "Jerusalem" hardly conjures up a vision of peace. Rather it reminds us of the realities of warfare, and above all *religious* warfare, which constantly undermines, gives the lie to, religious claims. Of all the cities of earth, this could be among the *most* fought over, among the most symbolic of human inability to live together in peace. The notion of a household of life, within whose precincts combatants can be invited to ask, *in the right way*, the questions that separate them, has everything to do with the strife that goes on in today's cities.

Such a household is extraterritorial to the issues over which we human beings struggle, but not as something "religious" distinguished from something called "secular." For us, the "religious" and the "secular" realms are distinguished in principle, but, ironically, lethally interrelated in practice. In the promised fulfillment both the theoretical distinction and the lethal combination are transcended.

On the evidence of Revelation 21, the realms of *ekklesia*, and of God's reign in human affairs, finally coincide in a *polis* standing for justice and peace. In the end, God gathers one people to the holy city, a community in whose life the contrast between "secular" and "religious" no longer applies. Neither one of these realms, nor the two of them in combination, can now provide the pretext for destructive violence. The "secular" and the "religious" as we understand them today are *constructs* belonging to an unfulfilled world, distorted by their incompleteness and shot through with anxiety. But in John's representation of the beloved community, all such penultimate distinctions and anxieties are transcended: between the natural and the supernatural, between the clerical and the lay, between theological language and other language.

We are told of "a new heaven *and* a new earth." The two have apparently become a single habitation for the saints of God. Here, by the power of the Spirit, is the enactment in space and time of the vision of the household in which God "dwells." What are the implications of this imaginative picture of the end-time? Here is the fulfillment of the original divine purpose sketched in Genesis 3: the creation of humankind *to be* God's "image" in creation and history.

The entire human community is here called to make God's "glory," in Hebrew the *kabodh*, or *shekinah*, present to the universe. Instead of the ark of the covenant, the Holy City becomes the *locus* of this presence, this glory: the place where God *dwells* (Greek *skenosei*, literally "tents") in the *midst* of God's people, to *be* their God. This fulfillment of the *imago Dei* is thus the living presence of God, Godself, who gathers and constitutes the community of the end-time. *This* fulfilled "image" ceases to be a mere sign which refers to, or substitutes for, something absent. This "image of God" *is* that to which it points, rendering God present by being the actual *locus* of God's reality. The holy city (not only the elements of bread and wine) becomes *sacramental* in the fullest sense.

Our distinctively ecclesial language then becomes one with the constitutive language of the household in which God dwells with God's people. In the consummatory vision there is no longer any special faith-language separate and distinct from the discourse that constitutes the beloved community itself. On the way to that end, church and theology fulfill their function by keeping space open in the human community for the seeds of this fulfillment—those possibilities hidden in the human community's grace-enabled capacity to respond to God's calling—to take root and grow.

In this penultimate time, *our* human time, any confusion between the faith in which we are ecclesially formed and our devotion to worldly causes runs the risk of works-righteousness, or even idolatry. But when the end is attained, the special functions of "theology" and "church" will have been fulfilled, and *as such* they will have disappeared. In the heavenly city, the distinction between ecclesiology and ethics, or even the existence of these as distinct categories, will have become inconceivable. Humanity itself will have become a moral community. There—as in the Trinity that *already* incorporates our humanity in the ascended Christ—God will be all in all.

Notes

Preface

1. J. Bryan Hehir reports that Bernanos "was once quoted as saying" these words, but does not indicate a source. See "Personal Faith, the Public Church, and the Role of Theology," *Harvard Divinity Bulletin* 26, no. 1 (1996): 5. I have found this article helpful even as I read its fundamental premise in a different theological frame of reference.

2. Compare Stanley Hauerwas, "The very way we have learned to state the problem is the problem." *After Christendom? How the Church Is to Behave if Freedom, Justice, and a Christian Nation Are Bad Ideas* (Nashville, Abingdon Press, 1991), 99. But my way of stating the problem differs from Hauerwas's, as these pages will show.

3. Hehir's concept of the "premoral" is based on philosophical and doctrinal presuppositions which he finds reflected in the people's basic consciousness as formed in the Roman Catholic tradition. He calls these the "incarnational," "sacramental," and "social" principles. Hehir then proceeds to call for "natural law" links between the theological and political fields of discourse. My argument parallels Hehir's along an ecclesiological, rather than a natural law, path. I see no natural law bridge categories through which Christians can think *for* the world by clarifying the world's own assumptions. But congregations can express their being in practices that, in turn, open *space* for persons engaged in the public world to think thoughts more generous, compassionate, imaginative, and even visionary, than they would otherwise.

4. The inquiry in question has been a joint effort of Units I (Unity and Renewal) and III (Justice, Peace, and Creation) of the WCC, carried out in three international consultations supported by preliminary study documents. A meeting at Ronde (Aarhus, Denmark) consultation in 1993 produced a text entitled *Costly Unity*, subsequently transmitted to the Fifth World Conference on Faith and Order at Santiago de Compostela in August of that year. A subsequent, 1994, consultation in Tantur, Israel, took up the issues again. The Tantur findings were published in 1995 as a booklet entitled *Costly Commitment*. A third document, *Costly Obedience*, reports the work of a June 1996 meeting in Johannesburg,

South Africa. The reports of all three meetings, with several further critical essays, have now appeared as a single volume: Thomas F. Best and Martin Robra, eds., *Ecclesiology and Ethics: Ecumenical Ethical Engagement, Moral Formation, and the Nature of the Churches* (Geneva: WCC Publications, 1997).

5. These have been the watchwords of a program of study and action now focused in WCC Unit III. "JPIC," as this focus is called for short, will be described more fully later in the book.

6. Charles C. West, in private correspondence, quoted by permission.

7. Dietrich Bonhoeffer, *The Communion of Saints: A Dogmatic Inquiry into the Sociology of the Church* (New York: Harper and Row, 1963), 134, 146–47.

8. Glenn Tinder, "Can We Be Good Without God?" *Atlantic Monthly*, December 1989, 76.

9. In private correspondence, quoted by permission.

10. In private correspondence, cited by permission.

11. The already published materials are "Ecclesiology and Ethics in Current Ecumenical Debate," *Ecumenical Review* 48, no. 1 (January 1996): 11ff., German translation "Ekklesiolgie und Ethik in der laufenden ökumenischen Diskussion," *(ö)kumenische Rundschau* 45, Heft 3 (Juli 1996): 270ff.; *Renewing the Ecumenical Vision*, ed. Joseph D. Small, Occasional Paper No. 7 of the Theology and Worship Unit of the Presbyterian Church (USA) and *Costly Obedience*, reporting the Johannesburg Consultation of June 1996 (in Best and Robra. eds, *Ecclesiology and Ethics*, 50ff.). See also "Faith, Ethics, and Civil Society," in the report of the WCC Consultation on Theology and Civil Society *God's People in Civil Society: Ecclesiological Implications* (Loccum, Germany: Loccumer Protokolle 23, no. 95 [1996]: 135ff.). The experience of drafting, with a committee, the message of the 23rd General Council of the World Alliance of Reformed Churches in Debrecen, Hungary, August 1997, as well as the "Declaration of Debrecen" (*Reformed World* 47, nos. 3 and 4 [September and December 1997]: 224ff.) also influenced my thinking.

12. The paragraphs in question are from part IV of the Johannesburg document "Costly Obedience" published in Best and Robra, eds., *Ecclesiology and Ethics*, 72ff. This section was, by agreement, completed after the close of the Johannesburg meeting, circulated by mail and fax to the participants, extensively revised, and recirculated for approval. One critic, not himself part of the study process or present for any part of it, has suggested that this section of the Johannesburg document still represents the views of the drafter more than it does the views of the committee. I can only say that here, as in the earlier parts of the Johannesburg text, I tried faithfully to find words for what I heard. The materials in question could not have been written apart from that meeting. They represent a direction of thought that ran strongly through the discussion. But it is all the more appropriate that I should acknowledge responsibility for these paragraphs now that I have revised them further in the light of helpful commentary.

13. Geneva: WCC Publications, 1996.

14. Geneva: WCC Publications, 1996.

Chapter 1

1. The meanings of terms such as "conservative" and "liberal" of course depend on the point of view from which these tendencies are described. By "conservative" I mean

doctrinally orthodox, traditionalist, and evangelical positions of all kinds. I use the word "liberal" here not in the classical individualistic sense in which it overlaps with much that would be considered "conservative" today, but simply to mean the leftward, but not radical, end of the opinion spectrum, where it has something in common, although by no means identity, with the 19th-century "liberalism" or theological accommodationism criticized by Karl Barth and others. However described, each camp also has its own *internal* spectrum of opinion: so much so that some think such terms conceal more than they clarify. I am well aware, as Max Stackhouse has urged me to recognize, that people can be conservative on some issues and progressive on others. Conservatives, without seeing any contradiction, can simultaneously be strongly opposed to abortion and in favor of capital punishment. Liberals or progressives can be in favor of social welfare and foreign aid, yet be conservatives where management issues are at stake. Yet these words represent persistent tendencies in human affairs, and ceasing to use them would only mean having to invent something new for the same purpose.

2. Stanley Hauerwas, *Truthfulness and Tragedy* (Notre Dame: Notre Dame University Press, 1977), 142f.

3. Hauerwas, *After Christendom?* 93ff.

4. Dorothy C. Bass, ed., *Practicing Our Faith: A Way of Life for a Searching People* (San Francisco: Jossey-Bass, 1997).

5. See Stephen L. Carter, *The Culture of Disbelief: How American Law and Politics Trivialize Religious Devotion* (New York: Basic Books, 1993), 8, et passim.

6. Jeffrey Stout, *Ethics After Babel: The Languages of Morals and Their Discontents* (Boston: Beacon Press, 1988), see especially 163ff. I am aware that I may have juxtaposed incommensurable categories: what Stout wants is probably not what Hauerwas has to give. Or is it? Stout hopes that the moral theologian will *not* merely echo what the secular liberal ethicist has to say, and Hauerwas certainly avoids doing so with a passion.

7. See, for example, Adam Seligman, *The Idea of Civil Society* (New York: Macmillan, Free Press, 1992). Seligman argues that conceptions of human relationships having a religious origin are indispensable to contemporary attempts to reason out the basis of a moral public realm. Similarly, Georgia Warnke argues in *Justice and Interpretation* (Cambridge: MIT Press, 1993) that contemporary political and moral philosophies are not in fact self-standing arguments, but rather interpretations of bodies of public conviction in which, presumably, residual, sometimes religiously grounded, notions of virtue still reside.

8. The results of this WCC study are published as Best and Robra, eds., *Ecclesiology and Ethics*.

9. See Konrad Raiser, "Ecumenical Discussion of Ethics and Ecclesiology," *Ecumenical Review*, 48:1, (January, 1996), 3ff.

10. See the action of the World Alliance of Reformed Churches at Ottawa in 1982 suspending the membership of two South African Reformed bodies on grounds of their theological defense of apartheid and refusal of communion to blacks. The technical term is *status confessionis*, a declaration that a position taken by a church on some issue, often a moral one, threatens the integrity of the faith itself.

11. In this case, the Serbian Orthodox Church. The WCC Central Committee launched an inquiry into that church's "ambivalent, or at any rate insufficiently forthright, statements on the war in the former Yugoslavia and human rights violations by the Serbian army" (Raiser, "Ecumenical Discussion," 3).

12. Such a debate occurred at the WCC Canberra Assembly in 1991 on a motion by Konrad Raiser, not yet elected as WCC General Secretary. The motion was narrowly defeated.

13. The exception has been the position of the churches of the left wing of the Reformation such as the "historic peace churches" and others. Here ecclesiology has been intimately tied to a notion of discipleship in which certain moral principles and practices are paramount. See Raiser, "Ecumenical Discussion," 7.

14. Ibid., 4.

15. A sign of the times is the republication of James B. Nelson's *Moral Nexus: Ethics of Christian Identity and Community* (Louisville: Westminster/John Knox Press, 1996). Nelson has supplied a new introduction in which he says, "we are necessarily concerned with the formation of persons within those communities that express visions of the good in specific images and stories" (xiv). He goes on to speak of "the important connections of narrative ethics to the church as moral community." Moral "agency" in the world, he concludes, is grounded in "formation" (xiv).

16. Alasdair MacIntyre's role in making these points, as well as his influence on theologians, is well known. See *After Virtue: A Study in Moral Theory* (Notre Dame: University of Notre Dame Press, 1981, second ed. 1984).

17. Charles Taylor says that the arguments often offered in support of these secular moral agreements are more likely, on careful study, to undermine them, or give them a bad name, because of their inadequacy as grounds for the large conclusions they are called upon to support. Taylor suggests that the modern moral identity "is much richer in moral sources than its condemners allow but that this richness is rendered invisible by the impoverished philosophical language of its most zealous defenders. Modernity urgently needs to be saved from its most unconditional supporters" (*Sources of the Self: The Making of the Modern Identity* [Cambridge: Harvard University Press, 1989], xi).

18. We can, John Rawls says in his best-known book *A Theory of Justice* (Cambridge: Belknap Press of Harvard University Press, 1971), reason out a conception of justice without reference to *any* communally maintained traditions of the good life. The shape of Rawls's argument, at least in *Justice*, makes graphic the exclusion from consideration of cultural identities, communal traditions, or religious doctrines. A group of persons is imagined meeting behind a "veil of ignorance" that brackets out of consideration all factors having to do with their identities, backgrounds, viewpoints, economic status, and the like, so that they can concentrate on bargaining out the minimal terms of a just society in which they would be willing to live.

19. Richard Bernstein makes just this point about the philosopher Richard Rorty. "If by relativism we mean epistemological behaviorism, that there is no other way to justify knowledge claims or claims to truth than by appealing to those social practices which have been hammered out in the course of human history and are the forms of inquiry *within* which we distinguish what is true and false, what is objective and idiosyncratic, then Rorty advocates such a relativism" (Bernstein, "Philosophy in the Conversation of Humankind," in *Philosophical Profiles: Essays in a Pragmatic Mode* [Philadelphia: University of Pennsylvania Press, 1986], 41).

20. John Gray, "Why Irony Can't Be Superior," in *Times Literary Supplement* (November 3, 1995), reviewing Norman Geras, *Solidarity in the Conversation of Humankind: The Ungroundable Liberalism of Richard Rorty* (London: Verso, 1995).

21. Raiser, "Ecumenical Discussion," 8.

22. See, for example, my book *Why Is the Church in the World?* (Philadelphia: Presbyterian Department of Church and Society, 1967), which was written in collaboration with a committee to consider what justification the church as institution had at that time for becoming involved with matters such as the American civil rights movement or opposition to the war in Vietnam. Now the question of involvement as such is largely moot. With the discovery by the American "religious right" of the allure of political activism, the question is no longer *whether* the church shall take public stands. It is, rather, who shall control the public stands the church takes.

23. The world confessional bodies have not been unaware of the need. The 23rd General Council of the World Alliance of Reformed Churches in Debrecen, Hungary (August 1997), did some distinguished work on global economic ethics under the leadership of Milan Opocensky, Kim Young Bok, and others.

24. Raiser, "Ecumenical Discussion," 8.

25. See Jack B. Rogers, *Claiming the Center: Churches and Conflicting Worldviews* (Louisville: Westminster/John Knox Press, 1995) 2ff., et passim.

26. These positions are articulated in directives to the hierarchy and to Catholic teachers of ethics telling them to think in accordance with officially sanctioned notions of moral truth. I think especially of *Veritatis Splendor.* I have written an analysis of this encyclical commending its sophisticated argumentation and innovative use of the natural law tradition (see Lewis S. Mudge, "Veritatis Splendor and Today's Ecumenical Conversation," *The Ecumenical Review* 48, no. 2 [April 1996]: 158, and articles by other writers on the same subject in that issue). Still, this papal pronouncement places Catholic moral thinkers under strict guidelines, ruling out, for example, the use of "consequentialist" or "proportionalist" theoretical models, often found in non-Catholic or secular ethical writing.

27. The wording of this 1997 Presbyterian enactment is as follows: "Those called to office in the church are to lead a life in obedience to Scripture and in conformity with historic confessional standards of the church. Among these standards is the requirement to live either in fidelity within the covenant of marriage of a man and a woman, or chastity in singleness. Persons refusing to repent of any self-acknowledged practice which the confessions call sin shall not be ordained and/or installed as deacons, elders, or ministers of the Word and Sacrament."

28. Ironically, on almost the same day that the Presbyterian vote on "fidelity and chastity" was announced, the Board of Orthodox Rabbis in America announced that Jewish identity is to be equated with rigorous fidelity to every one of the just over 600 commandments in the five books of Moses, or Torah. This, not birth from a Jewish mother, not commitment to the preservation of Jewish civilization, not religious commitment as such, not integrity of personhood in conversation with the tradition, is now to be the standard of Jewish identity. This deliverance purports to exclude from the Jewish community most members of the Reform and Conservative movements as well, no doubt, as inducing unconscionable anxiety among some of the Orthodox themselves. It is no doubt a coincidence that just about the same number of commandments are found in the Torah as there are references to specific sins in the Presbyterian *Book of Confessions* to which the "fidelity and chastity" amendment refers.

29. At a certain Eastern university the student honor code in the early 1950s is said to have run to just under two pages and to have relied on common understanding of what it

meant to be "a scholar and a gentleman." Now the same document has expanded to over 100 pages detailing every possible nuance of infraction and retribution.

30. As final revisions are made to this book, a proposal to replace the previously mentioned enactment effectively prohibiting the ordination of gay and lesbian persons in the Presbyterian Church (U.S.A.) is being voted on by the presbyteries. The proposed wording is as follows: "Those who are called to office in the church are to lead a life in obedience to Jesus Christ, under the authority of Scripture and instructed by the historic confessional standards of the church. Among these standards is the requirement to demonstrate fidelity and integrity in marriage or singleness and in all relationships of life. Candidates for office should acknowledge their own sinfulness, their need for repentance, and their reliance on the grace and mercy of God to fulfill the duties of their office." This text is in fact a centrist formula, among other things reflecting more accurately than the previously adopted text the historic hierarchy of authority in Presbyterianism from Jesus Christ, to Scripture, to the confessional standards. That the proposed wording is seen by many as "liberal" in a pejorative sense is evidence of the passionate polarization of moral perception that afflicts this denomination and many others.

31. Johann-Baptist Metz, "Messianic or 'Bourgeois' Religion?" in *Faith and the Future: Essays on Theology, Solidarity and Modernity* (Maryknoll, NY: Orbis Books, and London: SCM Press, 1995), 23.

32. John Milbank, *Theology and Social Theory: Beyond Secular Reason* (Oxford and Cambridge, MA: Blackwell Publishers, 1990), 2.

33. Ibid.

34. Jeffrey Stout, *Ethics*, 182. To be fair, I must add that Gustafson has not been without means to reply to this sort of complaint. The central point, as I see it, is that Stout's neo-pragmatism has no resource to offer apart from the personal integrity of its proponents when the modest moral platitudes they have to offer are challenged by tyrants or torturers. Gustafson's Christian perspective is made of sterner stuff.

35. John P. Burgess, "Can't Stop Talking About Sex," *Christian Century* (July 28–August 4, 1993): 732ff. See also Burgess, "Sexuality, Morality, and the Presbyterian Debate," *Christian Century* (March 5, 1997): 246ff.

36. Ibid.

37. Hehir, *Public Church*, 4.

38. See Jack B. Rogers, *Claiming the Center: Churches and Conflicting Worldviews* (Louisville: Westminster/John Knox Press, 1995).

39. Douglas John Hall, *The Future of the Church: Where Are We Headed?* (Toronto: United Church of Canada Publishing House, 1989), 62–63.

40. Ibid., 56ff.

41. Ibid., 65.

42. Ibid., 84.

43. Loren B. Mead, *The Once and Future Church: Reinventing the Congregation for a New Mission Frontier* (Washington, D.C.: Alban Institute, 1991).

44. See Carter, *Disbelief*, 3ff. et passim. But there are very recent signs, if popular TV programming as well as news reporting in America are any indication, that ignorance of and disdain for "religion" are beginning to diminish. Still, attitudes toward religion in the public media remain mostly conventional and stereotypical, with a few notable exceptions.

45. Nicholas Lash, "The Church in the State We're In," *Modern Theology* 13, no. 1 (January 1997): 126.

46. See Robert N. Bellah, "How to Understand the Church in an Individualistic Society" in *Christianity and Civil Society*, ed. Rodney L. Petersen (Maryknoll, NY: Orbis Books, 1995), 10.

47. Stanley Hauerwas makes this point vividly in *After Christendom?*: "The world, which I think we can call liberal, has become the presupposition of most Christians as well as most Christian theologians. We believed our task was to make such a world work" (31). He continues, "Yet it is my contention that Christians would be ill advised to try to rescue the liberal project either in its epistemological or political form. The very terms necessary for that project cannot help rendering the church's challenge to the false universalism of the Enlightenment impotent" (35). Here the word "liberal" does not mean moderately left wing, but rather refers to attempts to base a democratic order on the basis of a logic of individual human autonomy, as illustrated by Rawls's *A Theory of Justice*.

48. William T. Cavanaugh, " 'A Fire Strong Enough to Consume the House,': The Wars of Religion and the Rise of the State," *Modern Theology* 11, no. 4 (1995): 400, quoted in Lash, "Church in the State We're In."

49. Bellah, "Church in an Individualistic Society," 4ff. Bellah credits a conversation with Bryan Hehir for the suggestion that the Treaty of Westphalia opened a distinctive period of relationships between church and society, a period now drawing to a close.

50. Lash, "Church in the State We're In," 127.

51. Lash writes, "As the power and autonomy of nation-states decline, the forces of 'globalization' and 'localization'—one operating at a level 'above', the other 'below', that of the state—gather strength. Information and the money markets all 'spin beyond the control of any government'. On the other hand, as the diminishing power of the nation-state renders it increasingly incapable of answering 'the most basic questions of human identity, so we see larger societies disintegrate into religiously, culturally, or ethnically defined entities' " ("Church in the State We're In," 128).

52. I have in mind the work of such writers as Hans Frei, George Lindbeck, James McClendon, Douglas John Hall, William Placher, Stanley Hauerwas, John Howard Yoder, and many others. However diverse in detail and specific outworking their positions may be, these authors seek to recover the integrity of the community of faith with its distinctive stories and doctrines in a world as much in fragments epistemologically as it is morally.

53. Philip Selznick, *The Moral Commonwealth: Social Theory and the Promise of Community* (Berkeley: University of California Press, 1992), 12f. Selznick goes on to write, "History is discarded as irrelevant; all is foreground, all surface, and multiple surfaces at that. Continuities of place and experience are lost forever in a world of homogeneous settings and replaceable modules. A ceaseless barrage of images and 'sound bites' undercuts the capacity to make sense of public and private life. Consumerism reigns, and with it a transformation of things properly valued for themselves into fungible commodities." Selznick continues, "In the postmodern perspective, all ideas are products of subjective interpretation, uncontrolled rhetoric, or political domination. They are radically contingent and without foundations. Human experience is best understood as 'discourse' about 'texts' which are patterns of life as well as words. Because the worlds we inhabit are products of human artifice, they are arbitrary 'all the way down,' that is, fundamentally and irredeemably" (13).

54. Lash, "Church in the State We're In," 123.

55. Ibid., 128.

56. Lash, ibid., quoting Andrew Marr, *Ruling Brittania: The Failure and Future of British Democracy* (London: Michael Joseph, 1995), 75, 321. Marr piles on the phrases. "Com-

munity" is "the watchword for the nineties, the intellectually respectable form of nostalgia." Lash comments that the word "is in danger of becoming so over-used that it is subsiding into bland nothingness."

57. Bass, ed., *Practicing.* Acknowledgment is given Craig Dykstra for having had the insight that led to the book. Dykstra in turn credits Alasdair MacIntyre.

58. The practices presented in *Practicing* are honoring the body, hospitality, household economics, saying yes and saying no, keeping Sabbath, testimony, spiritual discernment, shaping communities, forgiveness, healing, dying well, and singing our lives.

59. Lash, "Church in the State We're In," 122.

60. The power, indeed the indispensability, of the "creative minority" for bringing about historic change has been evident througout history. Julio de Santa Ana has reminded me of the profound reflections of the Italian philosopher Antonio Gramsci on this subject. While ecumenical practice should be among the practices of every Christian congregation, Santa Ana senses, and I agree, that passionate commitment to ecumenism, combined with a grasp of all its ramifications, characterizes a remarkably small group of people across the globe today. I would think no more than several thousand at the outside. If this observation is accurate, one must ponder its implications for the moral difference we seek.

Chapter 2

1. Kenneth Scott Latourette, *A History of Christianity* (New York: Harper and Brothers, 1953): "the greatest century which Christianity had thus far known" (1063). Latourette adds, realistically, yet with a hint of triumph, "It was paralleled by movements which seemed to threaten the very existence of the faith and by challenges which called forth all its inner resources" (1063). Latourette's treatment of the post-1914 period combines continuing confidence with an awareness of new challenges. It is entitled, "Vigor Amidst Storm" (1347).

2. The slogan "the evangelization of the world in this generation" was in fact the late-nineteenth-century watchword of the Student Volunteer Movement for Foreign Missions, but it clearly animated many at Edinburgh in 1910.

3. Geiko Müller-Fahrenholz, *God's Spirit: Transforming a World in Crisis* (New York: Continuum, and Geneva: World Council of Churches, 1995), 111.

4. Latourette, *History*, 1063.

5. Attempts to grasp the meaning of the new ecumenical situation are also to be found in several other recent publications. See *Ecumenical Review* 42, no. 1 (January 1991), entitled "The Ecumenical Future and the WCC," in which the present writer has an article, "The World Council at the Crossroads?" A short summary of current obstacles to ecumenism, as well as of numerous opportunities for new departures, can be found in the report—drafted by Michael Kinnamon and a committee of which the writer was a member—of the Ecclesiology Study Task Force to the General Assembly of the American National Council of the Churches of Christ, Washington, D.C., November 1997.

6. David J. Bosch, *Believing in the Future: Toward a Missiology of Western Culture* (Valley Forge, PA: Trinity Press International, 1995).

7. Konrad Raiser, *Ecumenism in Transition: A Paradigm Shift in the Ecumenical Movement?* (Geneva: World Council of Churches, 1991). 8. It is worth noting that the word *ecu-*

menical was appropriated at a time when the movement bearing that name represented mostly Protestant churches of North Atlantic origin. This appropriation seemed to ignore the much more ancient Christian usage focused on the seven ecumenical councils of the undivided church. To have used the term *ecumenical* at a time when Roman Catholics and Orthodox were not yet involved seems in retrospect to have been at least presumptuous. And, of course, the conditions of a truly ecumenical council remain unfulfilled.

9. Philosophical readers will at once recognize the phenomenological term *intention* as well as the verb *to constitute*. I do not mean to invoke the fullness of technical meaning these terms have in the thought, say, of Edmund Husserl, but nevertheless take over from him a useful way of speaking. Roughly put, we "constitute" our world of perception and activity, i.e., put it together in a meaningful way, in accord with our purposes and objectives.

10. To my knowledge, the suggestion that the term *oikoumene* can and should now be connected with organized perspectives and global movements other than the Christian one first came in an address by José Miguez-Bonino at the meeting of the WCC Plenary Commission on Faith and Order in Lima, Peru, in 1982. I follow his example despite Martin Cressey's admonition (in private correspondence) that the term, grammatically, can only be singular. It is certainly so in biblical Greek. But what counts is the intention with which this singular world is constituted as an action-field. Note Luke 2:1, "that the whole world (*oikoumenen*) should be enrolled" where the constituting intention is enumeration for purposes of taxation. And see Hebrews 2:5, "the *oikoumene* to come." Here alone the notion of "world to come" is expressed with this term rather than the word *aion*, suggesting that, at least in this sense, there is more than one *oikoumene*, ours and God's. The identity of the *oikoumene* depends on who rules it. In short, the "inhabited world" is in principle one, but we have many ways of *constituting* it in intentional imagination. God's reign is the definitive constituting intention for the *oikoumene*. We try to discern and approximate that intention in the practices which constitute the world as theater of our moral imaginations today. I have resisted the temptation to invent an English plural form of the word *oikoumene* to make the point that there are ways of constituting "the inhabited world" other than this one. To add an English plural ending to a Greek word would in any case be a linguistic barbarism, justly placing me outside the civilized *oikoumene* as the Greeks understood it!

11. "Colonization" is Jürgen Habermas's term for the phenomenon in which state and market "systems" not only invade but settle down within, begin to inhabit, the human "life-world." See *The Theory of Communicative Action*, 2 vols., tr. Thomas McCarthy (Boston: Beacon Press, 1987) vol. 2, 318ff.

12. I acknowledge the influence of several authors on my discussion of global economics. See especially M. Douglas Meeks, *God the Economist: The Doctrine of God and Political Economy* (Minneapolis: Augsburg Fortress, 1989). I have been helped also by Ulrich Duchrow's *Global Economy: A Confessional Issue for the Churches*, tr. David Lewis (Geneva, WCC Publications, 1987), written from a German perspective, and Duchrow's *Alternatives to Global Capitalism: Drawn from Biblical History, Designed for Political Action*, tr. Elizabeth Hicks, Keith Archer, Keith Schorah, and Elaine Griffiths (Utrecht, the Netherlands: International Books, and Heidelberg, Germany: Kairos Europa, 1995). For a symposium of differing viewpoints, see Max L. Stackhouse, Peter L. Berger, Dennis P. McCann, and M. Douglas Meeks, *Christian Social Ethics in a Global Era* (Nashville: Abingdon Press, 1995).

13. Gary Becker, *The Economic Approach to Human Behavior* (Chicago, University of

Chicago Press, 1976). My attention was drawn to this book by Larry Rasmussen's *Moral Fragments and Moral Community: A Proposal for Church in Society* (Minneapolis: Fortress Press, 1993), 49.

14. See George Soros, "The Capitalist Threat," *Atlantic Monthly* (February 1997), 45ff. Soros argues that allowing the free market to decide the kind of society we shall have "undermines the very values on which open and democratic societies depend" (45), and therefore eventually destroys the social conditions needed for the market to flourish in the first place.

15. See Robert D. Kaplan, "The Coming Anarchy," *Atlantic Monthly* (February 1994). See also Anthony Lewis's reaction to this piece, "A Bleak Vision," Op-Ed page, *New York Times*, March 7, 1994, 16. See Julio de Santa Ana, "Areas of Convergence and Areas of Questioning," in *Civil Society*, Loccumer Protokolle 23, no. 95 (1996), 184.

16. See Bert Hoedemaker, "Introductory Reflections on JPIC and *Koinonia*," and Lukas Vischer, "*Koinonia* in a Time of Threats to Life," in Thomas F. Best and Wesley Granberg-Michaelson, eds., *Costly Unity* (Geneva: WCC, 1993), 1ff. and 70ff. See also Raiser, "Ecumenical Discussion," 3ff.

18. Jonathan Schell, *The Fate of the Earth* (New York: Alfred A. Knopf, 1982).

19. Hoedemaker, "Introductory Reflections," 5ff.

20. Again, it is good to be reminded of the etymological connection between the Greek word *oikoumene* and the English word *economics*. Both refer to the world ordered or arranged in a certain way, for certain purposes. An economic vision of the human realm occurs as early as the Christmas story in the Gospel of Luke. See Luke 2:1. The Orthodox tradition employs the notion of "economy" in the sense of "household" arrangements to meet specific conditions or situations. See the illuminating treatment of this word-group and its far-reaching implications in Meeks, *God the Economist*.

21. Paulo Freire, *Pedagogy of the Oppressed: New Revised 20th Anniversary Edition*, tr. Myra Bergman Ramos (New York: Continuum, 1993).

22. Robert MacAfee Brown, *Kairos: Three Prophetic Challenges to the Church* (Grand Rapids: Eerdmans, 1990).

23. Of course something more than common theological formulas or conceptual parallels between theologies developed in different cultures is needed to generate relationships between human beings that deserve the name *solidarity*. Perhaps only working side by side within a particular situation for a particular cause can produce genuine solidarity, and even then possibilities for the emergence of serious differences are always also at hand.

24. I recall meeting a pastor from Rostok in the former East Germany not long after the collapse of the Berlin wall who brought me up short by saying, "You have not defeated socialism: you have taken away my country!"

25. Gustavo Gutiérrez's book on the 16th-century saint of Spanish America Bartolomé de las Casas (1484-1566) clearly shows this move away from class analysis as such toward concern for the integrity of the cultures of the poor (*Las Casas: In Search of the Poor of Jesus Christ* [Maryknoll, NY: Orbis Books, 1993]). But at the same time, Gutiérrez lifts up Bartolomé's recognition of the impact of Spain's greed for gold on the Indians of the New World, an estimated 20 to 25 million of whom died because of wars, disease, and hard labor. Central to Las Casas's existence was his conviction "that in the Indian, as the poor and oppressed, Christ is present, buffeted and scourged" (18).

26. While in the early years there seem to have been many persons active in both

arenas, in more recent times leadership has tended to specialize in one area or the other. The extent of the early crossover can be ascertained by checking the duplication in participation lists of the Stockholm and Lausanne meetings in 1925 and 1927 and the Oxford and Edinburgh conferences of 1937. These can be compared with rosters of more recent years showing a reduced duplication of names. Of course, in the case of the Oxford and Edinburgh meetings, the overlap might be explained by the fact that these events occurred within days of one another the same summer, and only 300 miles apart.

27. See my discussion of this formula in ecumenical reflection in *The Sense of a People: Toward a Church for the Human Future* (Philadelphia: Trinity Press International, 1992), 44f., 170ff.

28. For a detailed treatment of this subject up to 1978, see Geiko Müller-Fahrenholz, *Unity in Today's World: The Faith and Order Studies on "Unity of the Church—Unity of Humankind"* (Faith and Order Paper 88, Geneva: WCC, 1978).

29. Faith and Order Paper 151 (Geneva: WCC, 1990).

30. Ibid., 39.

31. *Christians in the Technical and Social Revolutions of Our Time* (World Conference on Church and Society, Official Report, Geneva: WCC, 1967), 202.

32. Best and Robra, eds., *Ecclesiology and Ethics.*

33. Max L. Stackhouse, "Conclusion: Joining the Discussion," in *Global Era*, 128.

Chapter 3

1. The term "thick description," popularized by the anthropologist Clifford Geertz, is now widely used by human scientists to refer to the study of the full and multilayered complexity of cultures. It admirably links up with the concept of "formation." We are "formed" in rich and enveloping environments, not merely by the "thin" concepts scholars derive from those environments. See Geertz, *The Interpretation of Cultures: Selected Essays* (New York: Basic Books, 1974), 3ff.

2. Nelson, *Nexus*, 3ff.

3. Mark Johnson, *Moral Imagination* (Chicago: University of Chicago Press, 1993).

4. Ibid., ix.

5. Ibid., 12.

6. See my discussion of the relations between imagination and power in *Sense*, 95ff.

7. See Roger G. Betsworth, *Social Ethics: An Examination of American Moral Traditions* (Louisville: Westminster/John Knox Press, 1990).

8. See Gene Outka and John P. Reeder Jr., *Prospects for a Common Morality* (Princeton: Princeton University Press, 1993), 3, et passim.

9. "Ironic" in a philosophical, rather than a rhetorical, sense. Ironists say we have no metaphysical or epistemological foundations for the ways we choose to live together. We do the things we do because they are there to be done. Human cultures are contingent, without relationships to any fundamental order of being. Persons live in sympathetic identification with particular forms of life whose local and contingent character they freely acknowledge. Writers such as Richard Rorty indeed argue that societies based on ad hoc solidarities rather than claims to foundational principles are likely to be better, more stable, more humane.

There may be something to this, especially if renouncing philosophical certitudes and adopting pragmatic attitudes reduces the temptations of self-righteousness and fanaticism.

10. The notion of "colonization" of civil society by the forces of government and the market is a favorite formula of Jürgen Habermas. See chapter 2, note 11.

11. This city and territory newly under Chinese rule will for the next few years be a testing ground for the relationships between political and economic rights. Polls seem to indicate that many citizens of Hong Kong are content to let political rights go if they can prosper in the economic realm. The Chinese seem ready to exploit such attitudes. We will see what happens.

12. Michael Walzer's book *Spheres of Justice: A Defence of Pluralism and Equality* (New York: Basic Books, 1983), has brought out the extent to which "justice" means different things depending on the context of life in which it is considered.

13. This is John Rawls's conception of the roles of "reasonable comprehensive doctrines" in a just secular society as he understands it in *A Theory of Justice* and *Political Liberalism*. Beyond the limited or "thin" public agreement about what justice is, all other questions of value are left to private individuals and groups. Rawls believes that people will commit themselves, in a profusion of ways, to "comprehensive doctrines" concerning the total meaning of life in which notions of the good can be set forth. But they will be prevented from imposing their comprehensive doctrines on others. Instead, comprehensive doctrines will be urged to be "reasonable," i.e. contributing in a civil manner to the resolution of public issues. (Some doctrines, of course, will never be reasonable in this sense and will always need to restrained.) The reasonable doctrines, Rawls opines, will "overlap" with others in their practical effects to constitute a common culture supportive of the thin universal notion of justice as fairness, but not definitive of it nor able significantly to modify it. Religious groups are in effect invited to join with others to play this supportive role, influencing the content of the "overlap"—or common ground between comprehensve doctrines—to the extent that they can.

14. The paragraphs that follow have been freely adapted by permission from my article "Ecclesiology and Ethics in Current Ecumenical Debate," *The Ecumenical Review* 48, no. 1 (January 1996): 11ff.

15. Rodney L. Petersen, editor's foreword to *Christianity and Civil Society* (Maryknoll, NY: Orbis Books and the Boston Theological Institute, 1995), xvii.

16. I owe these examples to a conversation with Robert Bellah.

17. Bellah, "The Church in an Individualistic Society," in Petersen, ed., *Christianity and Civil Society*, 9.

18. Ibid.

19. Robert Bellah, "A Response," in Lewis S. Mudge, *Traditioned Communities and the Good Society: The Search for a Public Philosophy* (Berkeley: Protocol of the Colloquy of the Center for Hermeneutical Studies, New Series, no. 3, 1993), 28.

20. In the paragraphs that follow, I have adapted materials from my previous book *Sense*, 90f.

21. Ibid., 170f.

22. See Wolfhart Pannenberg, *The Church*, tr. Keith Crim (Philadelphia: Westminster Press, 1983), 142ff.

23. Nancy Duff writes of Paul Lehmann's understanding of social transfiguration: "transfiguration indicates a turning point in human events that creates entirely new struc-

tures for human relationships. In Lehmann's words, transfiguration indicates that one has broken out of 'old dehumanizing confinements into the direction of liberating possibilities' " (*Humanization and the Politics of God: The Koinonia Ethics of Paul Lehmann* [Grand Rapids: Eerdmans, 1992], 121, quoting Lehmann, *The Transfiguration of Politics* [New York: Harper and Row, 1975], 76).

24. Vigen Guroian, *Ethics After Christendom: Toward an Ecclesial Christian Ethic* (Grand Rapids, MI: Eerdmans, 1994), 39.

25. Larry Rasmussen, "Moral Community and Moral Formation," in *Ecclesiology and Ethics: Costly Commitment*, ed. Thomas F. Best and Martin Robra (Geneva: WCC, 1995), 56. This paragraph is in debt to this page of Rasmussen's article.

26. This paragraph is freely adapted from Mudge, *Sense*, 90.

27. The English term *mind* here translates the Greek *nous*, in this context meaning "mentality" or "worldview." Compare Philippians 2:5: "Have this mind in you (*touto phroneite*) which you have in Christ Jesus."

28. Adapted, once again, from Mudge, *Sense*, 90f.

29. See, for example, Charles Taylor, *Sources*, 211ff.

30. There are also spiritualities related to the great world religions, spiritualities representing indigenous religious communities, and spiritualities promoted by individual teachers who operate, as it were, at large. Christian spiritual-moral formation in today's world needs not only to draw upon the riches of the great traditions of Christian faith but also to meet, understand, grasp its differences from, as well as learn from, spiritual traditions outside Christianity.

31. Robert Bellah et al., *Habits of the Heart* (Berkeley: University of California Press, 1985), 20.

32. Jeffrey Stout has criticized the Bellah team for pursuing philosophical agendas in these "Socratic" interviews, which did not give respondents space to make the kinds of "second language" statements and connections with "first languages" they may have wanted to make. See *Ethics*, 193ff.

33. See Gadamer, *Truth and Method*, second revised edition (New York: Continuum, 1989).

34. See Habermas, *Communicative Action*.

35. This paragraph parallels the Johannesburg conference report "Costly Obedience" published in Best and Robra, eds., *Ecclesiology and Ethics*, para. 57, p. 68. The drafter acknowledges the special role played by Vigen Guroian at this point in the Johannesburg discussion.

36. See Best and Robra, eds., *Ecclesiology and Ethics*, 61ff. Part II of "Costly Obedience," dealing with formation and malformation in relation to warfare between nation-states and recent South African experience was drafted by John de Gruchy. These sentences are in debt to that part of the Johannesburg report.

Chapter 4

1. I am grateful to Larry Rasmussen for persuading me, in private correspondence, that distinctions between "inner" and "outer" history, "private" and "public" realms, the "ethical" and the "political" worlds, often tend to confuse rather than clarify discussions of this kind. Such categories do indeed "run and melt into one another." I have been helped,

too, by Elizabeth M. Bounds's new book, *Coming Together/Coming Apart: Religion, Community and Modernity* (New York: Routledge, 1997), in which, among other things she sorts out the ways different social theorists deal with distinctions and relationships between economic, political, and cultural "orders" and "spheres."

2. This Greek word means "communion" or a common sharing of holy things. It is currently a key term in ecumenical discussions.

3. Preliminary report of the Tantur Consultation to the Faith and Order Standing Committee, in *Minutes of the Faith and Order Standing Commission*, Aleppo, Syria, January 5-12, 1995 (Faith and Order Paper 170), 97f., paragraphs 69 and 70. The corresponding paragraphs in the *Costly Commitment* (Tantur) report (Best and Robra, eds., *Ecclesiology and Ethics*, 24ff.) are 72 and 73, which have essentially the same content but have been edited to include cross-references within the latter document. I use the Aleppo text for its clear focus on the issue at hand.

4. One wonders how far the average local congregation (if there is such a thing) in North America, or Europe, or Africa, or Asia, would agree that these ecumenically achieved moral agreements are now to be taken for granted. My suspicion is that several would still be controversial.

5. These words are, in fact, the subtitle of Hauerwas's book *After Christendom*.

6. Ibid., 27.

7. See Kenneth Arrow, *Social Choice and Individual Values* (Cowles Commission for Research in Economics: Monograph no. 12, 1951). Arrow summarizes: "Methods of symbolic logic are applied to the question whether a social valuation of alternatives can be consistently derived from given, partly conflicting, individual valuations." I am indebted for this reference and for the argument contained in it to Dr. Austin Hoggatt, professor emeritus in the Haas School of Business at the University of California, Berkeley, and a member of the February 1997 discussion group at Montclair Presbyterian Church in Oakland, California.

8. I understand that Hehir would not accept this notion of inaccessibility, because he is speaking from the tradition of natural law ethics as understood in the Roman Catholic Church. This tradition presupposes the possibility of moral propositions understandable both within the religious community and outside because they have to do with universally accessible truths about nature and human life-experience.

9. See William Werpehowski, "Ad Hoc Apologetics," *Journal of Religion* 66 (July 1986): 282ff. The description of Werpehowski's position is adapted from Mudge, *Sense*, 208ff. See also Mudge, *Traditioned Communities*, 24f.

10. Ibid., 291.

11. Given the successful outcome of a process of public or practical reasoning, Christians can claim they have "the better argument" for having done what was done. Not "the better argument" in Jürgen Habermas's sense, which presupposes an Enlightenment-style agreement about the nature of rationality, but "the better argument" for explaining transcendentally what is involved in something already pragmatically agreed. In several ways this proposal resembles Habermas's vision of "communicative action." But what confessional presupposition best warrants such a dialogical view of human life?

12. Werpehowski, "Apologetics," 293.

13. I John 4:1ff. is of course the classical passage for discerning the spirits. "By this you know the Spirit of God: every spirit which confesses that Jesus Christ has come in the flesh is of God, and every spirit which does not confess Jesus is not of God" (RSV).

14. Foucault used the term *subjugated languages* to refer to ways of seeing and talking about the world which have been suppressed by dominant Western political, commercial, and academic worldviews, styles of analysis, and forms of speech. Thus, the ways asylum inmates, prisoners, poverty-stricken campesinos, or imprisoned and tortured black Africans under the *apartheid* regime see the world are very different from the way Western academic sociologists see it. Foucault spoke of an "insurrection of subjugated knowledges," meaning that oppressed peoples the world over are now demanding the right to be heard in their own terms and that Western knowledge paradigms had better take account of what they are saying. See *Power/Knowledge: Selected Interviews and Other Writings*, ed. Colin Gordon, (New York: Pantheon Books, 1980), 81.

15. Hoedemaker, "Introductory Reflections," 2.

16. Avishai Margalit, *The Decent Society* (Cambridge: Harvard University Press, 1996), especially 115ff.

17. Niebuhr, *Moral Man and Moral Society* (New York: Scribners, 1932), 258.

18. Originally issued under the title *The Care of the Spitfire Grill*, Gregory Productions: Forrest Murray producer, Lee David Blotoff director and screenwriter, distributed by Castle Rock Entertainment, 1996.

19. Selznick, *Moral Commonwealth*, 426n.

20. The philosophers in question were Jürgen Habermas, Ronald Dworkin, Thomas Nagel, Michael Sandel, Bernard Williams, Amy Gutmann, and Rawls himself.

21. Ironically, the one who did not was Jürgen Habermas, the philosopher whose work has attracted the most attention from theologians and who professes not to understand the reason for the interest. He certainly does not reciprocate it.

22. It is increasingly realized that what has in the past been taken as pure practical reasoning (e.g., utilitarian thinking, or Kant's derivation of the "categorical imperative" from the rational person's alleged inability to live with the inner contradictions entailed in violating the duty implied in that principle) is often no more than an attempt to generalize, or universalize, the essence of some widespread tradition of moral or spiritual formation. John Rawls now admits in his book *Political Liberalism* that his theory of justice is not for everyone on earth but rather reflects, if in a new way, the moral traditions built into mid-twentieth century American liberal society. See especially 134ff.

23. John Milbank, *Theology and Social Theory* (Oxford, UK and Cambridge, MA: Blackwell Publishers, 1990) 2.

24. For Rawls, a rationally conceived and shared idea of justice is all we need to maintain a decent public world. Under its umbrella human beings of every conceivable persuasion are free to seek the good life as they conceive of it. They are free to pursue "reasonable comprehensive doctrines" (e.g., philosophical schools, forms of religious faith) that please them. It is Rawls's hope, expressed in his more recent work *Political Liberalism* (New York: Columbia University Press, 1993) that among these "reasonable comprehensive doctrines" there is enough practical "overlap"—that is, similarity in the ways different faiths lead people to behave in public—to undergird the rationally derived idea of justice: to make it work in the real world.

25. For a philosophical and legal analysis of forgiveness and mercy see Jeffrie G. Murphy and Jean Hampton, *Forgiveness and Mercy* (Cambridge: Cambridge University Press, 1988). This work illustrates particularly well the possibility that Christian faith can make moral space for secular philosophical argument to move in a particular direction. Jean Hampton writes: "I come to grips with the Christian teachings and texts from outside the tradition

of theological reflections on those subjects. But I hope that my perspective is of some interest to theologians and others, who may be intrigued by the treatment of biblical teachings as suggestive of reasoned arguments" (12). Can biblical teachings really suggest "reasoned arguments" to secular thinkers who are able to move in the directions they do by the presence of faith communities that embody these teachings in practice?

26. This, we remember from chapter 1, is Jeffrey Stout's complaint in *Ethics* about the distinguished Christian ethicist James Gustafson.

27. Peter Steinfels's *Beliefs* column, "A Language Barrier at the World Population Conference Involved Much More than Words," *New York Times*, September 24, 1994.

28. See Donald W. Shriver Jr., *An Ethic for Enemies: Forgiveness in Politics* (New York: Oxford University Press, 1995.) Shriver deals, among other things, with the relationships between Germans and Americans after each of the world wars, and between Japan and the United States after World War II. He also considers the relation between justice and forgiveness in American race relations. Summing up, he writes: "I have arrived at the belief that the concept of forgiveness, so customarily relegated to the realms of religion and personal ethics, belongs at the heart of reflection about how groups of humans can move to repair the damage that they have suffered from their past conflicts with each other. Precisely because it attends at once to moral truth, history, and the human benefits that flow from the conquest of enmity, *forgiveness* is a word for a multidimensional process that is eminently political" (ix).

29. Duncan Forrester, in a paper presented to the 1993 meeting of the International Society for Practical Theology in Princeton, New Jersey.

30. I have little doubt that this is what Georges Bernanos was writing about in *The Diary of a Country Priest*, and indeed what Bryan Hehir had in mind in quoting him. See the first page of the Preface to the present book.

31. I am thinking, for example, of the sort of depth hermeneutic of contemporary assumptions supplied by Charles Taylor's *Sources*. See also Taylor's *Ethics of Authenticity* (Cambridge: Harvard University Press, 1992). To discover where modern individualism comes from (among other sources, from the seventeenth-century Protestant "affirmation of everyday life") is to identify forms of it (e.g., radical personal autonomy irrespective of other claims and values) that fail to do justice to the complex richness of the idea. While Taylor does not say this, one may be more likely to make such a discovery by being in touch with a community living out a richer, more deeply grounded, idea of personhood drawing on the classical Christian sources than in reading intellectual history in a university.

32. One may thus think of the "household" as a people both within and beyond the borders of the organized church to whom ecclesiastical institutions in a deeper spiritual sense *belong*. The theologian Joseph Haroutunian used to speak of "the people of God *and* its institutions." His point was that the community of the Holy Spirit is largely invisible, but that God has provided certain institutions whose calling is precisely to make the invisible become visible: to "mark" the presence of such a larger community in the world. I have discussed Haroutunian's proposal in more detail in *Sense*, 10f., 24f. See Joseph Haroutunian, *God With Us: A Theology of Transpersonal Life* (Philadelphia: Westminster Press, 1965), 48ff.

33. Ronald Dworkin, *Life's Dominion: An Argument about Abortion, Euthanasia, and Individual Freedom* (New York: Alfred A. Knopf, 1993), 68ff.

34. I recognize the contribution of aspects of natural law theory as taught and practiced

by Roman Catholics to the clarification of issues in public debate. Bryan Hehir, in his immensely attractive idea of asking questions in the right way, no doubt has the formulas of Catholic ethics in mind. The power of such reasoning has been demonstrated by at least two of the pastoral letters issued by the American Roman Catholic Bishops' Conference: on nuclear deterrence and the economy. The encyclical *Veritatis Splendor* has since restated a form of natural law theory as intrinsic to the Catholic teaching that the magisterium is bound to promote. On offer to the world here is a specific way of thinking, which may, to some, appear to have dogmatic strings attached. Rather than contributing certain conceptual formulas to the world as religious teaching, my proposal is that the church constitute itself as a space-making community of trustworthy *practice*: a "household" in relation to which public argumentation is rescued from ideological superficiality and encouraged to find more profound directions.

35. Emmanuel Levinas, *Totality and Infinity: An Essay on Exteriority*, tr. Alphonso Lingis (Pittsburgh: Duquesne University Press, 1969).

36. I am indebted to Prof. Joshua Mitchell of Georgetown University for these observations offered in private correspondence.

37. Rebecca S. Chopp, *The Praxis of Suffering: An Interpretation of Liberation and Political Theologies* (Maryknoll, NY: Orbis Books, 1986), referenced in Peter Hodgson, *God in History: Shapes of Freedom* (Nashville: Abingdon Press, 1989), 181.

38. John W. de Gruchy, *Christianity and Democracy: A Theology for a Just World Order* (Cambridge: Cambridge University Press, 1995), 199ff. I am indebted to Prof. de Gruchy's book for this example as well as for the accompanying observations concerning South Africa.

39. Lest we become too romantic about these "transitions to democracy," it is important to note that democratic revolutions can be sidetracked and that the role of the church in a postrevolutionary period can become far more complex and difficult than it was when the only issue was ridding a nation of oppression. Speaking of Germany, John de Gruchy writes in a paper presented at the 1994 meeting of the American Academy of Religion, Chicago, "The revolution of 1989 only led to the 'incomplete liberation' (quoting Huber, in Witte, *Christianity and Democracy*) of the GDR. With the reunification of Germany the revolution was in a sense hijacked by the architects of liberal, capitalist democracy who, in many ways, proceeded to strip the country of its assets and undermine some of its achievements."

40. In this effort black South African church leaders were aided by declarations from the Lutheran World Federation and the World Alliance of Reformed Churches declaring the theological defense of apartheid to constitute a *status confessionis*, i.e., a matter in which the integrity of the faith was at stake.

41. De Gruchy, *Christianity and Democracy*, 212.

42. See Geiko Müller-Fahrenholz, *The Art of Forgiveness: Theological Reflections on Healing and Reconciliation* (Geneva: WCC Publications, 1997). This is a deeply *theological* book on forgiveness in the political realm, notably connecting the concept with the canceling of debt owed by impoverished nations in the international market. Müller-Fahrenholz writes, "the Bible understands forgiveness as a process which includes both the perpetrator and the victim. Forgiveness can occur when the perpetrator asks for it and the victim grants it. This mutuality is basic to an understanding of the biblical concept. Both sides are changed by this encounter. Much more than a word or a gesture, forgiveness is a genuine process

of encounter, of healing, of the releasing of new options for the future. A guilty and painful past is redeemed in order to establish reliable foundations for renewed fellowship in dignity and trust. Forgiveness frees the future from the haunting legacies of the past" (4).

Chapter 5

1. The WCC document *Costly Commitment* (Tantur) puts the issue with unmistakable clarity: "Is it enough to say that, if a church is not engaging responsibly with the ethical issues of its day, it is not being fully church? Must we not also say: if the churches are not engaging these ethical issues *together*, then *none of them individually is being fully church*" (Best and Robra, eds., *Ecclesiology and Ethics*, 29, para. 17, italics in the original)?

2. See John Zizioulas, *Being as Communion* (Crestwood, NY: St. Vladimir's Seminary Press, 1993) which argues this case. He writes, "Ecclesial being is bound to the very being of God" (15). See also the elaboration of closely related insights in Ion Bria, *Liturgy*.

3. The acts of worship during World Council of Churches assemblies and other major events have often had this sense about them. The writer remembers the eucharist celebrated under Protestant auspices under the tent at the WCC Sixth Assembly at Vancouver and the Syrian Orthodox archbishop who was asked afterward if he was not tempted to go forward to receive the elements. "Almost," he replied, almost!"

4. The English word *council* has two distinct meanings. It may refer to an event such as the "council" of Nicaea or to a modern "council" of churches. The former (A.D. 325) was one of the "ecumenical councils" of the undivided church whose work is today recognized as having been definitive in the formation of Christian doctrine. The latter means simply an organization in which separated churches cooperate to whatever degree they wish or are able. The distinction comes out more clearly in European languages that employ different terms where English has only one. In German a "council" like that at Nicaea is a *Konzil*, while the WCC is a *Rat* (like a town council that meets in a *Rathaus*). In French the Nicaea event was a *concile*, while the WCC is a *conseil*.

5. The paragraphs that follow from this point to the end of the chapter are adapted by permission from part IV of the original Johannesburg (1996) text, *Costly Obedience*, drafted in collaboration with others by the author of this book. The material in its original form appears in Best and Robra, eds., *Ecclesiology and Ethics*, 72ff. I take this opportunity to thank the members of the Johannesburg drafting committee with whom I worked. They were William Henn, Margaret Jenkins, Elizabeth Tapia, and K. M. George. Others involved in a very vigorous and rich discussion were Anna Marie Aagaard, Duncan Forrester, John W. de Gruchy, Mongezi Guma, Vigen Guroian, Margot Kässmann, and Frans Noko Kekane, as well as WCC staff members Thomas Best, Alan Falconer, Martin Robra, and Marise Pegat-Toquet. Many of the best ideas in these pages come from these good colleagues. The reconsidered version of this text incorporated in the present chapter is, of course, my own responsibility.

6. The *Costly Unity* (Ronde) document of the WCC study puts it this way: "The 'local' means different things in different circumstances. It may mean a neighborhood, or a nation, or a region of the world. And sometimes an issue may be global in its importance, yet not susceptible of any single explanation or formula so varied are its ramifications in different places. Sometimes a global issue is such that it comes to expression most clearly

in some particular locality, whose Christian people then have special responsibility for defining its significance for the rest of the *oikoumene*. Sometimes an essentially local issue can only be clearly seen when its global aspects are grasped" (Best and Robra, eds., *Ecclesiology and Ethics*, 14, paras. 35-37).

7. Foucault, *Power/Knowledge*, 81.

8. These ideas are adapted in part from the thought of Michael Welker, whose name surfaced several times in the Johannesburg discussion. See his article "The Holy Spirit," translated by John Hoffmeyer, *Theology Today* 46 (April 1989): 4-20. Welker writes that the Spirit "restores solidarity, loyalty, and capacity for common action among the people." Likewise it generates a realm of "poly-concreteness" in which there can be a "multifaceted, reciprocally strengthened and strengthening process of cooperation." This seems an excellent description of relationships within the *oikoumene*. See also Welker's *God the Spirit* (Minneapolis: Fortress Press, 1994), especially 239ff.

9. Larry Rasmussen, commenting on the original Johannesburg text, writes, " 'Costly Obedience' has taken a certain quiet, crucial turn here. It suggests, in effect, that linkages of ecclesiology and ethics are not effectively answered *at the normative level alone*. Differently said, the most promising way forward is not that of finding the language of normative common ground as that might be offered by theologians and agreed to by heads of communions. This understanding of ecumenical formation is essentially doctrinal and jurisdictional. The most promising way is arranging a common table, open to participation by the whole people of God, to see what emerges as living church when faith is freely shared on the burning issues we face" ("The Right Direction, but a Longer Journey," in Best and Robra, eds., *Ecclesiology and Ethics*, 107).

10. Terms such as *justice* and *peace* of course also have rich contexts of meaning in secular moral and political philosophy, as well as in the common parlance of journalists, politicians, and diplomats. While it is indispensable, as we have said, for Christians to be in touch with these secular worlds, there is danger that their terminology represents a covert hegemony of Western thought-categories in one way or another related to Western political and economic interests. The idea of deriving the meanings of "justice" and "peace" (and of course the "integrity of creation" as well) from an ecumenical sharing of contextual moral engagements is intended to help ecumenists escape the hegemony of political and economic interests disguised as moral principles.

11. This is what the WCC Commission on Faith and Order tried particularly to express in the preface to *Baptism, Eucharist, and Ministry* (Faith and Order Paper No. 111, Geneva: World Council of Churches, 1982). It asked the participating churches whether they recognized *in* the new language of the document "the faith of the church through the ages."

12. These oft-spoken words echo inexactly, and depart from the original meaning of the language of *Unitatis Redintegratio*, the "Decree on Ecumenism" of Vatican II: "For [those] who believe in Christ and have been properly baptized are brought into a certain, though imperfect, communion with the Catholic Church" (Walter M. Abbott, S.J., ed., *Documents of Vatican II* [New York: Guild Press, Association Press, America Press, 1966], 345).

13. Rasmussen takes exception to the original Johannesburg text at this point, arguing that "in the end it forecloses on its own process. It is still preoccupied with 'language.' Its bias is finding common ecumenical 'discourse' and 'voice,' not as the outcome of ecumenical process but as initial common ground." Rasmussen makes substantially the same

observation about the use of "the reality of our common baptism" as "the source of common moral content across churches." He continues: "But this subtlety, probably unwittingly, subverts the very promise offered. The bias toward finding common discourse and shared substance in the sacraments will sideline a more basic, and more promising effort. It will likely end up reinserting the need to agree upon theologically normative categories and criteria" (Rasmussen, "The Right Direction," in Best and Robra, eds., *Ecclesiology and Ethics*, 109).

14. In his presentation "The Search for Christian Unity and Common Moral Orientations: Three Case Studies" (Centro Pro Unione, Rome, November 14, 1996) Günther Gassmann has criticized the Johannesburg text for leaving the impression that moral communion and eucharistic communion are two different *kinds* of communion. That was never the intention, any more than one in speaking first of the "immanent" Trinity and then of the "economic" Trinity should be taken to mean that there are two *kinds* of Trinity. Many passages in *Costly Obedience* make the essential integrity of *koinonia* abundantly clear. See, for example, paragraphs 74, 82, 103. But ecumenical relationships can sometimes progress more rapidly in one dimension of *koinonia* than in the other. How does one talk about this reality and represent it tangibly in ecumenical relationships? The drafter nonetheless acknowledges that expressions vulnerable to Gassmann's interpretation can be found in the original Johannesburg document. The passages in question have been reworded in the present adaptation.

15. Deep and divisive ecclesiological issues are involved, and behind them lie philosophical questions concerning the relationship of act and being. It could turn out that such questions are not resolvable in the terms in which they are currently posed, and that only in sharing lives of sacramental-moral practice, validated by their mutual resonance in the Spirit of Jesus Christ, can we move beyond our current impasse.

16. Indeed, it appears that the intent of some went even further: to give affirmations growing out of the program on "Justice, Peace, and the Integrity of Creation" (the lineal descendant of the Life and Work movement within the WCC structure) a formal ecclesiological significance, i.e., to make moral commitments part of the *esse* of the church as theologically and juridically defined. It seems to have been, among other things, a recoil from this sort of commitment, seen as an unwarranted theological escalation of the meeting's original agenda, that led the Roman Catholic Church to withdraw from official participation in the Seoul meeting.

17. Margalit, *Decent Society*, 1ff.

18. My attention was drawn to these criticisms by Charles West in private correspondence.

19. Martin Robra, "Theology of Life: Justice, Peace, Creation," *Ecumenical Review* 48, no. 1 (January 1996): 35.

20. See, on the image of *oikodomé* or "mutual upbuilding," the treatment by Geiko Müller-Fahrenholz in *God's Spirit: Transforming a World in Crisis* (New York: Continuum, and Geneva: WCC, 1995), 108ff.

21. I see the idea of such a forum of Christian (and perhaps other) spiritual communities and centers of energy, open to participation without previously conceived juridical or theological requirements, as parallel at the world level to the communal process sampled by the "Theology of Life" conference near Nairobi in January 1997. Larry Rasmussen describes it: "The form was 'Sokoni,' the African market-place for exchanges of all kinds—

goods, information, ideas, networks and plans, stories, music, gossip and deliberation. Church groups of all kinds came from throughout Kenya to express in ways they chose— drama, music, study, testimony, conversation, dance—what 'being church' meant in their 'actual lived communities with their cultures' " (Best and Robra, eds., *Ecclesiology and Ethics*, 107f.). "Sokoni" seems to me to be one easily adaptable model for the kind of ecumenical gathering that would depend on a recognition of mutual resonance in the Spirit rather than conformity to definitional standards preconceived by the organizers. But there needs to be some, however minimal, *initial* basis for mutual trust. The Ten Affirmations have served that purpose in certain situations.

22. The original, October 1996, "Common Understanding and Vision" proposal of the WCC bore some resemblances to notions that the present writer and others have been proposing for some time. In particular, the idea that the world meetings of a number of ecumenical bodies occur at the same time and place to mark the turn of the millennia, but also as a practice for the future, was proposed in the writer's *Christian Century* article "An Ecumenical Vision for the Year 2000" (September 19, 1979), 96. See also *Sense*: "Could a Roman Catholic synod of bishops, an Assembly of the World Council of Churches, a pan-Orthodox Congress, a world meeting of evangelicals and Pentecostals, gatherings of the world confessional bodies, and perhaps other events take place at the same time in ways both independent and interrelated? Could there be an element of common agenda, as well as distinctive items of business, in these meetings? Could there be Kirchentag-type assemblies in which Christians of all communions could be joined by representatives of other world faiths? What new way of thinking about God's people might such encounters make possible, as well as meaningful for the human race" (17)?

Chapter 6

1. While recognizing the power of economic interest to shape both ideology and conduct, I mean here to deny that such determinism needs to be absolute. A state of affairs for which one faithfully prays, and holds onto as a regulative idea in all one does, can be as much a "standpoint" for envisioning horizons of possibility as the set of circumstances surrounding one's position in the so-called real world. One sets the just constellation of conditions for which one *strives* against the interests that go with one's particular position in life, seeking to discern the world and its possibilities from that imaginatively conceived, even if only fragmentarily achieved, point of viewing. In fact, I believe that this is what Rawls actually does. His "original position" behind the "veil of ignorance" is as much an imaginative construct, as much at variance with the world as it actually is, as is the notion of a call to membership in a household of life. True, the ideology connected with who one *is* (e.g., North American, white, male, middle-aged, middle class, and the like) may easily cloud the vision of the world that goes with the identity one prays for. Yet this is not a reason to give up trying, by the grace of God, to see the world—and act in it—in a new way.

2. By "end" I mean both fulfillment of history's purpose, i.e., *telos*, and also history's ultimate knowable boundary, i.e., *finis*. In biblical eschatology the two go together, although the meanings are clearly distinguishable.

3. Today, of course, such questions also need to be asked against the far vaster backdrop

of cosmic time and space which helps significantly to shape our understanding of ourselves as, among other things, organisms that have appeared at a certain rather recent moment in a multibillion-year process. But it is not yet clear what moral conclusions should be drawn from our apparent place in this cosmic story. Will the household of life one day become interplanetary, interstellar, or even intergalactic?

4. Richard J. Mouw and Sander Griffioen, *Pluralisms and Horizons: An Essay in Christian Public Philosophy* (Grand Rapids: Eerdmans, 1993).

5. The term *empty shrine* is the invention of Michael Novak in his books *The Spirit of Democratic Capitalism* and *Freedom With Justice* (New York: Simon and Schuster, 1983 and 1984). Mouw and Griffioen explain Novak's term this way: "Instead of a socially imposed vision of the good, capitalist democracy displays a 'reverential emptiness at the heart of pluralism' " (*Pluralisms*, 41, quoting Novak, *Spirit*, 68). They continue, "the reverential emptiness he has in mind occurs when a society, in a deliberate act of self-limitation, refrains from attempts to define and codify the meaning and purpose of human life" (*Pluralisms*, 41, see Novak, *Spirit*, 55).

6. Max L. Stackhouse, "Social Theory and Christian Public Morality for the Common Life," in Rodney L. Petersen, ed., *Christianity and Civil Society*, 39.

7. Gordon Kaufman's writings on the nuclear threat—something far from resolved today despite its relative retreat from public consciousness—make clear how seriously he takes factors that could bar us from any future at all.

8. Gordon Kaufman, *In Face of Mystery: A Constructive Theology* (Cambridge: Harvard University Press, 1993), 407.

9. Samuel P. Huntington, *The Clash of Civilizations and the Remaking of World Order* (New York: Simon and Schuster, 1996), quoted in William H. McNeil, "Decline of the West?," *New York Review*, January 9, 1997, 18.

10. Vischer, "Koinonia in a Time of Threats to Life," in Best and Granberg-Michaelson, eds., *Costly Unity*, 72.

11. Ibid., 72f., Vischer's italics.

12. The "household" figure in its ecumenical applications can first be found in several of Philip Potter's reports to the Central Committee as General Secretary of the WCC. It was further developed by Konrad Raiser in *Ecumenism* and by Geiko Müller-Fahrenholz in *God's Spirit* (New York: Continuum, and Geneva: WCC, 1995).

13. An impressive summary of the biblical evidence is to be found in Raiser, *Ecumenism*, 79ff., and in Müller-Fahrenholz, *Spirit*, 108ff.

14. The more deeply one goes into "household" imagery, the more one finds that *other* New Testament images, those of the suffering "servant" or "child" or "slave," for example, become clearer in their interactions. Relations between these different terms become more luminous when one realizes that the context is an imagined Greco-Roman household where all these figures have accustomed roles which are then transformed radically by the gospel.

15. Müller-Fahrenholz, *Spirit*, 109f.

16. The characteristics of the "household of life" named here are derived from Raiser, *Ecumenism*, 105ff., and from Müller-Fahrenholz, *Spirit*, 108ff.

17. See Ernst Lange, "The Malaise in the Ecumenical Movement: Notes on the Present Situation," *Ecumenical Review* 23, no. 1 (1971): 8, referenced in Raiser, *Ecumenism*, 108.

18. See Philip Potter's address to the 1983 Vancouver Assembly, *Ecumenical Review* 35, no. 4 (1983): 350ff., referenced in Raiser, *Ecumenism*, 109, n. 57.

19. See, for example, Reinhard Hütter, "Ecclesial Ethics, the Church's Vocation, and Paraclesis," *Pro Ecclesia* 2, no.4 (fall 1993): 433-34, quoted in Stanley Hauerwas, *In Good Company* (Notre Dame: University of Notre Dame Press, 1995), 30, n. 25.

20. This formula echos Augustine in the *City of God*, Book XIX. See Rowan Williams's interpretation in "Politics and the Soul: A Reading of the *City of God*," *Milltown Studies* 19, no. 20, (1987), 55ff. "Book XIX seeks to show that the spiritual is the *authentically* political. The saint is engaged in a *redefinition* of the public itself, designed to show that it is life outside the Christian community which fails to be truly public, authentically political" (58).

21. John Milbank clearly pictures this consummation as a swallowing up of secular social constructs into an essentially *ecclesial* nexus. In *Theology and Social Theory* he writes, ". . . the social knowledge advocated is but the continuation of ecclesial practice" (6).

22. So far as the writer knows, "household of life" terminology is not actually in use among the writers named.

23. Augustine, *City*, XIX, 21. See Williams, "Politics and the Soul," 59.

24. Augustine, *City*, XIX, 12. See Milbank, *Theology and Social Theory*, 392-98 (on René Girard).

25. Hauerwas, *Good Company*, 30.

26. The one unacceptable alternative among the six analyzed in Mouw and Griffioen's *Pluralisms and Horizons*.

27. My sense is that Stanley Hauerwas must ultimately believe something like this, however "alien" to the world he wants life in the "Christian colony" to be. He describes an animated conversation with students at Duke University about ethical implications of the US rocket attack on the headquarters of Libya's Colonel Quadaffi. His suggestion is that a proper Christian response to this dilemma might be for the United Methodist Church to announce that it is sending a thousand missionaries to Libya (*Resident Aliens: A Provocative Christian Assessment of Culture and Ministry for People Who Know That Something Is Wrong* [Nashville: Abingdon Press, 1989], 47f.).

28. I do not believe, for example, that Hauerwas, Milbank, and the others truly address the issues concerning the nature of God's activity in history raised by Van A. Harvey in *The Historian and the Believer* (New York: Macmillan, 1965). In Harvey's typology they would appear to represent a variant on Barth.

29. Hauerwas, *Good Company*, 30, quoting Hütter "Ecclesial Ethics," 435.

30. Konrad Raiser, *Ecumenism*, 65. Raiser further credits Thomas Wieser, ed., *Wither Ecumenism? A Dialogue in the Transit Lounge of the Ecumenical Movement* (Geneva, World Council of Churches, 1986) 35ff., and Bible studies on Genesis 11 and Revelation 21 by Philip Potter, 9ff. Raiser continues: "[The notion of a household of life] points away from the *oikoumene* as global system to the *oikoumene* of the house of life, of the habitable earth, which, if it is to remain habitable, will involve concrete human stewardship in solidarity. In this turning away from the deadly illusion of the global system and turning towards the messianic vision of 'God dwelling with humankind' (Rev. 21:3), we see the outline of a new paradigm beyond Christian universalism taking shape" (65).

31. The position described by Bert Hoedemaker in *Costly Unity* seems an unusually clear example of this viewpoint. Here the church is constituted when persons engaged in various forms of worldly moral struggle against contemporary threats to life come together seeking what help—and solace—they can find in Christian tradition and practice. The church is then virtually defined by the configuration of the political-moral efforts in which

its members are engaged. As Hoedemaker puts it, "the human moral struggle, with all its pressures, sorrows, and hopes, is a basic ecclesiogenetic power," and, further, "a confessional ecclesial tradition consists of a series of just such occasions of ecclesiogenesis" ("Introductory Reflections," 6).

32. Raiser, *Ecumenism*, 104f.

33. Jürgen Moltmann, *The Church in the Power of the Spirit* (New York: Harper and Row, 1977), 134.

34. Ibid., 163.

35. Ibid., 64f.

36. Latin for "a means of binding, fastening, band, bond, rope, cord, fetter, tie." In mathematics, "a straight line drawn over two terms indicating that these are to be considered as subject to the same operations of multiplication, division, etc., by another term" (Charlton T. Lewis, ed., *Elementary Latin Dictionary* [Oxford: The Clarendon Press, 1947], 921).

37. I believe, for example, that the "household" idea—extended in this manner to refer to relationships in the "public" as well as the "private" world—speaks to and helps to overcome the tension between "moral man" and "immoral society" set forth by Reinhold Niebuhr. Niebuhr, as Larry Rasmussen has reminded me, seems to have assumed that the private sphere would do the moral formation necessary to undergird a viable public world, and never quite saw the complex relationships between them. To speak of the public world as likewise a "household" (like speaking of the global community as a "village") at least rhetorically turns "household" into a mediating category between the "thick" and the "thin" contexts of life. The "household" discussion thus recognizes the inevitable interrelationships of issues in the private sphere with issues of public policy. See Ronald F. Thiemann, *Constructing a Public Theology: The Church in a Pluralistic Culture* (Louisville: Westminster/John Knox Press, 1991): "The line between private and public, between the personal and the political, can no longer be drawn with absolute clarity" (19). See also Williams, "Politics and the Soul": "Augustine makes it plain that the *pax* of the household is to be 'referred' *ad pacem civicam* (*City*, XIX, 16). The implication seems to be that the *civitas* is itself, like the household, ideally a creative and pastoral community" (64). It is not that private virtues translate directly into public ones, but considering the public world as "household" helps open the way to exploring precisely what the connections are.

38. Peter Hodgson, *God in History: Shapes of Freedom* (Nashville: Abingdon Press, 1989), 209.

39. Ibid., 208.

40. Ibid.

41. Welker, *God the Spirit*, 142f. I am indebted to Anna Marie Aagaard for suggesting the relevance of Welker's work at this point in the argument.

42. Again, I am grateful to Anna Marie Aagaard for this suggestion and for permission to quote from private correspondence.

43. I realize that here I am close to having redescribed the vocations of Faith and Order and Life and Work, respectively. Should not these two vocations, once they have really articulated their complementarity, be encouraged to pursue their functions in a revised WCC structure that insists on practical and conceptual coordination?

44. See, for example, Raiser, *Ecumenism*, 93.

45. The technical distinction is between the "immanent" Trinity in which the focus is upon the internal relationships of the three persons in constituting one divine hypostasis,

and the "economic" Trinity in which the focus is upon God's ongoing attention to and relationships with the human drama. The latter term, common in the texts of the Eastern churches, is derived, once again, from the Greek word *oikos*. God's "economy" or "household management," or "accommodation" to the details of human need, is matched by the church's own "economy" by which it adjusts itself to the pastoral necessities of actual experience.

46. Jürgen Moltmann, *God in Creation: A New Theology of Creation and the Spirit of God* (San Francisco: Harper and Row, 1987), 218.

47. Moltmann, *Creation*, 215ff.

48. I am indebted to my colleague Herman Waetjen for calling attention to the expression "new human being" as a translation for "son of man," and for building a contemporary christology around it in his own work. See *A Reordering of Power: A Socio-Political Reading of Mark's Gospel* (Minneapolis: Augsburg/Fortress Press, 1989).

49. For example, in the thought of St. Augustine. Despite its "immanent" or internal differentiation in three persons, the Trinity shows itself to us human beings as an undifferentiated unity, as divine sovereignty. The individual human subject stands before this undifferentiated sovereign God living out the dialectic of sin and grace.

50. Moltmann, *Creation*, 223.

51. Ibid., 242.

52. Ibid.

53. The transition from "household" to "city" has not yet claimed the attention it deserves in ecumenical study. But it is an essential move. As already mentioned, Augustine in *City*, Book XIX, seems to see the "city" in householding terms and vice versa. Rowan Williams speaks in "Politics and the Soul," of "the link which Augustine makes between *imperare* and *consulere*," adding that "*consulere* is spiritual nurturing" (63). Williams continues: "The natural order of family life is the primary locus for the exercise of such a [ruling] office: a dramatic reversal of what Hannah Arendt saw as the classical set of priorities" (64). One may plausibly object that the link between "household" and "city" is easier for Augustine to imagine because of his hierarchical assumptions about the family. All members of the typical Roman household are under the formational authority of the *paterfamilias*. See also the rich discussion of "*polis* or *oikos*" in Milbank, *Theology and Social Theory*, 364ff.

54. Karl Barth, "The Christian Community and the Civil Community," in *Against the Stream*, (London: SCM Press, 1954), quoted in Oliver O'Donovan, *The Desire of the Nations* (Cambridge: Cambridge University Press, 1996), 285.

55. O'Donovan, ibid.

56. See Aristotle, *Politics*, Book III, chapter ix, 8, 13, 14. (Barker translation, Oxford: Oxford University Press, 1946): "Any polis which is truly so-called, and is not merely one in name, must devote itself to the end of encouraging goodness. Otherwise, a political association sinks into a mere alliance, which only differs in space from other forms of alliance where the members live at a distance from one another."

57. I am indebted for this account of economic life in the Roman Empire to a Bible study given on several occasions by Philip Potter. This material now appears as part of Potter's article "The Global Economic System in Biblical Perspective," in Marc Reuver, Friedhelm Solms, and Gerrit Huizer, eds., *The Ecumenical Movement Tomorrow: Suggestions for Approaches and Alternatives* (Kampen: Kok Publishing House, and Geneva: WCC, 1993), 33ff.

Index